a manual for
Tumbling and Apparatus Stunts

a manual for seventh edition
Tumbling and Apparatus Stunts

Otto E. Ryser
Indiana University

James R. Brown
Indiana University

wcb

Wm. C. Brown Company Publishers
Dubuque, Iowa

PHYSICAL EDUCATION

Consulting Editor
Aileene Lockhart
Texas Woman's University

HEALTH

Consulting Editor
Robert Kaplan
The Ohio State University

PARKS AND RECREATION

Consulting Editor
David Gray
California State University, Long Beach

Copyright © 1961, 1968, 1976, 1980 by Otto E. Ryser

Library of Congress Catalog Card Number 79–55744

ISBN 0–697–07170–7

Printed in the United States of America

Contents

Foreword

Drawing from years of knowledge and experience first as a competitor, then as a coach, but always as a teacher, Dr. Ryser has compiled a comprehensive guide for both teacher and student of gymnastics. Having drawn from a wealth of experience, Dr. Ryser has trained many teachers and coaches who are successful today.

Because physical education classes are now being taught coeducationally, Ryser decided to include girls' work in this edition. He sought and obtained the help of Dr. James Brown for this endeavor. Dr. Brown has successfully conducted boys' and girls' gymnastics classes in a camp situation for years. The two men have worked together for over fifteen years in coaching and teaching situations.

This *Manual for Tumbling and Apparatus Stunts* is not only an excellent guide for the classroom teacher who needs a usable reference for class organization and skill technique, but it also serves very well as a guide for the coach of a competitive gymnastics team, providing competitive rules background information along with skill progressions on the various competitive events.

Seldom has a text shown such insight into the sport of gymnastics. Subjects such as gymnastics safety, conditioning exercises to prepare one physically for gymnastics performance, methods of motivation through the use of gymnastics games and contests often make the difference between an outstanding teacher/coach and an average one. Those subjects along with many more are dealt with thoroughly in this text.

The authors recognize the value of exhibitions and demonstrations in the promotion of the sport of gymnastics. Here again they draw from a wealth of experience in conveying to the reader a variety of ways in which successful demonstrations can be organized and performed, taking into account the age and ability level of the performers.

Of particular interest is the chapter on spotting. The authors have successfully synthesized the many considerations for proper spotting into a succinct list of guidelines with which a spotter can prepare himself mentally. The teaching of gymnastics skills through proper spotting is an absolute necessity for the proper teaching of gymnastics skills.

With a text of this scope and sensitivity, strides are being made towards better teaching of gymnastics skill through the use of proven skill progression, application of scientific principles, and a wealth of empirical knowledge seldom made available to the general teaching and coaching profession.

Roger Counsil
Professor of Physical Education
Gymnastics Coach
Indiana State University

Preface

The physical fitness phase of P.E. remains now as in recent past years one of the very important objectives of physical education. It is a well-known fact that gymnastics is a valuable aid in developing total body fitness with a special proficiency in increasing the strength and muscular endurance of the upper body—an area only slightly benefitted by many other physical education programs. This fact continues to increase the demand for gymnastics in all well-rounded physical education programs.

An added reason for the continuing popularity is the increase in the number and caliber of competitive teams in this country. In 1972, television and a tiny Russian girl, Olga Korbut, had much to do with this increase in interest. Television viewers fell in love with her and her amazing skill. When she and the Russian team (men as well as women) toured in this country in 1974 they appeared before 125,000 spectators in seven cities. Then in 1976 an even younger Roumanian girl, Nadia Comaneci, electrified the world by superb performances in the Montreal Olympics, scoring a perfect "10" five times in her twelve performances.

Now the U.S. is finally able to challenge the best and that too adds to the interest in gymnastics. Kurt Thomas and Bart Connor have already won gold medals in world competition and 15 year old Marcia Frederick scored a 9.95 in the World Championships in France.

In this edition an emphasis has been placed on the womens' skills and equipment usage. The addition of the womens' gymnastics follows the rise of gymnastics as an activity of interest in high school and college teams.

Why are Americans getting better? Better coaching, longer hours of practice, greater dedication, more scientific study of moves . . . sure. But also more interested people—participants and spectators alike. That means a greater demand for physical educators to teach gymnastics in the schools. Many private clubs and camps have sprung up to answer this demand but the schools too must do their part.

A factor that prevents an even more rapid development of gymnastics is the shortage of properly trained people who are capable of teaching. In fact, some teachers in dance schools are attempting to take advantage of this interest and advertise tumbling and gymnastics classes. The ability to adequately and safely conduct a program of this kind can be obtained only through a course specifically designed to prepare a teacher for that job. This book was developed to serve as a tool for such a course.

It is true that educational philosophies have changed and many educators frown on the traditional method of teaching. As the ad proclaims, "You've come a long way, Baby." But not *all* change is necessarily for the better. Sometimes the distance travelled by "Baby" is not in the best *direction*. The "do-it-yourself" trend in general education and "movement exploration" in physical education is not *safe* for gymnastics nor is it profitable in terms of expended time. Improper (even dangerous) techniques may become habit and lead to injury. For this reason, the old-fashioned teaching methods of *telling them how to do it* still persist in this edition.

The impetus for this revision stems from the fact that the implementation of Title IX means that boys and girls will be in the same physical education classes throughout their school life. Since they will be together, a text that covers both men's and women's events seems to be practical. Of course, there is a difference between men's and women's gymnastics but many of the stunts can be taught to both at once. This book tells how that can be done and tells how to adapt the different pieces of apparatus to both sexes.

New photographs and drawings have been added. The illustrations are of *good* performers but not of experts. It is felt that a top notch gymnast performs not only better but in a different manner than a novice. The beginner will find it impossible and even unwise to attempt to imitate the style and body positions of a world class performer. In many instances the directions include comments to the effect that advanced performers should try the maneuver with an "arch all the way" or "keep the shoulders behind the hands" while beginners are advised to "pike slightly" or "lead with the shoulders."

The idea for this text grew out of the author's own need for instructional aids in teaching his classes of physical education majors who were preparing for the teaching profession. For these students, mere mastery of stunts and proficiency in performance were not a sufficient goal. They had to learn to *teach* as well as to perform. Just as one learns to swim by getting into the water and going through the movements of swimming, one learns to teach by teaching.

In an attempt to give the students an opportunity to teach the stunts, the existing texts were examined and the best ones were issued to the students. However, it was noticed that not enough specific and detailed information for the performance of the stunts was given for a person with little or no background in tumbling and apparatus work. This was especially true in the description of spotting techniques. Spotting and assisting are of tremendous importance in the teaching of gymnastics, and these prospective teachers needed to learn just where to stand and how to grasp or support the performer to safeguard him and to assist in his learning of the stunt.

Furthermore, specific methods and techniques of teaching peculiar to this type of work required attention. Also, it was important that these pupils should believe in the worth of the activity so they would develop an interest in acquiring the necessary skills and an enthusiasm that would enable them to establish this sport in their own teaching situations. With this in mind, the chapters in this manual dealing with the values of tumbling and apparatus work and the special methods and techniques used to present this material were developed.

The author used this book in mimeographed form for over three years in his own classes. Assignments were given to class members, and they prepared and taught the assigned stunts to the rest of the class. Their teaching methods and techniques were discussed, and constructive criticism was given by the instructor and the class as a whole. The practice afforded by this method served them well, and much improvement in their manner of presentation was noted.

During this use in its original form, revisions and corrections were made as discovered. Various spotting methods were experimented with and adopted only after they proved themselves. This is a functional text; one based on use and not just on theory.

In a continuing effort to further improve this manual, comments were solicited from both teachers and students who used it as a text. Carefully made line drawings were copied (from actual pictures of performers) to illustrate and emphasize particularly important parts of the stunts. Since competitive gymnastics has become more popular and prevalent in the schools, this edition features a number of new stunts, slightly more difficult, and some of the less practical ones have been eliminated. Beginning and intermediate routines of from six to ten moves are provided for each event in order to acquaint the advanced beginner with the concept of gymnastics as a sport, rather than just a "trick" to be performed or a series of combined moves welded into a smooth-flowing picture of artistry and grace. Also, a chapter on the floor exercise event has been added as well as one discussing the problems of warm-up and conditioning. The rules and regulations governing competitive gymnastics have been brought up to date, but rule changes will continue to be made from year to year and the reader is advised to check the rules from official sources annually.

NOTE: This is still not intended to be a "coaching" manual. Its main purpose is to enable physical education teachers to conduct good, sound, safe gymnastics units on a class level that *may* lead to a varsity level program for the more advanced students in the class.

In preparing a lesson from this book, the reader is advised to read the descriptions of the stunts carefully and, at the same time, to study the pertinent drawings. He should then go through each position in his mind, doing the stunt mentally, and then picture the stunt being done in its entirety. This will help him develop a clear concept of the stunt and will enable him to describe it accurately when he teaches it. He should then go over each of the teaching hints and determine why each one is important. When preparing to teach a stunt involving a partner, he should picture himself in the role of one of the performers; this will help him in his interpretation.

The stunts are listed progressively according to difficulty in each section. Rather than starting at the beginning of a section and going through to the end, it is advisable to take the first few (10 to 12) of one type and then take the first few of another type for the next lesson. In other words, work on the beginning stunts in each category, then come back and add the next set of stunts from each category. This system will avoid getting into the most difficult work too early in the semester. The stunts are classified as they are to facilitate the locating of specific stunts.

In a normal school tumbling lesson for any one day, one would expect to find a couple of individual balance stunts, a few partner balance stunts, several individual tumbling stunts, plus some partner tumbling stunts, and perhaps even a simple stunt or two for good measure. This type of lesson would not be practical, for several reasons, in a "teacher training" class. Therefore, in this case it is suggested that each lesson be devoted to one classification of stunts. Of course, it is not necessary that the next lesson definitely come from a different clasification; sometimes a certain sequence of stunts is desired, and several lessons in a row might involve stunts selected from the same category.

Thanks is hereby expressed to the hundreds of physical education majors at Indiana University who served as "guinea pigs" for the experimentation connected with the writing of this manual and to the author's four sons, Larry, Terry Gary, and Barry for their willingness to try and retry stunts so that foolproof spotting methods could be worked out.

Appreciation for the helpful comments and suggestions offered by colleagues who were kind enough to review the book must be manifested. The author is deeply grateful to Roger Counsil, gymnastics coach at Indiana State University (winner of many NCAA gymnastics championships) chairman of the NCAA Gymnastics Rules Committee and Olympic coach, for his interest in the book and his kindness in writing the forword.

The progress made by gymnastics as a competitive sport and as a phase of a well-rounded physical education program is noted with pleasure. It is believed that a small part of that progress has been brought about by teachers who, as students, used this manual as a text in class. It is the author's fervent hope that this latest revision will make an added contribution to the field and that gymnastics will continue to grow.

O.E.R.
J.R.B.

Part I

Organization

1

Introduction

Friedrich Ludwig Jahn ("Father Jahn") is credited with being the originator of what is today known as gymnastics or apparatus work. His efforts were motivated by a political zeal and a burning desire to free Germany from French domination under Napoleon. It was his intention to build a strong, unified nation by developing the young men of Germany both physically and mentally so that they would be capable of free ing themselves.

He was teaching school in Berlin at the time (1810), and that spring he took a group of his boys out into the woods and fields to play, wrestle, jump, run, and climb. They met regularly and created their own apparatus from tree limbs and the like. During the winter some of the more enthusiastic boys continued to work indoors. The following spring the outdoor excursions intensified and other schools began to send boys too. Other crude pieces of apparatus were added. The boys invented stunts and tricks and dared others to try them. Jahn wrote down what was done and how the stunts were executed. In the winter they again moved indoors and this time brought their apparatus with them; more pieces were built and the stunts became more varied and difficult. Interest in the project was aroused and the movement spread. A number of organizations or "Turnvereine" were established to carry on this work. The apparatus was improved and subsequently manufactured commercially. The performers became more skillful; they devoted more time to practice. Gradually, competition in tumbling and gymnastics developed among the various Turnvereines, and thus our modern gymnastics competition was born.

In the 1820s a number of "Turners" (members of Turnvereines) came to this country to escape the political persecution in Germany, and they established Turnvereins in German communities in many of our larger cities. By the middle of the century the American Turnerbund (national organization of American Turners) was established. These Turners were also instrumental in introducing physical education into the American public schools—in some instances they even taught free of charge in order to get the program started. Since they followed the German system and program, apparatus work and tumbling had prominent places in the school physical education program. A number of other organizations helped in the spread of gymnastics and later aided in keeping the sport alive during the years when it was dropped from many school programs. Of these groups the YMCA, the Sokols (Bohemian equivalent of the German Turners), and the AAU were the most prominent.

At the close of World War I, a new philosophy of physical education evolved. Informal activities such as games and sports were emphasized. There was a general trend toward mild recreational activity for the majority though strenuous competitive activity was encouraged for the small minority. With the advent of this new philohopsy, gymnastics and tumbling, along with calisthenics, marching tactics, and rhythmics began to disapper from the school programs. This work was considered to be too formal, and the popularity pendulum swung over to the play and recreational type of activities.

The "progressive" faction threw out the so-called formal gymnastics. They failed to see the need for a balanced program. To be sure, informal play activities are a "must" in every program, but just as vital is a significant amount of body-building activities which can best be taught through the use of formal methods. The achievement of "total fitness"—social and moral as well as physical—demands adequately varied programs, varied in method as well as in content.

Now that the pendulum has swung back to a realization and reevaluation of the values that can be derived from participation in gymnastics, there are two principal obstacles to be surmounted before the program can function adequately on a nationwide scale. During the period when gymnastics was considered to be of little importance, school apparatus was relegated to the scrap heap. Now most schools find themselves inadequately supplied with this expensive equipment. The second problem is the short supply of physical education personnel with the training that will enable them to conduct classes in gymnastics. Fortunately, neither of these problems is insurmountable.

Though it is true that the cost of equipping a school properly for a program of this kind is quite high, the money seems to be obtainable when the school board becomes convinced of the need. A factor often overlooked when contemplating the purchase of such equipment is its durability. It will last for many, many years. Equipment purchases can be spread over the years. One or two pieces can be obtained each year and, in a short time, a well-equipped plant will result. If only a few pieces are available at first, the class can be divided; part of the class can work on the apparatus while the others are doing something else.

The gymnastics equipment companies are anxious to help in this matter. Several have developed a junior line of equipment that sells for approximately one-third the cost of regulation equipment. This equipment is not adequate for competitive work in the high schools or colleges, but it will serve for class work in elementary and junior high schools. It is suggested that if at all possible, the regulation apparatus be purchased for all levels, but if this cannot be done, the junior equipment is much better than none at all.

Even if no apparatus is available, a resourceful teacher can still find a way. Serviceable homemade parallel bars and vaulting boxes (used as a substitute for pommel horse vaulting) can be inexpensively constructed in the school shops. An outdoor horizontal bar is a simple matter: sink two posts in cement, bore holes through the posts and run a steel bar through the holes; set screws will keep the bar from turning. Tumbling may be done outdoors on turf or on sand pits covered with canvas. Indoors, freshly covered, used mattresses can be requisitioned. A number of blankets and quilts may be piled one on top of another and serve as a mat substitute. Then too, there are many simple stunts which can be performed without mats or any other equipment.

The lack of trained personnel is a greater problem. However, most of the teacher training institutions that grant degrees with a major in physical education now offer courses in tumbling and apparatus techniques. To take care of the teachers already in the field, a number of gymnastics clinics are being held and some school systems give in-service training under the direction of experienced gymnasts. In this way the teachers can become acquainted with fundamental work suitable for class participation. To coach competitive gymnastics, obviously much more work is required. For this type of work, competitive experience is almost necessary. Here, too, the picture looks brighter. Because of the recent large increase of competitive gymnastics on the college level there is greater opportunity for physical education students to participate. As these experienced gymnasts graduate and go out into the high school field, they start gymnastics teams in their schools. Many high school gymnasts are so impressed with the sport they decide to make a career of gymnastics coaching and so enter college to prepare for it. Thus, a continually enlarging circle develops. That this is true is demonstrated by the surprising increase in competitive teams, on all levels, all over the country.

Another development in recent years is the big increase in private gymnastics schools. TV publicity given to the Olympic Gymnastics and the United States tours of Russian, Roumanian, Japanese, and other famous gymnastics teams have done much to acquaint the American public with the value and beauty of gymnastics. Some high school and even several college gymnastics coaches have taken advantage of this interest and have started schools and clubs for pre-schoolers up to high school students. In some instances this has proved to be so profitable that individuals have resigned their public school positions in favor of full time concentration on their private schools. About 80% of the participants in these clubs are girls—probably due to the tremendous publicity given to Olga Korbut and Nadia Comanechi and the fact that girls seem to be more adept at gymnastics than boys.

Coeducational Gymnastics

This text is designed to enable the reader to conduct a safe, beneficial, enjoyable gymnastics class as part of a well rounded physical education program at the elementary, middle school, secondary school and college levels. Though it does not profess to be a coaching guide for competitive gymnastics, there is sufficient material and information to aid a beginning coach of a beginning team.

Since today's concept of education mandates co-educational classes at all levels and in all subject matter, both men's and women's gymnastics is covered. Despite the fact that there is considerable difference between the men's and women's programs (only two of the ten events are the same, and one of those differs in the position of the apparatus) at the advanced, competitive level, the two can work quite well together in a beginning or intermediate physical education gymnastics class.

For example, boys do not "compete" on balance beam but elementary school boys can enjoy and benefit from working this event. Girls and women do not work the pommel horse but they can vault over it with the boys. Though the horizontal bar is a men's event, many of the moves done there are performed by women on the uneven parallel bars. Tumbling, (a major part of the floor exercise event) is the same for both sexes. True, there are differences in the men's and women's floor event. The women's work is accompanied by music and is timed. Also, much of their work consists of dance sequences whereas the men's "floor ex" contains more tumbling, strength work, and static balance positions.

On the other hand, the tumbling and flexibility moves which are highly desirable for both men and women are pretty much the same. Then too, mechanical principles of performance are the same for both. Shortening the radius of a circle will speed up the movement whether it be a woman or a man performing. The same elements of good form are also considered: straight legs, feet together, toes pointed, and erect body carriage are important for both.

Another point to consider here is the fact that girls outdo the boys in gymnastics, both skillwise and in the number of participants. Competitively, girls teams far outnumber boy's teams and between 70 and 80% of the participants in private clubs are girls. Boys have an advantage in most sports but in gymnastics, especially in the elementary school, girls appear to do better and learn faster. This could be accounted for by their lower center of gravity and higher degree of flexibility.

The problems that will be faced in conducting a co-ed class will be covered in chapter 7, Methods of Organizing and Conducting Classes.

2

The Concept of Gymnastics: An Overview

To some, the idea of gymnastics as a sport or athletic even is a difficult concept to grasp. Sports are considered to be a direct striving of person against person or team against team; a situation in which one does his/her best to prevent another from achieving a particular goal. This aspect is very evident in contact sports such as football or wrestling and can be detected easily in the supposed noncontact sports of basketball and baseball. Even in truly noncontact sports where one is not permitted to interfere with his opponent's performance (tennis, volleyball) there is an offense and a defense. The offense attempts to hit the ball to an unguarded spot or draw the opponents out of position while the defense tries to "get the ball back."

There are, of course, athletic events where the defensive phase is less evident or even nonexistent. Track and swimming are examples. Uninformed spectators frequently miss the strategy of pacesetting in both of these events and that of running together to force opposing team members to swing wide to get around in track. Even in a short sprint where there is no finessing or maneuvering that can be classified as defense strategy the competition can be seen and felt. Each runner strives mightily to defeat the others. First, one is slightly ahead, then another.

In field events where athletes are competing one at a time, they are competing against something tangible—something that can be seen: a crossbar or a tape measure. If one high jumper knocks the crossbar off and the other doesn't, it is immediately clear to the spectators who has won.

In gymnastics—and in a few other sports such as diving and figure skating—not only is there no interference with the opponents' endeavors, but the striving against them is much less discernible. Oh, the competition is there all right, but in a more subtle or subdued form. In one sense, the contention is actually with oneself. An attempt is made to bring the body under such control that one can flawlessly complete the routine developed during months and even years of practice.

In order to get a clear picture of the sport, another difference between gymnastics and most of the other sports must be understood. Not only *what* one does but *how* he/she does it is important. The agonized expressions of strain on the faces of athletes who are exerting every iota of physical force to obtain their objective of winning are familiar to all who see sports pictures in newspapers and magazines. For a gymnast, however, it is imperative that the facial grimaces, the trembling muscles, the very suggestion of intense effort, be eradicated. If this is not done, points will be deducted from the score. The action must convey the impression of effortless ease. Elegance and security are the keywords for gymnastics.

Gymnastics requires an aesthetic quality akin to that displayed by the ballet dancer or figure skater. A sense of artistry must be part of the gymnast's makeup. A technically perfect but mechanically rendered performance will not score as high as will one displayed imaginatively in an ethereal manner.

The FIG (International Gymnastics Federation—the governing body for all international competition, including the Olympics) introduced a new idea for the 1968 Games to even further the aesthetic emphasis.

The new rule states that in the finals of international competition, a 9.4 is the highest score that can be earned by a *perfect* routine or exercise that meets all the difficulty and composition requirements (explained later in the chapter on judging) if it is performed in an ordinary or "stock" manner. Formerly, such a display would have earned the maximum 10.0 for the gymnast. The remaining .6 of a point can now only be earned by exhibiting risk, originality, and virtuosity above and beyond the ordinary. The N.C.A.A. has also adopted this rule.

At an international gymnastics coaches symposium in Macolin, Switzerland, in March 1969, it was the consensus that in addition to ROV (risk, originality, and virtuosity) a championship routine should contain an element of surprise. One person described it as being an element so startling as to cause a judge to drop his pencil. This is not (as yet) written into the rules, but it is something that the judges will be looking for.

Arthur Gander of Switzerland, president of the FIG in 1967, described gymnastics as a way of life, a discipline. He elaborated on the point to the extent of saying that a gymnast could be recognized even at 80 years of age by a characteristic erect bearing, a spring in his step, and a general optimistic outlook on life.°

We see, then, that gymnastics is a special kind of competition. It is a self-discipline. It is a philosophy— a mental attitude. There are, of course, those who engage in gymnastics who do not feel this way and are, perhaps, not even aware of this concept of the sport.

To become a gymnast one must keep the objective of complete routines in mind rather than having as his goal the learning of many tricks. Of course, the first step in the development of a complete routine is the mastery of the individual parts of the routine. However, when two adjacent tricks in a contemplated routine are learned, they should be put together and practiced in combination. The beginner should learn to work into and out of each part with the preceding and following parts. It should be noted that at least one prominent and successful gymnastics coach teaches most of his work in series. For example, his tumblers learn a round off, back handspring, back flip right from the beginning rather than learning each stunt individually and then putting them together. Though the majority of coaches feel that this procedure is unsound, he is a very successful coach and it is difficult to argue with success. When these combinations have been worked up and are moving fairly smoothly, all the parts should be combined into the whole routine and practiced in that way.

Frequently, a gymnast will encounter much difficulty when first trying to throw the routine as a whole. This could be true even though all of the sequences can be done without trouble. This is the result of the added factor of fatigue setting in. If one is used to doing three or four moves at a time, then resting and trying the next parts when freshened, it will be quite different going into the fifth and sixth parts with a tired body. This endurance has to be developed over a period of time. Additional nervous energy is also expended at a time like this because of the excitement of "going through the whole thing" for the first time. This, too, is a physical drain.

Another factor that adds to the issue is that the mind has been trained to deal with the points of emphasis of a few stunts at a time. Now, it suddenly has to come up with the next move and momentarily there is a blank. Naturally, this interrupts the smooth transition from stunt to stunt.

If a great deal of difficulty is encountered in working the whole routine, it will be wise to practice the first half, pause a moment to regain the breath and strength and to collect the thoughts, and then go through the second half. When this can be done fairly easily, the two halves should be combined.

In some instances, a rather difficult dismount is to be performed and the gymnast may still have a few misgivings. In this case, it is better to do all the routine except for the dismount. Then, after a very short rest, he should do the dismount. Sometimes the dismount should be done alone till confidence is gained. Then the trick preceding the dismount should be added; then two, three, etc., working backward till the whole routine is performed.

Even after the routine has been done a number of times, there will be weak parts in it. These parts can be given special emphasis during practice and, for awhile, be worked on individually, At times, the trouble lies *between* two parts, and though each of the stunts can be done well by itself, the fifth one cannot be thrown from the fourth one. Work must then be done on the finishing position of the fourth stunt so that

---

°From a speech at the Gymnastics Congress held by the United States Gymnastics Federation in Kansas City, October 1967.

the fifth one can be started without a break. This search for the trouble spot can be quite complicated. Perhaps the difficulty with the finish position of the fourth stunt is caused by an entirely unsuspected fault in the third stunt.

It is a quite normal urge to try to develop too fast—to try the harder stunts before the easier ones have been mastered. Besides the apparent safety hazard, there is the strong possibility of developing into a "circus performer rather than a gymnast. There is a tremendous difference between the two concepts. An added reason for mastering the fundamentals first can be found in the following example: A young man—a very good gymnast—was competing on the horizontal bar. He was in the middle of a very difficult and well-performed routine when he experienced a momentary break in the routine. He attempted to kip (a very elementary move) to resume his routine, and to everyone's surprise he failed to do the kip. He tried twice more, failing each time, and finally dropped off in disgust. In his training he had bypassed this stunt as being too elementary and useless to him. When he needed it in an emergency, he didn't have it. Gymnasts who are well grounded in the fundamentals can frequently "cover up" breaks more easily than can those who have simply learned a series of difficult tricks.

It was suggested earlier that both the coach and the gymnast should play a part in building or planning the routines. This is entirely true on an advanced level, but a beginner, having no idea of what can be done, would be completely lost. For that reason, specific routines on each piece will be outlined.

A wide range of abilities are very likely to be found in most classes. Some students in the class may be there because it is required, some out of curiosity, some because of a desire to build their bodies, some because they have a bit of a background and feel that they can earn an A in the course, and others because they like it.

To meet the needs of the students, one of the routines will be relatively easy and suitable for beginners. A second will be semiadvanced. For those who are quickly able to do both routines with good form and acceptable style, several advanced moves will be presented and opportunity given for the development of optional routines. Those with special ability should be encouraged to try out for the gymnastics team. If there is no team, a club could be formed which could eventually become a team.

The Gymnast

Following this concept of gymnastics, let's see what can be discovered about the temperament of the gymnast. What physical, mental, and psychological characteristics are found? First, his vital statistics: The average male gymnast is small and light, broad shouldered and narrow waisted. A composite Olympic performer would be 5'5" tall, weigh 137.64 pounds, and be 26.06 years old. These figures were obtained by averaging the heights, weights, and ages of the top twenty performers in the 1964 Olympic Games in Tokyo.

These averages were influenced greatly by the fact that many Japanese were in the top twenty and they, traditionally, are small in stature. The height extremes were 5'3" and 5'7". The weights ranged from 117.5 to 156.6 pounds. The youngest man was 21 and the oldest was 33. American teams will average somewhat taller and a little heavier, though they will be considerably younger. The American team at Tokyo averaged 5'6" in height, 143.6 pounds in weight, and 23 years of age.

This does not mean that a tall, relatively heavy man can not succeed in the sport. Outstanding proof of this was found in the 1952 NCAA Championship Meet held at the University of Colorado in Boulder, Colorado. A gymnast in that meet was 6'5" tall and weighed over 230 pounds, and he just missed making the finals in his event. Of course, that is unusual but many good men have been over 6' tall and close to 200 pounds. Some have been quite tall and very thin. So, nobody is necessarily excluded because of build. Generally, the same physical characteristics (small, light) hold true for women gymnasts as well.

Close to 100 percent of the good gymnasts are well above the average in strength for their height and weight. This is especially true in the upper body—arms, shoulders, chest, and upper back. They are much more supple than most other athletes and are especially well coordinated. A good kinesthetic sense is also a *must* for gymnasts. The usual concept of endurance, that involving the cardiovascular and respiratory systems, is not as important to a gymnast as to participants in some of the other sports. Another type of stamina, muscular endurance, is, however, of great importance.

Power, the ability to explode all at once with a tremendous burst of energy, is another vital factor. This ability is derived from a combination of two components: strength and speed. Without this explosive force, stunts such as the double back flip in floor exercise (or in tumbling) cannot be done.

A good sense of timing—the feel for the exact split second when a push, extension, or flexion must occur—in order to insure the completion of a trick—is also required.

A gymnast cannot become proficient without a well-developed feeling for balance. This goes hand in hand with kinesthesia, the perception of movement, position, and strain in various muscles. Immediate reaction and adjustment to the slightest imbalance at the *moment it occurs* is essential. This balance ability must be both static (the common concept) and dynamic.

Agility, or nimbleness, the quality that enables one to adjust in midair very quickly and with no wasted motions, is another attribute of a gymnast. Speed of movement, accuracy of movement, coordination, and reaction time are all involved in this quality.

A football player participating in a gymnastics class was once heard to remark, "Who said this is a noncontact sport?" Of course, gymnastics is not a contact sport in the true sense of the term, but frequently there is unplanned contact between the performer and the bar, horse, or mat. It was this contact to which the football player alluded. Thus, in the learning process, a gymnast must be prepared to "take it." Courage is a by-product of most forms of athletics. Even in tennis, where there is little chance of physical injury caused by an opponent, one must have the courage to force himself to play on though he may be worn out or hurt. In gymnastics, the development of courage is of a different nature. When learning a new and difficult stunt there is always the possibility of falling off, crashing into the bars, or straining a muscle or joint, and there are apt to be misgivings in the performer's mind. One must learn to "go" for the stunt wholeheartedly because there is danger in holding back after once making the start. The ability to make the effort without reservation entails a feeling of confidence in oneself, in the spotters, and in his coach's or teacher's judgment.

Still another side to this matter of courage is the need to take a chance on the possible disruption or "break" of a routine through the inclusion of a risky move that may possibly not present any physical danger to the performer but be of such a nature that if missed would cause the loss of the event.

To become a gymnast, one must also have perseverance. For many, progress is slow; there are many discouragements. At times, a stunt which had previously been learned is "lost" and has to be relearned. Stick-to-itiveness, to coin a word, is a necessary ingredient in the gymnast's makeup.

Creativity is another important facet. Since gymnastics is artistic in nature, the gymnast must possess the imagination and the creative instinct of an artist. Each year someone comes to a national or international meet with a new move; something that is distinctly and uniquely "his/hers." Frequently these innovations are named for the innovator.

Some feel that this type of ingenuity is not needed by the gymnast since there is a coach to tell what to do and how to build the routine. However, this should be the responsibility of both, since the gymnast must "feel" what he/she is doing just as much as a musical virtuoso feels the music. If he/she hasn't created —rather than simply going through the motions someone else has planned—the performance is apt to be mechanical rather than alive and vibrant. Each gymnast should attempt to individualize or personalize the performances with style and flair.

Strong self-motivation is another identifying trait of quality gymnasts. They have to push themselves to practice new and difficult tricks. If they depend on their coach to make them practice, they'll never get far, for they will probably be working with little enthusiasm. Even harder than working on new parts of a routine is the practice and repractice of old, already learned sequences in order to perfect them. Again, the artist is used as an example in the concept of perfection. A famous artist spent a great deal of time trying to correct one little detail in a huge painting. A friend commented on this and said, "No one will ever know about that." To this the artist replied, "I will know. I cannot leave it that way." It is true that all performers perform for the audience, but the best ones perform for themselves as well.

Gymnasts are frequently individualists and, for this reason, are sometimes difficult to coach. Though they should, and usually do, want their team to win, they are out there to beat their own teammates as well as the opponents. Despite this, the practice periods require and generate team work. Spotting (safetying) each other makes it important that team members work together. Also, since the present method of scoring converts each gymnast's scores into team points and a team winner is determined, usually all members feel a team responsibility and have an interest in their teammates' work. On most successful teams, a cooperative spirit is exemplified.

It is necessary that gymnasts have great confidence in themselves. They are out there alone, the focus of all eyes. The judges are watching them critically, ready to "deduct" at the bat of an eyelash. The psychological tension will break them down if they don't have self-confidence.

This confidence will also be reflected to their benefit in positive performances. It will create a feeling of elan which will be projected to the judges, resulting in favorable impressions on their parts. Without confidence, it is virtually impossible to maintain the poise which is so necessary to a first-class performance.

Emotional stability is also a part of all this. A gymnast must be able to concentrate. Though aware that he/she is the cynosure of all eyes, one must divorce oneself from the effect. While the overstimulation induced by such a situation may be advantageous in some sports where an all-out burst of energy is required (high jump, shot put, hitting the line in football), it could have a detrimental effect on a gymnast. A *too hard* thrust might result in an overspin which would cause a break or interruption in the routine.

Especially difficult performances call for special needs in the psyche of an individual. One must concentrate one's psychological powers of attention, speed of orientation, and special perception and thinking on the immediate task at hand. The crowd and the judges must be forgotten. All available sources of nerve-muscle strength must be mobilized, and all this must be molded into a smooth series of moves, each one flowing into the next.

Though friendliness, cooperation, and helpfulness are not necessary characteristics of good gymnasts, a surprising number possess these worthwhile qualities. This is evidenced during premeet warm-ups, aftermeet workouts, and clinic practice sessions where members of opposing teams work together and even help each other with problem spots in their routines. This conduct seems to be more prevalent in gymnastics than in other sports.

Now, must an individual have all these attributes—strength, flexibility, coordination, muscular endurance, courage, balance, kinesthesis, persistence, power, confidence, timing, agility, and creativity—*before* he starts the long, hard trail to becoming an expert gymnast, or will they be developed during the process of working out while one follows the trail? Probably the true answer lies on a continuum somewhere between the two extremes. The workouts are certainly conducive to the improvement of all these factors, but in order to reach a high state of proficiency, the natural talent must also be there.

It should be noted that these factors are all interrelated and that the proportions are not the same for all gymnasts. Also, we have been talking primarily about the all-around gymnast, the one who performs in all six of the international events for men or the four women's events.

All-Around versus Specialist

In most foreign countries all gymnasts work all around. In the United States the majority work only a few pieces of apparatus, many only one. For many years, there has been a difference of opinion among the leading coaches and gymnasts as to which idea is the better. As in all issues, there are valid points in favor of each side. Should we continue to develop the specialist, or should we devote all our energies toward building the all-around person? No attempt will be made here to settle the issue, but a few points will be brought out in favor of each side in order that the reader may become cognizant of the problem.

Proponents for the all-around contend that one who works just a few events is not, in truth, a gymnast. They claim that the physical benefits are far greater because the different events complement each other and thus contribute to more complete physical development. From a competitive viewpoint, they argue that in international competition only all-around performers are permitted to enter. The specialist is excluded. The all-around gymnast does not become bored with the work because he/she goes from piece to piece and is always faced with new problems. Learning a stunt on one piece makes it easier to learn a similar stunt on another; there is much carry-over from event to event.

Those who advocate continuance of our specialist program offer the following arguments: This is the United States—why should we abandon something that works here just to favor the very few that can expect to qualify for international competition? It takes a long time to make a good all-around performer. The Europeans start their gymnasts at a much earlier age than we do and, therefore, they can develop the all-around gymnast. Here, with a limited amount of time, this is not feasible. The specialist actually helps to improve our limited number of all-around men. The specialist has time to learn and perfect new stunts. The all-around man on the team is able to take advantage of the learning procedures of the specialist and thus can take shortcuts in his own learning. Since competition is stimulating, the all-around man will try to beat the specialist in each event, and this incentive of high standards and goals is bound to improve the work of the all-around gymnast. By using specialists, teams will be larger and more people will become interested in gymnastics (parents, brothers, friends, etc.) which will raise the status of gymnastics in this country.

Other arguments are advanced from both camps, but the above is enough to give the reader an idea of the problem. The NCAA Gymnastics Rules Committee has spent many hours in debate over this subject but is gradually supporting the case for the all-around performer. In 1969 they established the makeup of a team at two all-around and two specialists per event. In 1971 they changed to three all-around and two specialists with the top three men to count per event. In 1974 they retained the same numerical relationship but placed more emphasis on the all-around by stating that the top *four* men would count. This means that the scores of at least two all-around men will be used in each event for the team score. Though the rules regarding the all-around didn't change at the 1975 meeting, the pressure for going to an entirely all-around program increased. The present (1979) N.C.A.A. rules for men require four all around and two specialists which permits six men per event with the top *five* counting for team points.

As has been stated, the physical requirements for specialists are not as complete as for all-around men. Those who just work floor exercise do not need the strength for ring work, while ring men can get along very well without the flexibility that is so important in floor exercise. Not as much courage is needed to work the pommel horse as is required for the horizontal bar, but a better sense of dynamic balance is necessary for the horse. Floor exercise and vaulting require leg strength and power that are not needed for the other events.

Thus it can be seen that for general fitness the all-around program is the better. But, some people just aren't flexible, or strong, or they lack some other attribute of the all-around gymnast. Rather than deny them the pleasures and benefits of gymnastics, they should have the chance to become a specialist.

3

Values of Gymnastics

Proof that something has been lacking in our physical education programs of the past was found in the records of the induction centers during World War II. A definite and pronounced weakness was noticed in the shoulder girdles, arms, chests, and upper backs of the majority of the men inducted into the service. Additional evidence of this lack appeared in the mid 1950's. The Kraus-Weber Test of Physical Fitness and the AAHPER test given to American and European children demonstrated that our children were inferior to the Europeans in physical fitness. Games and sports programs can take care of the legs and the "wind" of participants, but the upp   body's development must not be neglected. Gymnastics does have a definite and necessary contribution   the students' welfare.

Participation in tumblin   may benefit an individual in the following ways:

1. By promoting health   through vigorous exercise which involves all parts of the body.
2. By increasing strength—   arms, shoulder girdle, chest, and upper back. (Weight training may be faster, but gy.   ables one to handle his own body rather than an object outside the body.
3. By developing neuromuscular coordination (timing—rhythm) which enables one to work and play with a greater conservation of energy. Good coordination helps one to better control the body and take care of oneself in dangerous situations.
4. By increasing flexibility and litheness. (A recent study indicated that gymnasts were the most flexible of all athletes and that pound for pound, they were the strongest.)
5. By developing precision and exactness of movement.
6. By developing a better sense of balance (dynamic as well as static) which lessens the danger of falling.
7. By developing a sensitve kinesthetic sense, a sense of location which helps one to know in which direction one is moving despite the position of the body.
8. By amplifying an appreciation of aesthetic values—grace, beauty, harmony of movement, etc.
9. By building power—explosive force (combination of strength and speed).
10. By providing conditioning for other sports. Many pole vaulters work out on the parallel bars. The ability to handle the body is a prime factor of success in any sport. The knowledge of how to "roll with a fall" is valuable in many sports and in life in general.
11. By encouraging quick, accurate decisions and actions.
12. By building a strong, good-looking body. The general body build of most gymnasts is well proportioned.
13. By serving as an enjoyable recreational activity.
14. By making available the acknowledged benefits of competition when engaged in as a competitive sport.

15. By providing a competitive sport in which smaller children can excel. Most of the other varsity sports place a premium on size and weight.
16. By offering physically handicapped individuals a chance to participate in and enjoy competitive sports. Poor eyesight, for example, would not lower a participant's efficiency. A number of gymnasts who have suffered infantile paralysis in the lower extremities have become champions. Several star performers have only one leg.
17. By providing an activity with carry-over value into family life. A father and son (or daughter) can do many of the partner balance stunts right in the home, and mother can join in the fun by spotting —or by performing too.

The above values are more or less inherent in the stunts, and their mere performance and practice are conducive to their being acquired to some extent by the performers. But there are other contributions to the student's well-being that the gymnastics program can and will make under the guidance and direction of a capable, experienced teacher. These outcomes are less tangible and objective than the others, but they are nonetheless real and valuable. A skillful teacher can use the stunts program to accomplish the following:

1. Develop resourcefulness, initiative, and originality by giving the performer opportunity to devise new stunts or create new combinations of old stunts. When one stunt is learned, a new one suggests itself or seems possible. There is no limit. In fact, extra points are awarded for originality in competition.
2. Develop perseverance, which is achieved by giving encouragement and help on a difficult stunt until the stunt is mastered.
3. Create an appreciation for the skill of others.
4. Educe the feeling and fun of *friendly* competition. In most sports an antagonistic emotion is frequently engendered because your opponent is actively engaged in trying to thwart your efforts, while in gymnastics there is nothing he/she can do to prevent you from doing your best.
5. Develop leadership, helpfulness, and habit of safety by placing various capable pupils in charge of squads.
6. Augment a spirit of cooperation through spotting each other and giving helpful hints.
7. Increase the pupils' confidence in themselves as the result of their gradual mastery of difficult stunts; this is made possible by good teaching and the use of a definite progression of stunts.
8. Discourage foolhardiness through insistence on proper safety precautions and proper spotting.

In addition to the above values to the participant, the program has other uses:

1. It adds variety, fun, and interest to a physical education program. Tumbling can easily be adapted to all age levels, to varying levels of skill, and to both sexes.
2. The simple stunts with forward motion (both individual and partner) can be used as the means of locomotion in relay races.
3. The miscellaneous simple stunts (both individual and partner) can be used to liven up a calisthenic drill. After a number of exercises, a few stunts can be attempted, and then back to the exercises.
4. It has excellent entertainment value. It can be used for exhibitions or demonstrations between halves of basketball games, P.T.A. meetings, etc.
5. It can be used as a self-testing activity and as such can serve as a partial determiner of final grades.
6. It does not demand a great amount of space.

4
Safety

If there is opposition to including apparatus and tumbling work in the school physical education program, one of the commonest arguments used is its supposed danger. When proper safety precautions are followed, this activity is no more dangerous than most of the other worthwhile physical education activities. Of course, one cannot guarantee that no one will be hurt; neither can a guarantee be given that a person walking down the street will not trip, fall, and break an arm.

Accidents are unplanned, unexpected occurrences usually having causes. Frequently these causes can be removed, greatly reducing the chances of having an accident. However, since there is the *possibility* of severe injury, the following safety precautions should *always* be observed:

SAFETY HINTS

1. Incorporate safety provisions in every gymnastics lesson plan. A good safety record does not come by accident.
2. Create a safe atmosphere by impressing upon the class members the need for safety precautions. (A gymnastics program can be used to develop safety habits and skills in other aspects of life.)
3. Post spotting hints and safety rules in the gym and locker room.
4. Institute a conditioning program several weeks before starting gymnastics to develop sufficient strength.
5. Conduct a brief but thorough warm-up period of calisthenics and running each period prior to the gymnastics work. Stress stretching.
6. Follow a definite progression in presenting stunts.
   a. Select stunts carefully. Be sure they are within the capacity of the students.
   b. Teach the stunts in sequence, progressing to others only after foundation stunts have been learned. If the "action" of a stunt can be learned on the floor, practice it there before trying it on the apparatus.
   c. Learn stunts first on a low horizontal bar before working on a high bar. Likewise on the parallel bars.
   d. Make the progression gradual. Use "lead up" stunts and the "part method" for difficult, complex stunts.
   e. Don't permit daring students to try stunts beyond their present ability.
   f. Have the pupils practice fundamentals.
   g. Place the stunts requiring a lot of strength toward the beginning of the period when the students are fresher.
7. Develop self-confidence in the performer by spotting. Fear is a safety hazard. Teach following through with the stunt—to not change the mind in the middle.

8. Don't permit students to work when overly fatigued. True, endurance can't be influenced positively until the body is brought to a fatigued condition and then the demands on it increased, but a program of work not requiring skilled responses should be instituted at this time. Work on *new* skills when the body is fresh.

9. Teach students to concentrate on the mechanics of the stunt rather than on the possible danger.

10. Correction of performance mistakes is essential for safety.

11. Good quality equipment is safer—and cheaper in the long run. Instruct in proper adjustment of equipment.

12. Use all available safety devices such as safety belts (both hand and suspended), mats, nets, spotters, crash pads, and pads on bars. It is not "sissified" to use this equipment—it is foolish not to do so.

   a. Butt the ends of mats together—do not overlap. Landing on the ridge caused by overlapped mats can cause a sprained ankle. Use "fitted" mats if possible around pommel horse and parallel bars.

   b. If two small mats are used for one large mat, secure them so they can't separate.

   c. Tape pieces of sponge rubber to parallel bars for stunts in which there is a possibility of landing on the bars.

13. Allow no horseplay. Do not joke with a performer when he is on the apparatus.

14. Be sure the performer has a clear and correct picture of what he is to do.

15. Use carbonate of magnesium on the hands to prevent their sweating, for this causes the performer to lose his/her grip. The magnesium must be sanded from the bar regularly for it cakes on the bar. If this is not done a piece of skin may be torn from the performer's hand.

16. Inspect the equipment *daily* to assure yourself that the ropes have not become frayed, that bolts have not worked loose, or that the apparatus has not been improperly adjusted. This is especially important if homemade equipment is used. Be sure that no one stands under suspended apparatus (such as rings) when it is being pulled up.

17. Teach the class to be *sure* that no one is in the way while anyone is performing.

18. Do not allow performers to follow each other too closely, especially vaulting. Everybody must await their turn.

19. Make sure that no balls or any other equipment can possibly get loose and interfere with the performers. If necessary, station guards to stop balls used by other groups from getting into the gymnastics area. Change guards regularly so that all can participate.

20. Avoid placing mats so that the ends are toward a bright window. Sunlight may momentarily blind a person at a critical moment.

21. Use gymnastics shoes (ballet slippers). If they are not available, use gym shoes and caution the performers to lace and tie them tightly. If gym shoes cannot be provided, work barefooted rather than in socks because socks cause slipping.

22. See to it that eyeglasses, rings, and necklaces are removed before participating.

23. Insist on a suitable costume, including a *supporter* for males. Do not permit loose, sloppy clothing. Remove all pins.

24. Be sure that the performers have nothing in their mouth (gum or candy).

25. Use trained spotters whenever and wherever they are needed.

26. Use homogeneous groupings. Place those who are highly skilled in one group, those of average skill in another, and those who are below average in another. This will permit pupils to work at their own rate of speed.

Attention to the details just enumerated should result in a reasonably safe experience in gymnastics.

5
Spotting

The art of "spotting" or assisting is an art indeed and should be emphasized. It serves primarily as a safety device but can also be used as an aid both in teaching and in overcoming the timidity of some pupils. The safety angle is concerned with catching, supporting, or adjusting the performer's position in order to prevent a hard fall when has has lost balance or has lost control of the body's momentum. The teaching aspect of spotting is brought about by the spotter actually putting or lifting the performer through the stunt to give him its "feel." This is called "manual manipulation." Even experienced performers should always have a spotter. Bela Caroli, coach of the world famous Olympic gymnastics champion, Nadia Comanechi, follows her every move as she works out and has his hands *on* her even when not lifting or supporting. The hands are removed momentarily as she maneuvers through her intricate routines but instantly replaced. He truly demonstrates the artistry of spotting as she personifies artistic gymnastics. For best results, the spotters should be specially trained in separate classes.

It is recommended that for a class of physical education majors who are being prepared to *teach* gymnastics, every person should have an opportunity to spot every stunt. As one finishes, he/she should spot the next performer. This spotting procedure is NOT recommended for children in the public schools. There, only the best spotters in the class should be used. Generally, one spotter should do all the spotting for the entire squad. Of course, the spotter should have the opportunity to perform the skill too, at which time the teacher or another competent person should spot.

The system of each performer spotting the following person is good for majors because it not only gives needed practice in spotting but also tends to stress the importance of spotting. Early in the semester individuals sometimes forget to spot the next person. When this happens, the next performer is instructed to loudly call attention to the fact that so-and-so forgot to spot. It isn't long then till spotting becomes habitual.

The following hints are *general* and are applicable in all spotting situations. *Specific* spotting assignments for specific stunts will be found accompanying the descriptions of those stunts.

THESE HINTS PERTAIN TO THE SPOTTER:

1. **Protection of the performer is the primary consideration.** The spotter can't afford fear. Hesitation due to thoughts of possible personal injury will render a spotter ineffective.
2. Maintain an active position, ready to move instantly.
3. Anticipate the need for spotting. A fall is *preceded* by a faulty move.
4. Stay close to the performer but do not hamper the movements. Spotting at arm's length cannot be effective.
5. Keep fingernails clipped close to avoid scratching the performer.
6. Be aware of all the movements made by the performer.
7. Don't joke with the performer as he/she works.

8. Check the performer's fall by adjusting his/her head and shoulders so that the landing will be on the feet. It is not always necessary to actually catch him/her.
9. Center the support near the head and shoulders.
10. Be sure that you know which stunt the performer is about to attempt and that you understand it fully. Analyze its mechanics and determine its danger points—the spot where the centrifugal force is greatest.
11. When possible, apply force in the direction the performer is moving. For example, lift during the move upward.
12. Coach the performer. Point out mistakes and what to do to correct them.
13. Don't use a small, weak person to spot a heavy performer.
14. Don't spot *over* the bars when spotting a performer on the parallel bars. Reach between the bars from below. Spotting is just as effective and the danger to the spotter is reduced.
15. Have confidence in yourself; this will instill confidence in the performer. Learn to recognize signs of timidity and fear and give special encouragement and help.
16. Don't allow your attention to be diverted *by anything* while the performer is attempting the stunt.
17. Don't be lured into an inattentive attitude by a long period of participation without an accident. A hand or foot may slip at *any* time. This is especially important when performers are following each other fairly rapidly.
18. Don't over spot. Let the performer do most of the work. Don't lift and hold her/him in place (except to give the "feel" of the stunt the first few times it is attempted.)
19. Use mechanical spotting devices when appropriate.

THE FOLLOWING HINTS ARE FOR THE PERFORMER:

1. Give yourself to the fall—relax. Don't kick or squirm. This makes it harder for the spotter to help you.
2. If you fall, absorb the shock of landing by rolling as you land.
3. Keep your palms downward and your fingers pointing forward when falling.
4. Always have a spotter present. Don't take unnecessary chances.
5. Follow through on each stunt. Don't change your mind in the middle of a performance.
6. Have confidence in your ability. Don't tense up in the middle of a stunt.
7. Have confidence in your spotter. Trust him/her.
8. Learn to work with your eyes open. Closing them becomes a bad habit.

To summarize, safety planning is vital; the program can be reasonably safe; attention to the listed details is imperative.

Warm-up Activities

General

1. Jogging is a good way to start. Begin loosely, lightly, relatively relaxed and gradually quicken the tempo—but not to a real fast pace. Run until mildly warm and until a slightly accelerated heart rate occurs.
2. If running in a group, vary the running patterns from time to time: circles, squares, ovals, serpentines, etc.
2. Vary the running styles: forward, backward, sideward, turning while running, etc.
4. Substitute skipping, leaping, hopping, or jumping for the regular running step.
5. Use ballet-type movements: jumps, leaps, tour jete (turning leaps), pas de chat (cat leap), etc. These movements can be worked into the floor exercise event in actual competition so they serve a dual function.

Stretching

After the general warm-up a stretching or flexibility program is advisable. First, general stretching is recommended.

1. Lie on back, arms stretched overhead. Stretch arms and legs in opposite directions as far as possible. Keep chin on neck and back on floor (don't arch the lower back). Hold for 4-5 seconds. Roll over and repeat while in front lying position.
2. Lie on back, arms sideward, palms on floor. Keep shoulders and back flat and twist legs and hips left, then right. Repeat several times. Roll over, arms overhead, and twist upper body while keeping hips flat on floor.

Next, work on specific joints: hamstring stretching.

1. From a stride stand, legs well spread, relax the trunk forward, keeping knees *straight*. Hold this position 2-3 seconds then force the trunk a little lower. Hold again, then lower a little more. Don't overdo. Expect a little discomfort.
2. Stride forward with the left foot and backward with the right. Turn the right foot to the right. Lower *slowly*. When it pulls, stop momentarily. Try to relax at that point, then lower farther if possible. Don't force *too* much. Repeat with the right foot forward.
3. From a sitting position, spread the legs as wide apart as possible. Have a friend pull them (gently) a little wider. Stretch the trunk upward by raising the chest and flattening the back (sit tall). With knees straight, slowly lower the flat back forward. Have a friend push gently on the back. Hold then go farther.
4. From a stand, spread the legs sideward as far as possible, lowering into a side splits. Follow the same format as the front splits. The goal for both splits is to be able to sit on the buttocks with the legs straight and be fairly comfortable.

The shoulder girdle also needs a lot of work. In some cases a gymnast can't hold a good handstand, not because he isn't strong enough or skillful enough, but because he is too tight in the shoulders.

1. From a prone lying position, arms overhead, keep the head on the floor while raising the *straight* arms as high as possible. The hands should be shoulder width apart. A friend may assist by gently lifting on the arms.
2. Move the arms sideward and repeat.
3. Place the arms at the sides and repeat. Keep the hands shoulder width apart.
4. Lie faceup on a bench, arms sideward and straight. Let them drop as low as possible, then slowly move them upward (toward the head) and downward (toward the feet). Keep them straight and as close to the floor as you can while moving them.
5. From a sitting position with the legs straight and together, back flat, chest raised, bring the arms overhead. A friend grasps the wrists, puts a knee in your back and gently tugs backward on your arms. This should also be done with the arms in a sideward and downward position.

6. Place the hands on a less-than-shoulder-high solid object and bend forward at the waist, keeping the arms and legs straight. Lower the trunk as far as possible, while keeping the hands on the object. Drop the head between the arms.

Gymnastics frequently calls for extreme flexibility in the upper and lower back.

1. For the upper back, lie prone on a mat with a friend sitting astride your back just at the bottom of the rib cage. Raise the arms, head, and shoulders as high as you can while the friend holds the rest of the body down. He may assist by pulling on the shoulders.
2. For lower back flexibility have the friend sit just below the hips (on the thighs) as you raise the entire trunk.
3. This can be reversed by his sitting on your upper back while you raise your *straight* legs as high as possible.

Wrist suppleness can be gained by pushing backward on the fingers of one hand with the heel of the other hand and then changing hands. Circling the wrists by rotating them in all directions will, in addition to developing flexibility, strengthen the forearms which is so necessary in pommel horse work.

As stated in principle No. 7 of the General Principles for Warm-ups, one can actually be working on specific skills to be used in competition while working on improving his flexibility. The arabesque or "scale" used in floor exercise routines (stand on one leg, body leaning forward, other leg extended backward parallel to mat, arms extended sideward) requires and develops flexibility as well as static balance. A beginner will usually have both legs partly bent, the back rounded instead of arched, and the rear leg pointing downward instead of being carried high. As he/she practices, she/he can gradually straighten the legs, arch the back, etc. The ability to hold a still position will also improve. Thus, flexibility practice enhances performance and performance helps to become more flexible. The forward and sideward splits are additional examples.

Strength and Endurance

Unlike warm-up work and flexibility exercises, strength and endurance maneuvers should come *after* the gymnastics workout rather than before. Since the SAID principle is involved here also, one must work until the muscles and body are really fatigued before benefits will accrue. Thus, if the body is fatigued before work on skills is begun, very little will be accomplished and a dangerous situation is apt to develop. When one's muscles are too tired to support, a fall and possible injury will result.

Strength and endurance are *not* the same but they are related, and work done specifically on either will have a positive effect on the other. Also, there are really two kinds of endurance—cardiovascular and muscular. The gymnast has a greater need for the latter than the former, though the cardiovascular system can't be neglected.

Some leaders in the gymnastics field advocate weight training in one or several of its various forms (weight machines, barbells, springs, rubber hoses) as a menas of increasing strength and muscular endurance, while others hold that working the various events to the point of weariness will build the strength and endurance needed and also benefit the gymnast inasmuch as he is learning to control his body as well.

The common chins, push-ups, dips, and swinging dips (see stunt No. 22, p. 144) can be used by beginners as well as advanced performers if weights are not available. The game "Chase" on page 38 can be used as an enjoyable and challenging means of developing endurance. Contests to see which gymnast can do the most circles on the horse, the most handstand push-ups, or to see who can hold a "planche" or front lever the longest are other ways to make this developmental program more interesting. Awards of a jelly bean or some such "valuable" prize can be given to the winners.

Training for holding a cross on the rings can be accomplished by having a gymnast assume a support position on the rings and lower into the cross position while someone gives some support by holding on to the ankles. The assistant gives just enough support so that the gymnast is exerting maximum effort to hold the position. Often the assistant will give a little more support than what is needed which will allow the performer to raise and lower his body a number of times before fatiguing. The arms should be kept perfectly straight when working on this. This type of work enables the performer to "feel" the correct position in which to hold the cross.

For a strong individual the normal push-ups would not do much for increasing strength, and it would take quite some time (until he got tired) before his endurance would be benefited. Therefore, someone should sit on the shoulders as he/she does push-ups. In this way he/she will gain some strength and reach the fatigue point much sooner so that endurance will increase.

Some running can be done, but a gymnast does not put much strain on his circulatory system since he/she usually finishes a routine in much less than a minute. Even the floor exercise event, which requires more cardiovascular endurance than the other events, seldom lasts much over a minute. Thus, the running need not be distance running at a relatively slow pace, but high-speed sprinting, Sprinting 60 yards, walking 25 yards, and sprinting again would be beneficial.

Strong legs with explosive power are important for vaulting and for the tumbling skills required in the floor exercise event. This power can be obtained by doing rapid, successive jumps for height or distance—or both. As proficiency is gained, do a series of "tuck" jumps. (Bring the knees to the chest and grasp the shins with the hands before landing. Keep the back straight and the head up.) The "tuck" jump can be alternated with "pike" jumps. (Raise the straight legs forward, parallel to the floor, and touch the toes with the hands while in the air.) The tuck and pike jumps can be alternated with forward or dive rolls down the mat. Work for good balance, but try to eliminate the pauses between the landings. Jumps with full twists can be substituted for the tuck and pike jumps in the roll series.

Another idea is to start in a front lying support position (push-up position) and squat through between the arms (stunt No. 14, page 69) to a rear lying support, turn or hop to a front lying support and repeat a number of times as rapidly as possible. As flexibility is gained, a "stoop" (knees straight) through rather than a squat through should be attempted.

Occasionally a device used by wrestlers to develop quickness and dynamic balance can be employed. One student gets on the hands and knees and another lays on him/her with arms and legs draped over, but not holding on. The bottom person squirms, twists, turns, and bucks in an effort to dislodge the top student. The person on top tries to stay with him/her, using only the weight, the legs, and a shifting of balance to stay atop. No holding on with the arms. If not used too often, this can add fun to the workout.

7

Methods of Organizing and Conducting Classes

The credit for success or the blame for failure in any class should go, of course, to the teacher. The effectiveness of a teacher's work depends on his/her teaching methods as much as on knowledge and skill as a performer.

Teaching methods should be based on the principles of psychology. The former formal method of teaching mere positions and movements on the apparatus is uninteresting and unchallenging. The presentation of informal, interesting stunts or routines that provide self-competition as well as competition with others—exercises that offer a challenge rather than those used just for the sake of exercise—will aid greatly in creating an interest in this activity.

The play method should predominate with youngsters. For children below the fourth grade no formal instruction in apparatus work should be given. Tumbling, however, may be started in the second grade, and many simple stunts can be taught in the first grade. Probably the only contact these children should have with apparatus is during a supervised "free play" period. On these occasions various apparatus (no rings) should be set up and the children allowed to climb on, over, and under the apparatus. The parallel bars should lose its individuality as a piece of apparatus and become simply an object to play upon. Mats must be under and around the apparatus and apparatus should be adjusted to their lowest heights. It is necessary only to watch children in a situation such as the one described above to realize that apparatus work does appeal to them.

Several equipment manufacturers have recently introduced modified apparatus for elementary school children. This equipment is made specifically for that age group and takes their needs and abilities into consideration. If this type of equipment is available, start youngsters on a gymnastics program—fit for their level of ability—much earlier than if standard apparatus only is available.

When instruction is begun, emphasis on good form (straight legs and pointed toes) should be incidental. The successful achievement of the stunt is the principal aim. It is important that beginners be successful in their first few attemps at stunts as success breeds interest. The instructor should keep this in mind when planning his lessons and should choose the easy stunts. In this way the pupil's interest will be aroused; it is a well-known fact that individuals like to do things which they can do well. Once interest has been kindled, a few failures will only tend to increase the determination to succeed. Here the element of competition may well be brought in. Care, however, must be taken to curb the too enthusiastic ones who wish to try stunts beyond their present abilities.

In addition to *succeeding* in their first few stunts, it is essential that students not get hurt while doing them. Even a slight bump early in their experience with this sport will tend to lessen the possibility of their liking it. Once interest has been manifested, however, minor bruises will not prevent them from enjoying it.

It may be necessary to give some of the pupils conditioning exercises to prepare them for working on the apparatus. This is especially true for work on the parallel bars. Special exercises such as push-ups, pull-ups, rope climing, etc., are particularly good.

The positioning of the pupils at the apparatus is an important aspect of class organization. All should be able to see the demonstration by the squad leader and the performances of the rest of the squad. All must be far enough from the apparatus so that they do not interfere with either the spotter or the performer. As the pupils finish their turns they should immediately step back into their places in the squads and the next pupils should be ready to perform. Always plan for maximum use of equipment and space. Without proper organization, pupils will spend too much time just standing, waiting for a turn. Admittedly, this is quite formal and not in accord with the newer ideas of teaching which allow for pupil exploration and experimentation. However, due to the nature of the activity it is felt greater control and more regimentation is necessary because of the possible danger to the students.

There are three fundamental methods of conducting tumbling and apparatus classes: (1) the traditional or formal method, (2) the squad method, and (3) the free play or exploratory method. There is no "best"method. The method used depends on the situation, pupils, equipment, ability of the teacher, etc. All three methods have advantages and disdavantages, and their use is dictated by the particular situation. Organization should be flexible so advantage of changing conditions can be taken.

The Traditional Method

In this method, the entire class is under the direct command of the teacher. The prescribed exercise or stunt is performed by more than one individual at the same time. In some instances (when teaching miscellaneous simple stunts, for example, or when sufficient mats are available) the entire class may do the stunt en masse. At other times, only one or two in each squad may perform simultaneously.

Yes, squads may be used in the traditional method. There is a difference, however, in the way the squads are handled here and in the squad method. All squads receive all their instruction and direction from the teacher in this method while in the squad method, they work independently, as will be shown. The number of squads used in this method usually depends on the number of duplicate pieces of available equipment.

This method of teaching is quite formal. The instructor explains or demonstrates a stunt, gives the signal for the first one in each squad to approach the apparatus and perform the stunt, and then gives the signal for his return to his squad and the approach of the next individual in line. The entire class is under the constant control of the instructor. The formality can be reduced to some extent by allowing pupils to approach the apparatus as soon as the preceding performer is finished instead of waiting for the instructor's signal to begin.

This method is primarily intended for beginners in gymnastics. It is also a good method to use at the beginning of the year's work on the apparatus, even for more advanced classes. It should precede the use of the more informal methods.

Advantages of the Traditional Method

1. Disciplinary problems are reduced since the entire class is under the direct control of the teacher.
2. Progress can be better observed, and the amount of practice on each stunt can be easily regulated.
2. The teacher's time and energy are conserved, and thus a better job of teaching should result. Demonstrations, suggestions, and corrections to the entire class can be given at the same time.
4. The instructor can conduct the class without the aid of trained squad leaders if they are not available.
5. The teacher can assure himself that all spotters are ready and in place before giving the signal for students to perform, and therefore it is safer. It cuts down the amount of "horseplay" which in turn reduces the possibility of accidents.
6. Equal participation by all is assured.

Disadvantages of the Traditional Method

1. It is too formal and therefore tends to be uninteresting. Formal methods are in disrepute.
2. It does not allow talented pupils to progress as rapidly as they are able, and it may cause poor performers to advance too rapidly, since the progression must be determined by the ability of the "average" performer.
3. It is not conducive to the development of leadership, initiative, or self-expression.
4. It tends to reduce the fun and spontaneity of the students.
5. It is not conducive to *real* discipline (self-control). The discipline in this case comes from subjection to authority.
6. It requires a number of duplicate pieces of apparatus. This is expensive and creates a space problem for storage.
7. It is not feasible in classes where there is a great variation in the ages and abilities of the students.

The Squad Method

As is implied in the name, squads are used in this method. The squads in this method, unlike those of the traditional method, are autonomous. The squad leaders do the teaching, demonstrating, and correcting. Each squad works independently and need not wait for the other squads to finish before moving on to the next stunt. Squads need not even be doing the same thing. One squad might be on the pommel horse, another on the low horizontal bar, another on tumbling, and another on the rope climb or long jump. The instructor moves from squad to squad, checking on the instruction, answering questions, and giving aid and advice.

There are three varieties of the squad method: (1) the fixed squad, (2) the rotating squad, and (3) the choice squad.

In the fixed squad method, the various squads may work on the same or different activities. Each leader has the lesson prepared for him by the teacher and he/she conducts the squad as though he/she were the teacher and the squad the whole class. The squads remain at their assigned spots for the duration of the period.

The rotating squad method is very similar. With this method, however, a given squad spends only a portion of the period at a particular apparatus. At the instructor's signal, all of the squads rotate to another piece of apparatus. The leaders remain at their original stations, and thus one who is exceptionally effective in teaching parallel bars stunts will be able to give the entire class the benefit of his/her instruction instead of just one squad. It should be pointed out, however, that this method does not allow the leader to become well acquainted with the abilities of the squad members, and that is a handicap to good teaching. Also, it prevents the leader from getting experience on the other pieces of apparatus.

In the choice squad method, the pupils are allowed to choose the squad in which they wish to participate. The apparatus is set up, and the squad leaders are stationed at their apparatus. At a signal from the instructor, students go the apparatus of their choice. The instructor decides beforehand just how many are to work at any one activity, and when that number is reached, the squad leader doesn't allow anyone else in the squad. This method is more informal, but the possibility exists that pupils may select the same piece of apparatus each time and thus fail to get a well-rounded experience. Some sort of combination of all three methods is best.

Trained squad leaders and written lesson plans for the leaders are prerequisites for the effective use of the squad method of teaching.

Advantages of the Squad Method

1. Experiences in democratic living are offered.
2. More work can be accomplished. The entire class is not held up by a few slow pupils.
3. Greater allowances for individual differences can be made. This method is especially good for use in classes in which there are wide ranges in ages and abilities.
4. Pupil leadership is promoted.
5. Individualized instruction is possible when capable squad leaders are in charge.

6. It is less formal than the class method and, therefore, it is generally more fun and more acceptable.
7. Duplicate pieces of apparatus are not needed which makes it less expensive.
8. Real discipline (self-control) is fostered rather than mere subjection to authority.

Disadvantages of the Squad Method

1. The class is more difficult to control because the instructor's attention is occupied by one squad at a time.
2. There is more danger since the instructor cannot make sure that each performer is spotted. Also, daring students may try stunts for which they are not yet ready.
3. Timid pupils, who need the work most, may intentionally miss their turns. Eager, aggressive boys may monopolize the apparatus or tumbling mat.
4. The teaching is not as effective since only one squad at a time is given the benefits of the instructor's knowledge and experience. There is actually an opportunity for students to get incorrect and even unsafe information.
5. It is wasteful of the instructor's time and energy since explanations and demonstrations will have to be repeated to each squad.

Methods of Dividing the Class into Squads

One of the problems facing an instructor who wishes to use the squad method is that of dividing the class into squads. There are a number of methods which may be used.

1. Students may be placed alphabetically into squads. This is poor since it makes no allowances for individual differences in ability, or preferences.
2. The squad leaders choose those whom they wish to have in their squads. This is poor since a gang or a clique may get together and cause many disciplinary problems. Also, there is apt to be little regard for differences in ability when choosing.
3. The students select the leader under whom they wish to serve. This is poor for the above reason, but it has the advantage of probable good cooperation between squad and leader.
4. The instructor selects the pupils for each squad according to their neuro-muscular ability. This method is good because homogeneity of ability can be secured. However, there is no assurance that the boys will work well with the leader of the squad to which they are assigned.
5. A combination of methods three and four. This is best, but the hardest to work out.

The Exploratory Method

This is sometimes called the free play method. It is not recommended for regular use. It is primarily a practice period or a period for checking aims. All the apparatus is set up at the beginning of the period and the pupils are allowed to go to any apparatus they choose and practice the stunts which were previously taught. If specific aims (stunts required on each apparatus) are set up by the instructor as a partial means of determining grades, the pupils can take their "aim charts" to the squad leader in charge of a particular apparatus and have the squad leader check the chart when or if the stunt is successfully passed. The instructor acts as a general supervisor and keeps things running smoothly, assisting those needing help. This method may also be used for a period in which pupils try to make up original stunts or combinations of stunts, either for their own pleasure or in preparation for an exhibition or demonstration.

This method is really the most difficult to handle in a satisfactory way. At first thought, it seems to be the easiest. However, the teacher must be in about 40 places at the same time, teaching, helping, encouraging, reprimanding, and in general, supervising.

Advantages of the Exploratory Method

1. It is very informal, and it creates a lot of fun for the pupils.
2. It gives each one a chance to practice on any stunt with which he/she has had difficulty, and one can spend an entire period on it if desired.

3. It may cause an individual to work more diligently because of the feeling of freedom which it creates.
4. It permits a maximum opportunity for self-control, initiative, and creativeness.

Disadvantages of the Exploratory Method

1. It does not permit much *teaching* to be done.
2. It allows opportunities for loafing.
3. It permits pupils to work on stunts they do well (to show off) instead of working on the stunts they do poorly.
4. It is dangerous unless the instructor is extremely watchful because there is opportunity for pupils to try difficult and dangerous stunts without spotters.
5. It tempts the instructor to "turn the pupils loose" and either sit down and take it easy or do some other work.

8

Techniques of Teaching

So much for the methods of organizing and conducting classes. The actual teaching procedure is another vital matter to be considered. Just as there is no "best" method of organizing a class, there is no best technique or set of techniques for teaching. A style or method used by one teacher might not be appropriate for another. The techniques used by an individual in one situation might not prove effective under other circumstances.

The teaching process is composed of many factors. To be an effective teacher it is first necessary to win the confidence and respect of the pupils. It is well to earn their affection and admiration too, if possible, but the first two items are essential. This is seldom an easy matter and often the difference between succeeding and failing in this respect hinges on some small incident. Certainly the principles of psychology should be employed. It is important to consider all of the following points: attitude, voice, enthusiasm, preparation, skill, lack of bias, personality and neatness, and discipline.

Attitude: To be a good teacher, one must like teaching and like children. The way one feels about them will be reflected in the associations with the pupils. They will be quick to sense the way the teacher feels about them and about his job. All concerned will be better off if a person who does not enjoy teaching leaves the field. Chances for success will be enhanced if the teacher makes the assumption that each child *wants* to learn something today.

Voice: The voice is frequently a reflection of one's attitude. If a teacher has a hard, rasping, voice, the students will tend to develop a dislike for the teacher, the subject, or perhaps school in general. The teacher must, of course, speak loudly enough for all to hear without having to strain, but he should not speak so loudly that his voice is a source of irritation. The goal is to speak pleasantly and distinctly, yet firmly. The quality of the voice should convey to the pupils the fact that the teacher likes them, but also it should indicate that he means what he says and expects to be obeyed. A moderate rate of speech should be used. Speaking too rapidly makes it difficult to understand; too slowly makes it boring and uninteresting.

If the traditional method of organization is being used, the teacher must be sure that he has everyone's attention before beginning to talk. The entire squad should be listening if the squad method is being utilized. When the listeners' attention has been secured, the teacher should personalize what he has to say by looking directly into the eyes of the various members of the class. He/she should let his/her eyes move from face to face instead of looking at the floor. In this way each student feels, "the teacher is speaking directly to me."

Sometimes it will not be possible to do this as you may have to be talking while demonstrating in an upside-down position. In such a situation, extra care must be taken to speak loudly and distinctly because the strain of the position will make talking difficult and will give an unnatural quality to the voice. Avoid talking with your back to some of the students. Do not talk from the *center* of a circle or square; work, instead, at the edge.

Providing goals: Both short and long term goals should be established. If the goals are not quickly met, interest will lag; if they are too quickly realized no challenge will be offered for sustained effort.

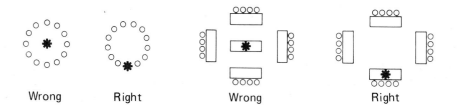

| Wrong | Right | Wrong | Right |

Making periodic evaluations: To determine the degree of achievement of goals, frequent evaluations should be made, using both written tests and performance tests. This will keep students apprised of their progress and serve as a motivator.

Enthusiasm: A good teacher can make almost anyone like almost anything. A teacher's enthusiasm for what is being taught is infectious. This enthusiasm will be mirrored in his voice, actions, and bearing. A word of warning here: be sincere. Youngsters are quick to detect sham, and a mere bubbling effervescence that is not based on a real appreciation of gymnastics will soon be noticed. Study the values of the activity—the need for it. If you as a teacher are enthusiastic about stunts and tumbling, you will have a good chance of creating enthusiasm for the work in your pupils.

Preparedness: One of the frequent causes of failure to gain the respect of the pupils—or to lose it if it has already been gained—is lack of perparation on the part of the teacher. The lesson must be well planned. You, the teacher, should know just how the mats or apparatus will be arranged, how many students will be in a squad, how the squads are to be divided, which stunts will be worked on and the order in which they will be presented, what teaching hints and devices will be used, how the spotting will be handled, how the demonstrations will be made (and by whom), how many will work at a time on each particular stunt, and which organization method (or methods) will be used. Select stunts that are interesting and challenging and those requiring a variety of skills for completion. Some balance, tumbling, and simple stunts should be included; both individual and partner.

Plan more stunts than you think you will use. It is better to have some stunts left over than to run out of things to do before the allotted time expires. Plan to stop in time so that the equipment can be put away properly and neatly.

Skill: Both children and adults tend to admire a person who does a difficult feat well. Personal skill in performance is certainly an asset. Try to master every stunt you teach. Practice much. However, though it is advantageous to be a skilled performer, this is not absolutely essential. It is possible for a teacher who is not able to do all the stunts to teach them successfully, as will be explained later.

Lack of bias: Having favorites or "teacher's pets" makes it difficult to gain the respect of the class. Try not to pick on any one person or give only a small group of persons special praise, coveted tasks, or other honors. Admittedly it is difficult to keep from doing this because a few participants just seem to stand out. If you look hard enough, however, you can find some action even in the "bad boy" of the class that is worthy of commendation. Be fair and impartial in all your dealings. This is especially important in giving grades.

Naturally, you will want your best performers to demonstrate the difficult stunts, but sometimes the poorer students can serve as bottom men, spotters or in some other special category.

If trouble starts, do your best to determine the facts and then mete out punishment to "fit the crime," regardless of the fact that the guilty party may be one of your favorites. Don't be too quick to lay the blame at the foot of the chronic troublemaker. This time he *may* be innocent.

Personality and neatness: Personality is defined as the sum of one's qualities of body, mind, and character. It is sometimes hard to change, especially in later life. Some people are naturally more likable than others. However, a neat appearance, erect posture, confident bearing, and a friendly attitude create an atmosphere that invites respect.

Discipline: Strangely enough, a teacher who expects and gets good discipline in his classes is more likely to be respected—and even liked—than is the teacher who lets the students do as they please and get by with things they shouldn't be doing. No talking or horseplay should be tolerated while explanations are being given, but a reasonable amount of talking and joviality can be permitted while the class members are performing. Care must be taken, however, because of the safety angle. Any conduct likely to lead to injury should be curbed at once.

Wholehearted effort on the part of the pupils should be demanded. It should be pointed out, however, that there are differences in the members of the class. Though all may be giving 100 percent effort, some will not succeed. Their body structure may be such that it is impossible for them to touch the floor with their hands without bending their knees. If they go down *as far as they can* the teacher should be satisfied.

There are other principles of teaching that do not have as direct an impact on the creation of a feeling of respect for the teacher but they are not any less important in getting the job of teaching done efficiently and well. These principles follow:

Combine demonstration and explanation: It has been said that a picture is worth a thousand words. That may or may not be so, but certainly if the picture (demonstration of the stunt) and the words (explanation of the stunt) are *both* given, this will be more effective than either one alone. These two phases of the presentation should be given together to save time. Children want action and should have it. The less time taken for explanations, the better.

The explanation should be clear and complete but as brief as possible. Class interest lies in activity and not in standing around listening to a long lecture. The demonstration should be as perfect as the teacher can make it so that the students will get a correct picture of what they are supposed to do. To combine the two, the teacher gets into the starting position for the stunt as he/she talks about it. Then he/she goes through the stunt slowly (if it can be done slowly) and assumes each position during the description. The common faults should be pointed out and the important teaching hints emphasized as the stunt progresses. To illustrate how this works, assume that you, as the teacher, are teaching the head balance. Choose a spot where all can see, get down on your knees and place your hands on the mat, shoulder width apart. As you do this, explain about the importance of making a triangle with the head and hands. Then point to a spot in front of the hands and say that the head goes there. Next point to the top of the forehead and inform the class that the top of the forehead, not the top of the head is placed on the mat. As you say this, place the top of the forehead in the proper position. Then explain about drawing the feet up close to the hands and raising the hips and do so as you talk about it. Continue in this way, thus providing all of the hints for the stunt.

Isolate important features: If possible, explain by using mechanical illustrations. For example, the importance of the triangle base explained above can be driven home to the students by attempting to stand a 5-by-8-inch card on its edge. After several attempts, fold the card in half, allow the two edges to separate slightly, and now stand it on edge. Ask for comments from the class as to the lesson they can learn from this. They should readily recognize the importance of the triangle base.

The need for a rounded back for a forward or backward roll can be depicted by comparing the roll of a round object (ball, piece of chalk, pop bottle, etc.) with the attempt to roll a flat object (eraser, book, block of wood). Ask why one rolled and the other didn't. Let the students discover the principle you are working on by themselves. To establish the need for bent knees (feet close to the hips) when finishing a forward roll, pair off the students, have one of the pair sit with legs straight and the other try to pull him to his feet by pulling on his hands from the front. Then have the sitting person bring his feet in close to his hips and again have the partner pull. The difference between the straight leg and bent leg positions will immediately be apparent.

It is sometimes possible to demonstrate a stunt effectively without doing it in reality. Leg circles on the pommel horse, for instance, can be clearly shown by standing behind the horse and using the arms to represent the legs. The arms can be swung back and forth and held in any position for as long as is necessary to comment about them. Since the body is held in support by the arms when actually performing the stunt, the legs cannot be held in the various positions due to the force of gravity.

To demonstrate a dismount from a piece of apparatus, it is effective to pause in the middle of the stunt by placing the feet or legs on the apparatus. Then proper positions of the body (hips extended, flexed, head turned, etc.) can be emphasized and any hand shifting can be slowly shown and explained. Finish the dismount by removing the legs and continuing. The dismount should be shown in its entirety (without pause) either before or after this phase. Some dismounts can be shown and practiced on the floor instead of on the equipment. In this way, the entire class can work at the same time.

Use pupil demonstrators: Usually the demonstrations are performed by the instructor as this saves time. Nevertheless, there are a number of reasons for selecting a pupil to give the demonstration. The advantages of pupil demonstrations are:

1. The teacher may be unable to demonstrate due to injury, illness, age, or lack of skill in performance.
2. The teacher will be able to point out the important features of the stunt as it is being done.
3. The teacher can hold the pupil in a certain position and discuss the reasons for certain actions while the class observes. This is especially important.
4. The pupils, seeing a member of their own group perform, will gain confidence in their ability to do the stunt, whereas if the teacher does the demonstrating, the pupils might think the stunt too hard for them. This is especially true in the case of complicated stunts and in those that appear dangerous.
5. The teacher can point out the reason or reasons for failure if the student fails to do the stunt. After being told how to correct his mistakes, as the demonstrator tries again and is successful, the class members can see the value of following directions to the letter.
6. The teacher can demonstrate the proper methods of spotting and assisting as the pupil goes through the performance. This will save time since he/she can't show the spotting while doing the demonstrating.
7. In partner stunts, the teacher may be too big or heavy to work with a member of the class. Therefore two students of the same size should be called to demonstrate. The pupil demonstrators need not always be the best performers in the class. Instead of using the same few students over and over again, it is better to spread the "honor" around and use many different ones. No harm is done if the person selected is unable to do the stunt without aid as the effectiveness of the spotting can then be shown.

Ask for questions: At the conclusion of the explanation and demonstration, ask if anyone has a question about the procedures. If there are questions, you can clear up any doubt or misconception in their minds. The entire organism is used in the learning process. Minds as well as bodies learn. Both must be used. Be careful, however, not to make the mistake of prolonging a discussion or allowing the class to prolong it. Remember that pupils tend to become unruly when not kept active.

Individualize instructions: Even when using the traditional method of instruction, the teacher must realize that the class is made up of individuals. Try to catch a glimpse of each performance despite the fact that a number of persons are working at the same time. This skill can be learned through practice. Many students will swear that the teacher has eyes in the back of his/her head because they have been caught in some misdemeanor while they thought the teacher wasn't watching. A good teacher will be aware of each performance and work personally with each individual in the class.

Learn to discover the timid ones in class early and then personally spot and encourage them. In this way you will help them to gain confidence in themselves. It is sometimes wise to put a few such cases off by themselves under the guidance and direction of the best leader in the class and let them practice and re-practice the easier stunts.

Offer constructive criticism: The majority of the students will not know what they are doing wrong. It is up to the teacher to tell them what is wrong and to indicate how to correct their mistakes. It is not enough to say, "That's wrong" or "You're lousy." No teacher should be sarcastic in commenting on performances. One of the most common points of weakness in a beginning teacher is his failure to correct poor work.

Corrections can be made both generally and individually. If a fault seems prevalent, it is best to stop the class and go over the point that is causing the trouble. If only one or two are making a mistake, the teacher should go to those individuals and, without drawing everyone's attention, work with them till they get the idea.

It is important also to commend good work. Sometimes instructors are so concerned with condemning the bad that they fail to recognize the good. Everyone likes a pat on the back, and if the pats are given when merited, this will encourage better work.

When an individual is working, keep your talk to a minimum. If the student is not used to it, it will be distracting because many can't concentrate on what you are saying and what they are doing at the same time. With a stunt that requires a sudden movement of some sort (push, kick extension, etc.) at a specific phase of its performance, a teacher can help the performer by calling out "Now" at the proper moment. The performer must be advised of this beforehand and be expecting the signal.

Use the "part method" when necessary: Some stunts can be broken into parts and each part taught separately. When all the parts have been learned, they can be put together into the whole stunt. There is no need to break some stunts into parts; for others, it is not only better, but safer. It is advisable to show the entire stunt first, though, before having the pupils work on its parts. By doing this, pupils will gain a clear picture of what they are working toward.

In some instances a stunt can be practiced on the floor before being tried on the apparatus. For example, the Front Dismount Right with a Half Twist Right (on the parallel bars) can be started from a front leaning support on the floor. A number of advantages can be realized in this way: (1) time saved by entire class working at the same time; (2) students less fearful since they can't fall and (3) they can go through the movements slowly—even on command and thus get the "feel" of the stunt.

Use manual manipulation: The "feel" of the stunt can be gained by having the instructor or squad leader lift or otherwise put the performer through the desired movements of the stunt. This is called manual manipulation and is a great aid in teaching many stunts. Because it gives the learner confidence, he loses his inhibitions and this too is very helpful. In the general spotting hints (Chapter 5) it is stated that "over spotting" should be avoided. In a sense, manual manipulation *is* over spotting but it can be justified during a performer's first few attempts or when he is having an unusually hard time learning.

Demonstrate spotting: When teaching a new stunt, always show just where to stand, how to grasp the performer, and whether to lift, pull, hold, or shove. This should be shown slowly, clearly, and emphatically. Then you must watch to see that the students do it correctly. It is not enough just to *tell* how the spotting is to be done; it must be *shown* as well. Also, be sure to correct student's faulty spotting procedures.

Use visual aids: Diagrams and pictures of gymnasts in action are excellent devices to use in teaching stunts. A series of pictures of a stunt in various phases of completion will give the pupils a good idea of the exact positions of the various parts of the body as the stunt is performed. The examples in this text may be so utilized. The motion picture is another great teaching aid. With this medium, the phenomenon of "slow motion" can be used to advantage. Action can be slowed down and even stopped so that the movements, or segments of movements, can be studied more precisely than when done at normal speed. Many stunts can't be done slowly; their action is so fast that an untrained eye fails to catch the details. These movements can be studied on film in slow motion. Instant replay via video tape is another great teaching aid. When students *see* their problems as they are being made it is much more effective than for the teacher to simply tell them about them. The teacher should point out the errors as the student watches.

In addition, films can be an excellent motivational device. Interest in tumbling and apparatus work can be generated by their use. Furthermore, the work of nationally known experts is available on film and the perfection of their demonstrations will go far beyond that which can be accomplished by the average teacher.

Combine stunts: When a number of the stunts have been learned, have the pupils put two or more together in a combination or short routine. The difficulty of the stunts is increased by doing this. Though there is an abundance of material for relatively advanced performers to work on, there is a lesser amount of material for beginning gymnasts. The number of beginning stunts can be increased by practicing various combinations. Then too, this permits the development of creativeness on the part of the students if they fashion their own routines. Longer routines increase physiological stimulation and develop endurance. In addition, competitive gymnastics requires the performance of stunts in a series. If the class work is intended to lead to competition, this kind of training will be excellent.

Use the gymnastics program: To get the maximum benefit from this program, both for the student and the school in general, exhibitions and demonstrations should be worked up and presented. Some of the numbers should include everybody—even fat little Sam, who has difficulty in doing a forward roll. Other numbers should be presented by a select group of participants who can demonstrate advanced work. The special group can be developed into a club or even a competitive team to represent the school in interscholastic competition.

These "shows" can be used for convocations, PTA meetings, civic club meetings, between halves of basketball games, and so forth.

9

Games and Contests Involving Gymnastics

Tumbling and apparatus stunts are, in themselves, fun and interesting to do for most students. Some however, do not enjoy participating in this activity. For most of these people, excitement and interest can be generated through the wise use of games and contests. Indeed, even those who are already captivated by working with the stunts can have their interest heightened by this means. The aroused competitive spirit will cause an even greater expenditure of energy by the gymnasts, thus increasing the benefits. Nor should the occasional use of a games program be overlooked even in the training of competitive gymnasts. A break from the usual routine of work will add zest to the workouts.

Some degree of proficiency in performance should be attained by the students before they participate in the games. The thrill of a contest frequently excites students to the degree that they are less sure of themselves and some body control is lost. Some, in the spirit of competition, will throw caution to the winds in an all-out effort to win, thus taking chances on stunts they would not ordinarily attempt. For these reasons it is imperative that exact rules and controls be established by the teacher regarding which stunts can be performed and which ones can't be tried. Keep equipment at low heights and use plenty mats and spotters.

Though one of the main purposes of the games is to have fun, the instructor must see that students don't just fool around. When participants get silly and laugh and giggle as they "make like a clown," they lose control of their own actions and joking spotters are not ready for emergencies. A joyous, fun-filled period can be experienced without losing sight of the need for caution and the practice of safety measures.

Even after the students have become skillful enough to participate in the games, the games periods should be used only occasionally. Little instruction is given at these times, and it is not advisable to try to learn new tricks or even to perfect skills previously learned. So, though they are valuable and definitely deserve a place in the total program, and though the pupils themselves will frequently ask for "more," these periods should be used sparingly and judiciously.

The following games and contests are recommended. Your ingenuity can devise others.

Add One

Traditionally this game is played on the trampoline, but there is no reason why it cannot be adapted for use on the other apparatus. Its use can facilitate the building of routines; the development of skill in going from one stunt into another; the development of stamina, originality, and creativeness; and it certainly can add more fun to the program.

The first member of the squad approaches and does a stunt on the trampoline (it could be a mount on any other piece of apparatus). He/she gets off and the next in line does that stunt (or mount) plus another stunt and then gets off. The third member performs the first two and adds one more stunt to the series. This continues until all have had a turn, at which point the first one in the squad returns and continues adding to the series.

Each member must do the stunts in the exact order indicated. It is advisable, therefore, for each player to silently repeat the stunts as they are being performed. If a person omits a stunt, performs one out of the proper order, or fails to add one to the routine, that person is eliminated from further competition in that game. The game continues until all but one are eliminated. This player is declared the winner and a new game is begun. If several pieces of apparatus are being used, the winners from each squad can be brought together for a grand championship game.

Care should be taken to avoid waste of time while changing performers, especially on the trampoline. The next person to go should be ready as soon as the preceding performer gets off.

Horse

This game is almost identical to the one above, Add One. The difference lies in the manner of dealing with those who miss a trick, miss the proper sequence, or fail to add a new trick. Some contend that it is a bad policy to eliminate anyone from participation—especially the poor participants who need the most work and who invariably are the ones who miss early in the game.

In Horse, when a person misses the first time, he acquires the letter *H*. The game then proceeds, but no one is eliminated. If a person misses again, the letter *O* is added to the *H*. The next time he misses he gets an *R*. This continues until one individual has missed five times and has received all the letters of the word horse. He is designated as the loser and a new game is begun.

Chase

This is a dual contest that is a lot of fun and will do much to improve cardiovascular endurance and stamina. It is usually played on the parallel bars as there are two ends to work on, but it may be adapted to other pieces of equipment if duplicate pieces are available. Two contestants stand at the parallel bars, one at either end, in a cross stand frontways (see chapter on nomenclature for description) with their hands on the bars. At a signal, they both jump up, do a rear dismount right (or any stunt selected by the instructor) and run to the opposite end of the bars where they repeat the maneuver. This continues until one performer is able to catch the other, due either to superior speed or greater endurance.

The same idea can be carried out with two (or more) pommel horses. Two (or more) men stand in a side stand frontways, one at each horse, and do a squat vault (or another stunt) over the horse. Upon landing, they each run to the next horse and repeat the vault. This continues until one is able to catch up with and tag the person in front of him.

Where only one of each piece of apparatus is available, the different pieces can be set up and the same plan followed with different stunts being done. Care must be taken in the selection of stunts for if one stunt than can be finished rapidly is followed by one that takes much longer to finish, the race may be over quickly because the contestant on the first event may catch the one in front before he/she completes the first trick. Each stunt, consequently, should take about the same length of time.

Keep the equipment at relatively low heights and be sure that the area is well covered with mats because when the contestants are equally matched the contest can go on until both are extremely fatigued and thus would be more prone to falls. In connection with the safety factor, judicious selection of stunts is also important. Stunts involving inverted positions of the body are contraindicated because of the fatigue, excitement, and speed factors. Should a slip occur, the body should be in an upright position. Since not all students would be involved in the chase at the same time, each man at each apparatus should be correctly and carefully spotted.

Relay Races

Relay races can be set up using any of the simple stunts with forward motion or any of the tumbling stunts—either individual or partner—as the means of locomotion. For example, a class of twenty-four could be divided into four teams of six men each with each team lined up in single file in front of its mat. The first person could do three forward rolls down the mat and then three backward rolls, touch off the second who would do the same, etc. The fact that each one has to use the mat coming back reduces the possibility of the next one starting before the predecessor has finished. The same type of race could be set up on the apparatus.

Contests

Any number of contests could be arranged. For example, each one could see how many successive swivel hips he could do on the trampoline. The one completing the highest number would win. If a trick were used that some of the class members could do almost indefinitely, it would be wise to set a limit and say, "let's see how many in the class can do twenty." This would prevent the monopolizing of the apparatus by a few class members. Another way of handling such a situation would be to see who could do the most in a specified period of time: twenty seconds, thirty seconds, etc. Should any of these contests involve strength and endurance as a limiting factor more than skill (such as swinging dips on the parallel bars), it is suggested that they be held toward the end of the period rather than at the beginning. In this way, the fatiguing effects of the contest will not slow down the learning of new skills that might be presented in the lesson.

Obstacle Course

The various pieces of equipment can be set up in the gymnasium and the class can be directed under, around, over, and through the apparatus using pertinent mounts, stunts, dismounts, and vaults. When this is done against a stopwatch and the youngsters are trying to set a record, a very vigorous workout can be achieved quickly. Used in this way, an obstacle course becomes an excellent conditioner.

Meet

Another type of contest is between teams. The class can be divided into two (or three) teams. Four, five, or more consecutive stunts can be worked into routines by each team, and then the routines can be judged by the instructor. The routines can either be compulsory (each gymnast does the same series of stunts which has been made up previously by the instructor) or optional (each one makes up his own sequences).

In the compulsory routines, only the form (execution) is judged. If optional routines are used, the difficulty of the stunts and the combinations also will have to be taken into consideration. The teacher may want to conduct the meet on two levels—those with poorer skills can perform a relatively simple compulsory routine while the better performers can compete among themselves using optional routines.

Several days, the number dependent on the time allotment, should be set aside to let the students practice and attempt to perfect the routines before the meet is held.

Rush

This game is played with two teams and two identical pieces of apparatus. Each team is numbered consecutively and stands in front of its apparatus on a line about fifteen feet from it. The instructor calls off a number and the name of a stunt. The two (one from each team) with the number called, rush to their apparatus, perform the named stunt and rush back to their line. The first one to cross the finish line scores a point for his/her team.

The numbers should be called at random and each contestant must be alert and ready to move as soon as the number is called. The name of the stunt should be called immediately after the number. Since no one knows what stunt is to be performed until after starting to the apparatus, quick reaction time and mental quickness are as important as speed of movement.

All the stunts which are used should already have been well learned before playing this game. Stunt names might be printed on cards, the cards shuffled and then the stunts called out in the order they turn up.

The number on each team should not be more than eight to ten. If the class is large, form three or four teams.

Whistle Stop

This game is patterned after the game of Musical Chairs. Arrange three or four pommel horses (or other equipment) in a large circle. The apparatus can either be all the same or different. Line the class up in front of one of the horses and have the students follow the leader in a vault or a mount and dismount over each of the pieces. The teacher (or another person) blows a whistle and those who are either in flight or on the apparatus as the whistle blows are eliminated from the game (or have a point scored against them). Only those who are on the floor at the time the whistle is blown are safe. The line must keep moving. No one may hesitate in front of a piece of apparatus in anticipation of the blast of the whistle. The whistle blower should either be blindfolded or have his back to the group playing the game.

Stunt Golf

Designate 9 (or 18) areas in the gym as "holes." At each hole have the name, picture, or description of a stunt on a card. Divide the class into twosomes or foursomes and have each group go around the course, attempting the assigned stunts at each hole. Those who succeed on their first attempt get one point (or stroke). If they fail the first time but succeed on the second, they get two points. If they fail again they get one more try, scoring three points for success. If they again fail, they move on to the next hole, having scored *five* points. The one with the *lowest* score wins.

Challenge (Classroom Game)

This is a team game in which two teams are selected. A member of team A comes to the front of the room, performs a stunt, and challenges "Jim" from team B to duplicate it. Team A gets a point if Jim fails to do it. (The teacher is the judge as to whether or not Jim succeeds.) Then Jim does a stunt and challenges a member of team A to do it. No one can be called more than once in any one game. This will prevent teams from calling the poorest performer on the other team all of the time.

The stunts to be performed can be stated by the teacher or left up to the individuals (with certain restrictions imposed by the teacher).

10

Squad Leaders

Utilizing pupils in the role of squad leaders is an important phase of instruction. If at all possible, a "leaders' class" should be organized. This is a prerequisite for the adequate functioning of a class being conducted by the Squad Method and is a valuable adjunct to the functioning of a class using either of the other methods.

Pupil assistance is valuable because it—

1. enables the instructor to conserve energy,
2. allows the effectiveness of the teacher's instruction to spread and extend,
3. permits greater individualization of instruction,
4. provides another means of developing the character and personality of the pupils who serve as leaders,
5. encourages a "spirit of service,"
6. promotes closer cooperation between the class and the instructor and tends to lessen disciplinary problems,
7. provides a corps of workers who can set up equipment beforehand and see to it that all needed accessories are at hand,
8. provides trained people for demonstrating stunts,
9. provides trained people for spotting,
10. encourages the development of leadership qualities.

There is some basis for the statement, "Leaders are born, not made." However, even if the leadership qualities are there, they must be nurtured and trained. This is necessary if the individual is to realize his/her full potential as a leader and if leadership abilities are to be pointed in an acceptable, worthwhile direction. The development of leadership qualities is one of the aims of general education, and the gymnasium "laboratory" is one of the best places to strive to reach that goal.

A special time should be set aside for the training of the leaders. The leaders' class may be considered as an extracurricular activity and function as a club or team, or it may be a class for which extra credit is granted. In this class, the potential leaders must be taught more than mere mastery of the stunts. They must learn how to *teach* and how to *spot* each stunt. They must be shown just where to stand or kneel for each stunt and where and how to hold, lift, or catch each performer. Also, it is necessary for them to know whether the part or whole method should be used when students are learning, and what particular teaching hints and techniques should go with each stunt. In addition, they should be able to assist in the evaluation of a pupil's performance and officiate in class competition, though the instructor of the class has the ultimate responsibility for assigning grades.

The problem of selecting squad leaders is an important and usually difficult one. Following is a list of desirable qualities for squad leaders. They should—

1. be proficient in performance,
2. be able to teach stunts to others,

3. be strong enough to spot effectively,
4. be courageous enough to spot effectively,
5. be democratic and fair,
6. be well liked and able to command the respect of their classmates,
7. be tactful and patient,
8. be reliable and honest,
9. be dependable (to be useful and effective they must not miss either the leaders' class or the regular classes to which they are assigned).

In short, the squad leaders should have all of the qualities of a good teacher save those of professional training and experience.

Various methods of selecting leaders are in use. These include—

1. appointment by the instructor,
2. election by the class or squad,
3. selecting volunteers,
4. appointment after demonstration which tests their skill and knowledge.

It is advisable to give leaders a distinctive uniform or emblem both as a reward for their services and as a badge of their authority. The degree of authority, responsibility, and duties of the squad leaders must be mutually understood by the teacher, the leaders, and the other pupils. Frequently, the boys and girls, in the leader's class or club can be formed into an exhibition team or developed into a varsity team for competition.

11

Lesson Plans

Lesson plans are needed in order to insure the maximum attainment of objectives. The first procedure is to determine the amount of work that should be covered during the pupil's entire school career. The elementary, the middle school, the junior high, and the senior high school should cooperate closely in this planning. The amount of work to be covered in each of the levels then should be decided. From this, a further breakdown should be made for each year and semester. Progression must be maintained throughout the years if a satisfactory program is to result, and it is only through the construction and use of lesson plans that this progression can be assured. Repetition of the same few stunts year after year is not conducive to the enjoyment of the activity.

It is necessary to keep in mind the final, overall picture; daily lesson plans directed toward this final goal must be made out. Lesson plans that contain all the needed information, down to the smallest detail, will help to keep things running smoothly.

Factors to be considered when constructing a lesson plan are the following:

1. The previous gymnastic experience and ability of the group.
2. The most advantageous use of time, space, and equipment.
   a. The best size for squads is six to eight.
   b. If insufficient equipment is available, it is best to organize half the class into another activity that needs little supervision so that the teacher can devote his time to the group in gymnastics. The following day, of course, the two groups would reverse activities.
3. The warm-up period which should be placed at the beginning to avoid pulled muscles.
4. The selection of a wide range of stunts.
   a. Do not sacrifice mastery for variety.
   b. Select stunts which take care of various body parts rather than a series of stunts which overwork one muscle group.
5. The avoidance of monotony.
   a. Do not repeat an already well-learned stunt too often.
   b. Do not work too long *at one time* on a difficult stunt. Rather than spend an entire period on the stunt, spend about 10 minutes each day for a number of days.
6. The arrangement of stunts in progressive order (from easy to difficult).
7. The maintenance of *all* safety standards.
8. The teaching techniques to be used for each specific stunt.
9. The listing of all materials and equipment needed for the lesson and where they should be placed.
10. The listing of the definite steps needed to present the lesson with minimum delay and maximum efficiency.
11. The availability of teaching aids.
12. The provision for ways of measuring progress.

Devise various tests, both written and performance (skill) tests, both formal and informal.

12

Testing and Grading—Evaluating

Since the beginning of formal schooling the matter of "grading" has been a problem. Many systems have been invented, tried, evaluated, discarded, and resumed. Few people feel that their method takes care of all their problems or answers all their questions. Some advocate abolishment of grades entirely. Others suggest grading on a pass-fail basis only. Much research has gone into the problem and still there is little agreement as to which system is the best.

What factors should be considered in arriving at a grade? Is attendance important? How about cleanliness and neatness? Should a skillful child who happens to be disruptive in class receive a higher grade than one who is clumsy but a model of deportment? Another consideration is effort. How does a poor performer who tries and tries and never gives up compare to a "natural" athlete who never breaks a sweat and yet performs much better?

Then too, one must know the objectives of the class. Determining marks for physical education majors who are preparing to teach gymnastics to school children requires a different set of standards than those that will be used by those majors when they are faced with the problem of evaluating the youngsters they teach. Since nobody yet has devised a system that satisfies everybody there is little hope that following suggestions will meet with unanimous approval. However, some guidance should help a little.

Evaluating the Prospective Gymnastics Teacher

Skill in performance is a valuable aid to a teacher. One who can "show" a student how it should be done is more effective than a teacher who can only "tell" how it should be done. Using both together (showing and telling) is more effective than either one alone. A master teacher ought to be able to "demonstrate" well.

Some will argue that skill in performance is not needed but it is difficult to gain the respect of the class members if they know that you are a poor performer.

A second important ingredient in the make up of a good gymnastics teacher is the ability to "spot" the gymnasts and to manipulate their bodies in such a manner as to give them the "feel" of the stunts. If they have confidence in you as a spotter they will be more relaxed in their attempts and be less reluctant to try. Also, if you are able to put them through the movements while supporting them, they will learn much more quickly.

Thirdly, an able teacher must understand and be able to apply sound teaching techniques. It is one thing to be able to *do* the tricks and quite another to be able to get *someone else* to be able to do them. Occasionally, a gifted gymnast may be able to accomplish very difficult maneuvers without really understanding "how" he does it and be unable to teach them to another. One must have knowledge of the proper progressions and correct lead-up procedures. Some apparatus moves can be learned on the floor then moved up to the apparatus and taught by the part method. Tied in with the technical knowledge is that nebulous quality often called personality; the capacity to "get along with" others.

A fourth quality found in better than average gymnastics teachers is a wide knowledge of the sport itself. Students will ask questions and the teacher should be able to give correct answers. Of course, no one knows everything. There are times any teacher will have to admit he/she doesn't know. However, the fewer times this is necessary the easier it is to gain and retain the respect of the students.

The last element and perhaps the one that helps to integrate all the components into a unified whole is the "attitude" of the prospective teacher. Just how interested in learning, teaching, and helping is the major? Sometimes, those who rate very high in the skill category may feel that since they can already execute the moves there is no reason why they should do them. They may fail to see the importance of working with the less skilled and refrain from showing and explaining to them. This is the very experience they should be acquiring to help them to become good teachers. At the other end of the continuum is the clumsy, uncoordinated individual who just stands around and doesn't try. There are several possible reasons for this lack of participation:

1. Fear of injury
2. Embarassment—fear of being laughed at
3. Frustration
4. The feeling of "What's the use? I'll never get better."

Other worthy objectives of physical education (social, emotional, personal growth) are not included in this discussion because they are not germane to the issue and because they are so difficult to measure. Any instructor who wishes to consider them in arriving at a grade may, of course, do so.

Now, if we agree on *what* to measure, *how* do we measure these divergent qualities? Again, there are differences of opinion as to how it should be done. Let's consider several.

Skill: Skill can be measured by having the class members take a proficiency or performance test. The test items (stunts) should be selected and listed for the students. Usually a period or part of a period is allowed for special practice on those skills because the purposes of testing and grading include furnishing an inducement to improvement as well as determining the present ability of the testee. After the practice, the students perform the stunts one at a time and are graded by the teacher.

A scale of "0" for complete failure, "1" for poor performance, "3" for average and "5" for excellent is suggested. This is more flexible than a system of 0, 1, 2, 3 because it allows for a situation in which the performance is not really poor, yet not quite average and also when the instructor can't quite decide if it's average or excellent. A prerequisite for use of this scale is the establishment of standards for each degree of perfection. The standard may be written and published to the class or merely in the mind of the instructor.

Since the majors will one day be faced with the task of assigning marks to their students it is good to have them evaluate each other's performance. Discussions can then be held as to why the student awarded a "5" while the professor gave a "3" for a particular performance. Granted, this procedure will take considerable time but it will be a valuable training device for the prospective teachers.

Some authorities recommend scoring routines rather than individual stunts because competitive gymnastics does deal with routines. That is a good method and the reasoning is sound, but it takes longer to learn routines and routines are learned one skill at a time anyway and then combined. Teachers do not usually demonstrate routines, especially for physical education *class* gymnastics. Of course, routines are more important for coaching teams.

Spotting: It is recommended that evaluation of the majors' "spotting" skills be done in two ways: 1) Observation of their spotting competency, alertness, and knowledge during class work-out times and 2) a written examination on the techniques of spotting selected stunts. By having all the students spot their classmates everyone will have to demonstrate their spotting. During the semester the instructor can arrive at a pretty accurate estimate of each student's spotting proficiency.

The written test should contain questions about general spotting (covered in chapter 5) and specific spotting (hints accompanying the descriptions of the stunts). The spotting exam may be incorporated in the regular "end of the semester" exam or given separately.

Teaching: We learn to teach by teaching. Therefore, the class members should teach each other for practice. Preparation for this is made by studying assigned stunts and then teaching them. Subjective judgement on the part of the professor is used to evaluate the teaching act in terms of completeness (including spotting instructions) clarity, poise, voice projection, ability to answer students' (and professor's) questions, etc. The "tricks of the trade" covered in chapter 8 should be displayed by the student teachers. As the class works on the stunt taught, the student teacher should correct, spot, offer advice, answer questions, and, in short, act as though he/she is the hired instructor of the course.

After the class members have gone through the skill a few times the professor should request comments on the teaching performance. The remarks (both praise and critique) are aimed at solidifying strong points and improving weak points so that this phase becomes a "learning" as well as a "grading" occasion.

Obviously, the class would move faster and more stunts could be covered if the instructor did all of the teaching, but then the purpose of the course would not be met as well if the students didn't get this teaching experience.

Gymnastics Knowledge: Determination of a grade for this element can be made by administering either a written or oral examination or both. The questions here should be cognitive as well as rote memory. Questions such as "What would happen if a gymnast extended early in . . . ?" or "What are two causes of a performer spraining a wrist while doing . . . ?" are examples.

Attitude: To measure students' attitudes we must again fall back on the subjective judgment of the instructor. A reasonably valid measure can be obtained if the instructor is cognizant of the importance of this phase and consciously observes the students for the qualities that reveal their attitudes. This should not be a "one shot" affair but an ongoing study throughout the whole semester.

What are the characteristics that distinguish persons with good attitudes from those with poor or undesirable attitudes? Certainly the amount of time and effort spent in class related activity during the period is a good indicator. What do the students do when not spotting or performing? Do they watch the other performers, offer suggestions, ask questions, tell those having trouble with a skill how to improve? Are they always ready for their turn to practice? Do they offer to demonstrate? Are they eager to learn? Do they come early and stay late? (Instructors should be aware that some students can't do this because of other obligations before and/or after class.) A student who is genuinely interested will reveal that fact in his/her actions.

Another thought on evaluation is to have every member of the class select the two or three best (in their opinion) gymnastics teachers in the class and the two or three poorest. Each one should eliminate his/her own name from consideration at either end. The reasons for the selection of best and poorest should accompany the list.

Making the selections and giving the reasons for them will cause the students to think about the qualities of a good teacher (and a poor one) and most will think about where they rank in the list. It will also give them practice in this important phase of teaching. Another benefit lies in the fact that the instructor can compare his/her evaluations with those of the students. In most cases the results will confirm his/her opinions. In a few, where there are divergencies, it may cause a restudy of the factors involved. The restudy might result in a change of opinion and thus a change in grade.

Evaluating School Children in a Gymnastics Class

The purpose for this class is quite different from the situation above. Therefore the grading procedure will be different. They will not be teaching so that factor will not be considered. Only a few will be spotting (see chapter on Spotting) so that too is eliminated. Knowledge of mechanical principles, how competition is conduced, what to look for when watching a meet, etc. is of some importance from the standpoint of interest so a short written examination is appropriate. However it should not be weighted very highly. Attitude can be counted in much the same way as with the major students.

Skill in performance should receive the highest value. It can be measured as suggested for the majors or as follows: The stunts and combinations desired for each event are listed on a "check-off" sheet. When a student feels ready to perform a specific stunt he/she goes to the teacher (or a previously trained squad leader) and performs the move. If the performance is acceptable, that stunt is checked off and the student works on another skill. A separate check list is kept for each person. At the end of the semester the skill grade is determined by the number or percentage of stunts checked off. This is informal and allows the children to work on any of the skills they choose. The informality makes it enjoyable for the participants.

The check-off system can be used once a month, once a week, or every day. Once a week is probably best. It is important to set up standards for earning a check mark on each stunt.

13

Rules of Competitive Gymnastics

Men's Rules

The present increased interest in gymnastics has prompted a great increase in the number of competitive gymnastics teams in high schools, colleges and clubs. Because of this, a chapter dealing with the rules of competition is included here despite the fact that the majority of stunts presented in this book are of a beginning nature and the major purpose of this book is to aid the teacher in conducting gymnastics stunts in the regular physical education program.

It was stated earlier that an exhibition or competitive team should be an outgrowth of such a program. The differences between classwork and competitive work lie in the length of combinations, the increased difficulty of the stunts, the form, style, or perfection with which the stunts are executed, and the fact that the routines (combinations of stunts) are evaluated and a "winner" declared.

In gymnastics, as in other sports, there are different sets of rules made up by different governing bodies. The main national groups are the National Collegiate Athletic Association (NCAA), the National Association of Intercollegiate Athletics (NAIA), the Association of Intercollegiate Athletics for Women (AIAW), The United States Gymnastics Federation (USGF), the Amateur Athletic Union (AAU), and the National Federation of State High School Associations (NFSHSA). Various collegiate conferences, local AAU groups, and state high school athletic associations deviate somewhat from the rules set up by these national organizations. They often decide on special rules for *intra*conference competition, but national championship meets must follow the national rules. *Inter*conference competition also follows the national rules unless the coaches of each of the schools agree upon a given divergence. However, there is more unity than one would suppose since the International Gymnastic Federation (FIG) published its *Code of Points* in 1968. This code forms the basis for the rules of the various groups mentioned above and the divergences have been slight.

In addition, the rules committees of these organizations meet each year to consider possible rule changes. It is not possible, therefore, to include a set of rules and say, "These are THE RULES of gymnastics." Instead, a brief résumé of the commonly accepted rules will be given. It should be noted that even the names of two of the events have recently been changed—though not accepted by everyone. The side horse is now called the "pommel" horse, and the long horse event is simply called "vaulting" and will be referred to in that way in this text.

Rules Summary

Events and Order of Competition

Men and Boys	Women and Girls
1. Floor Exercise	1. Vault
2. Pommel Horse	2. Balance Beam
3. Rings	3. Uneven Parallel Bars
4. Vault	4. Floor Exercise
5. Parallel Bars	5. All Around
6. Horizontal Bar	
7. All Around	

The All Around event is not counted toward team score in collegiate dual meet competition but is frequently used in high school dual meets. The All Around is always contested in championship meets on all levels.

Men's Event Specifications

Floor Exercise: The mat is 42' x 42' and a minimum of 1" in thickness. (Before 1965 this event was performed on the bare floor. Because of the expense of the mat, many high schools compete in "strip" floor exercise, using a tumbling mat 60' x 5'). An area 39'4½" x 39'4½" is marked off by white lines on the regulation mat and points are deducted if the gymnast steps on or over any of the lines. A time limit is specified in international and USGF competition, but not in high school or collegiate contests. The routine consists of a combination of stunts or moves displaying balance, strength, agility, and tumbling skills. The whole routine is tied together with rhythmic transitional movements and ballet type leaps and turns making up a smoothly flowing, coordinated routine that covers all or most of the prescribed area.

Pommel Horse: (Formerly called "side horse"). This is a leather covered cylindrical body 64" long and 14" wide, supported by two uprights (sometimes four legs) at a height of 45¼". Two pommels (handles) are fastened to the horse about 17" apart. They are 4¾" high making the top of the pommels 50" from the floor. The left end is called the "neck" the middle (between the pommels) is the saddle, and the right end is called the "croup." In competition, stops or hesitations result in point deductions. The performer is required to move to and work on all three areas (neck, saddle, croup) of the horse. Both regular and reverse scissors must be executed (one of which must be done twice in succession) and double leg circles must predominate.

Rings: The rings are suspended from cables from the ceiling or from a ring rig 18'4½" above the floor. The cables are 19½" apart and the rings are 8'6½" from the floor. Competitive rings are made of wood, but some gyms have iron rings covered with either rubber or leather. At least two handstands are required, one obtained by strength, the other by swinging into it. An additional strength move is also required but the swing type moves should outnumber the strength skills. The rings themselves must not swing forward and backward. Points are deducted if this occurs.

Vaulting: The regular pommel horse may be used for this event by removing the pommels. The holes for the pommel shafts should be plugged or covered with tape to prevent the vaulter's fingers from entering. The horse is placed with the croup toward the vaulter and is set at 53" in height. A ½" wide white line is taped or painted around the middle of the body to separate the croup and neck grip zones. If the vaulter's hands touch this line, 0.5 point is deducted. Only one vault is permitted. Each vault has a specific difficulty rating ranging from 7.0 to 9.8. A spring board is used to aid the vaulter.

Parallel Bars: (Frequently called "P" Bars) To wooden (or fibre glass) bars supported by four posts connected by a frame. The width and height of the bars are adjustable. The bars are 11'6" long, 5'7" to 5'9" high and 18" to 20" in width. "Hold" moves (static positions) are limited to a maximum of three per routine. The performance of a stunt with a simultaneous release of both hands to a simultaneous re-grasp of both hands is required. The strength move which used to be required is no longer needed, but most good routines still use one.

Horizontal Bar: (Often referred to as "High" bar.) This is a steel bar supported by uprights at a height of 8'4⅜". The bar is 7'10½" in width from pivot point to pivot point. For a maximum score, the gymnasts must perform a move with a double (simultaneous) release and regrasp and either work in an "el" grip (hands everted) or in a dorsal suspension (back toward the bar) for a full 360° rotation. Both in bar (body close to the bar) and out bar (body extended at arms length away from the bar) work must be executed and no stops or pauses are allowed.

Women's Event Specifications

Vaulting: This is the same as for the men except that the horse is turned sideways to the vaulter and lowered to a height of forty seven inches. Each of the possible vaults has a predetermined value of up to 10 points. Judges award points up to the maximum score of the vault by evaluating the preflight, support, after-flight, and form and technical execution of the vault. Women perform two separate vaults, counting only the better of the two attempts.

Floor Exercise: The equipment for this event is identical to that used for the mens' event. The requirements, however, for men and women differ markedly. Women's routines are choreographed to music; therefore, dance type skills including leaps, turns, and body waves are important to the composition of the routine. Strength movements are not required but tumbling/acrobatic skills are necessary elements and allow the gymnast to perform in the entire area of the mat. The duration of the event must be between a minute and a minute and a half.

Balance Beam: This piece of equipment is a 16'4" wooden beam rising 3'11¼" above the ground. It is 3⅞" wide with the edges rounded, and the top surface may be padded for the comfort of the gymnast. Dance, balance, and acrobatic skills are used to meet the requirements of the event. The gymnast must perform high and low on the beam, and at some time cover the entire length of the beam. This event is similar to performing floor exercise on a narrow beam, and as such places great emphasis on balance.

Uneven Parallel Bars: The name describes the event. The two bars are parallel, but one is higher than the other. The upper bar is 7'6½" above the floor and the lower bar is 4'11" high. The width of the bars is adjustable to a maximum of 2'9⅞". This event has evolved from mens' even parallel bars. Although women at one time performed on parallel bars, the event was not satisfactory because of the necessary emphasis on strength. The bars were, therefore, made uneven so that the emphasis could be changed from strength to swinging type movements. Circling, kipping, and somersaulting movements are used to work above, below, and between both bars. The gymnast must also perform changes of direction and grips. Movements must be continuous and pauses are penalized accordingly.

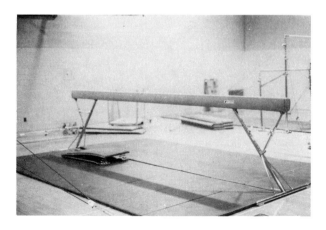 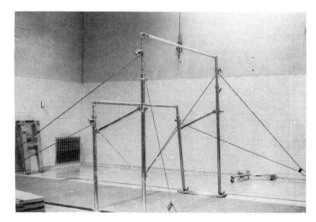

14

Nomenclature

Terminology in gymnastics is quite confusing. Identical stunts are known by different names and even the names of the pieces of apparatus are not completely standardized. An attempt has been made to standardize nomenclature (system of names used to describe stunts, systems of gymnastics, apparatus, and methods of teaching) by the Committee on Nomenclature of the YMCA. The AAU has also done some important work on this problem. However, there still is little standardization due probably to the fact that so many sources have contributed to the development of gymnastics, and also because those in different sections of the country refuse to give up the nomenclature with which they grow up and are therefore used to. There is at present a move to turn to international nomenclature as promulgated by the FIG.

The following definitions and explanations of terms and names are used throughout this text.

Relationship of Performer to Apparatus

In order to describe a performer's position in relation to the apparatus, it is necessary to establish two axes. One, the performer's axis, is represented by an imaginary line running from shoulder to shoulder and extending beyond them indefinitely. The second is the apparatus axis, and this is represented by an imaginary line running the length of the apparatus extending indefinitely. For example, a performer facing East would have his axis running North and South. A parallel bar with the ends facing North and South would have its axis running North and South (through the length of the bar).

When the performer's axis crosses the axis of the apparatus, the performer is in a *cross* position. If the axes are parallel, he/she is in a *side* position. This is true whether standing, sitting, hanging from, or supported by the apparatus.

Further, the surface of the body that is toward the apparatus is also considered when naming the position. For example, a performer standing in front of the pommels of the side horse would be in a *side stand* (the two axes are parallel) frontways (the front surface is toward the apparatus). If the right side is toward the side of the parallel bars it is a *cross stand right*. If the right side is toward the end of the bars he is in a *side stand right*. When facing away from the end of the bars he/she is in a *cross stand rearways*. The stand is always named first and then the position, according to the body surface.

Stands—A stand is a fixed position in which the body is supported by the feet either on the floor or on the apparatus.
  a. Squat stand—knees bent.
  b. Straddle stand—legs spread (feet apart).

Supports—A support is a position on the apparatus in which the weight is borne by the hands, the forearms, or the upper arms with the shoulders *above* the point of support.
  a. Straight arm support—The hands suport the weight and the arms are straight.
  b. Bent arm support—Same as above but the arms are bent.

c. Forearm support—The forearms support the weight (used on parallel bars).

d. Upper arm support—The underside of the upper arms bear the weight. The hands grasp the bars in front of the point of support (used on parallel bars).

e. Leaning support—A support in which the weight is supported by the hands and another part of the body (the thighs, toes, or heels).

f. Balance support—The body is in an "L" position (hips flexed) both arms supporting and the legs straddling one of the arms (used on the pommel horse).

g. "L" support—The body is in an "L" position (trunk upright, legs parallel to the floor) with the legs either together or straddled and the weight being carried on the hands. (Used on floor, parallel bars, and rings.)

Hangs—A hang is a position on the apparatus in which the weight is borne by the hands, knees, or toes with the shoulders *below* the point of support.

a. Straight arm hang—The hands support the weight and the arms are straight.

b. Bent arm hang—Same as above but the arms are bent.

c. Inverted hang—A hang with the head downward and the rest of the body extending upward. It may be:

    (1) Knee hang—The weight is supported by the knee joint while the rest of the body hangs downward.

    (2) Toe hang—As above but the toes support the weight.

    (3) Inverted hang—The hands support the weight and the shoulders and trunk are below the hands while the feet and legs are above the hands.

    (4) Inverted squat hang—Same as above, but the knees and hips are flexed.

    (5) Kip position—Same as 4, but the knees are straight and the legs are parallel to the floor.

Grasps—The ways of holding onto the apparatus with the hands are referred to as grasps. Unless otherwise specified, the thumbs should be on the undersurface of the bar (rings or pommels) when the fingers are on top, and on top when the fingers are below.

a. Overgrasp (or upper grasp)—The palms are on top of the bar, rings, or pommels.

b. Undergrasp—The palms are under the bar.

c. Mixed grasp.—One hand has an undergrasp and the other an overgrasp.

d. False grasp—The grasp is high on the heels of the hands. The palms do not contact the apparatus.

e. Reverse grasp—The hands are twisted or rotated from their normal position. The thumbs are turned away from the body.

Balances—An *inverted* support position of the body in which the weight is borne by the hands, upper arms, forearms, or head. The shoulders are above the point of support and the feet and legs are extended upward.

Seats—A position on the apparatus in which the weight is supported by the thighs or buttocks.

a. Straddle seat—A sitting position in which the body is supported by the inner or lower surface of the thighs, one on either side of a divided surface such as a parallel bar.

b. Riding seat—A sitting position in which the weight is borne by the buttocks or by the inner surface of the thighs, one on either side of an undivided surface such as a horse.

c. Side seat—A sitting position in which the weight is borne by the buttocks and both legs are on the same side of the apparatus. The performer's axis is parallel to that of the apparatus.

d. Cross seat—A seat on one thigh with both legs on the same side of the apparatus and the performer's axis crossing that of the apparatus.

Feints—A movement in which one or both legs are swung in one direction momentarily in preparation for a movement in the opposite direction. (Used primarily on the pommel horse.) Feints are not permitted in competition (points deducted if used) but beginners find them useful in learning stunts.

a. Single feint—From a side support frontways, swing one leg over the horse to the other side without releasing either hand. If the right leg is used for the feint, the right arm bears most of the weight. The body is turned to face toward the saddle.

b. Double feint—Both legs are swung over the end of the horse and rest again the wrist of the supporting arm.

Body Positions

a. Tuck—Hips and knees completely flexed.
b. Pike—Body bent at the waist, legs straight.
c. Layout—Body extended (arched).
d. Head up—Eyes straight ahead, head in line with body.

Mount—A stunt that moves the performer from a stand on the floor to a position on the apparatus.

Dismount—A stunt that moves the performer from a position on the apparatus to a stand on the floor.

Vault—A stunt that moves the performer from a stand on the floor, over the apparatus to the floor again in which a momentary support and push-off from the hands is obtained.

Jump—A stunt from a stand on the floor, over the apparatus to the floor again without touching the apparatus.

Routine—(exercise—combination—sequence)—A grouping of more than one stunt into a continuous series. A routine is used in competitive gymnastics. The routine is judged on form, continuity, and difficulty. It starts with a mount, has intermediate stunts, and terminates with a dismount.

Part **II**

Stunts

15

Simple Stunts

Not all of the "simple stunts" are easy. The term is used to differentiate between the tumbling stunts which usually start in one position, revolve, and then return to the original position, and the stunts classified as "simple" which are found in this chapter.

Simple stunts require and develop agility, flexibility, strength, balance, and coordination. They may be performed in open order as part of a calisthenic lesson or in squads. They can be used as activities in story plays and mimetics. Some may be used as a means of locomotion in relay races. Some stunts may serve as self testing devices, and may be used as a partial determiner of grades. Several are usable as transitional moves and skills for beginning floor exercise routines. No equipment is needed for most of the stunts so they can be used in programs with small budgets. Many of these stunts are suitable for first graders. In the lower grades, permit the children to have fun and add reality to their animal imitations by barking, crowing, growling, etc.

Classifications of Simple Stunts:
1. Individual stunts with forward motion
2. Partner stunts with forward motion
3. Self testing stunts
4. Transitional floor exercise stunts

Individual Stunts with Forward Motion

(Excellent for Use in Relay Races)

1. **Dog Walk**—Bend forward and place the hands on the floor about 24 inches in front of the feet. Walk or run forward on all fours, keeping the body at slightly oblique angle to the forward path.
   Hints: a. Keep the head up and the arms straight.
   b. Distribute the weight equally on hands and feet.
   c. Start slowly and then gradually increase the speed.
2. **Crab Walk**—Bend the knees and place the hands on the floor behind the heels. Move the feet forward until the hips can be raised high. Walk or run forward, then backward in this position.
   Hints: a. The arms should be slightly more than shoulder width apart.
   b. The fingers should point backwards.
   c. When moving forward, move a hand first and then the foot on the same side.

3. **Wet Cat Walk**—Assume the "Dog Walk" position and then raise one of the feet from the floor. Move forward on the hands and one foot and occasionally shake the free leg. Try changing the raised foot while in motion.
   Hints: a. Keep the head up.
        b. Move the hands forward first and then hop forward with the supporting foot.
        c. Keep the free leg loose and relaxed when shaking it.
        d. Take short hops to prevent overbalancing.

4. **Chicken Walk**—Assume a full squat position, place the arms between the legs and reach around them to place the backs of the hands on the top of the feet. Walk forward in this position without removing the hands from the toes. Try running in this position.

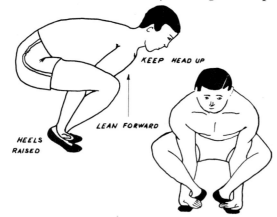

KEEP HEAD UP

LEAN FORWARD

HEELS RAISED

     Hints: a. Lean slightly forward but *keep the head up.*
        b. Raise the heels from the floor.
        c. Keep the hips fully flexed.
        d. Take short steps.

5. **Duck Waddle**—Assume a full squat position with the knees spread wide and bend the elbows, placing the hands under the armpits. The arms serve as wings. Walk forward in this position and flap the wings as each step is taken.
   Hints: a. Lean forward slightly for balance.
        b. Rotate the left foot outward (pivot on the ball of the foot) when stepping forward with the right foot.
        c. Keep the knees spread wide.
        d. Stay close to the floor. Don't raise the hips.

6. **Kangaroo Jump**—Assume a full squat position and hold the hands in front of the shoulders, elbows against the sides. Jump upward and forward as far as possible in this position. Do not extend the legs very much. They should be somewhat flexed all the time. Continue hopping rhythmically.
   Hints: a. Take small hops while learning the stunt.
        b. Lean forward slightly.
        c. Keep the head up.
        d. Flex the ankles, knees, and hips completely when landing.

7. **Frog Hop**—Squat and place the hands on the floor with the arms between the knees. Move forward by placing the hands a few feet forward and then bringing the feet up to the hands again. Hop rhythmically.
   Hints: a. Keep the head up—look forward.
        b. Take short hops.
        c. Do not move the feet forward until after the hands have been placed on the floor.

8. **Rabbit Jump**—Squat and place the hands on the floor slightly in front of the feet. Reach forward with the hands and at the same time leap forward from the feet. Land on the hands and bring the feet to the floor just behind them. Continue to hop rhythmically.

   Hints: a. The hands must not contact the floor until after the feet have left it. There must be a period of flight.

        b. Stretch out as much as possible during the leap.

        c. Take up the shock of landing by bending the arms gradually and bring the knees forward.

        d. Be sure that the reaching of the hands precedes the leap.

        e. Keep the head up throughout the stunt.

9. **Seal Crawl**—Assume a front leaning support position (body supported by the hands and feet, back straight) and propel yourself forward by stepping forward with the hands and dragging the feet.

   Hints: a. Place the hands shoulder width apart, fingers pointing sideward.

        b. Keep the head up and the back straight.

        c. The shoulders should be slightly ahead of the hands.

        d. The toes should be extended backward.

        e. Shift the weight to the right when moving the left hand.

        f. Keep the arms straight.

10. **Turtle Creep**—Assume a front leaning support position (as in No. 9), but bend the arms so that the chest is an inch or two from the floor. The body should be straight, with only the hands and toes touching. Move forward by taking short steps with the hands (keeping the arms bent) and by moving the toes forward, one foot at a time. Don't bend the knees.

   Hints: a. Keep the hands fairly close together.

        b. Bring the left foot up (scoot the whole left side of the body forward) when moving the left hand. Then repeat with the right.

        c. Keep the head up.

11. **Bear Walk**—Bend forward, *keeping the knees straight,* and place the hands on the floor in front of the feet. If possible, place the palms flat on the floor. The arms must bear part of the weight and be about 12 inches from the feet. Walk forward in this position without bending the knees.

   Hints: a. Practice for this stunt by bending and touching the floor several times without bending the knees.

        b. Move the left hand and left foot together and then the right hand and right foot.

12. **Measuring Worm**—Fall forward to a front leaning support position. Keep the hands where they are and move the feet up to them by taking short steps forward. The *knees must be straight.* When the feet get about twelve inches from the hands (the hips are flexed), move the hands forward a step at a time while the feet remain in place. The body again lengthens into a front leaning support. Repeat this several times.

   Hints: a. Take short steps.

        b. When moving the feet forward, place most of the weight on the arms. Lean forward with the shoulders.

        c. Bring the feet up as close to the hands as possible without bending at the knees.

        d. Keep the head up.

        e. Warm up for this stunt as for the "Bear Walk."

13. **Novelty Walk**—Circle the right leg around behind the left leg and then as far to the front of it as possible. Step onto the right foot and swing the left leg entirely around the right leg and to the front, placing the weight on the left foot. Now again bring the right leg behind and then to the front of the left leg. Continue walking forward in this manner.

Hints: a. As the right leg moves forward on the left side of the left leg, bend the left knee to allow the right leg to move further forward.
   b. The legs should be crossed as far above the knees as possible.
   c. Rock up on the left toe and lean forward as the right foot is placed.
   d. Start very slowly and gradually increase the speed.
   e. Concentrate on swinging each leg behind the other before moving it forward.

14. **Stump Walk**—Start in a kneeling position *on the mat.* Reach back with the hands, grasp each ankle, and draw the feet up from the mat. Walk forward on the knees without letting go of the ankles.
   Hints: a. Pull the feet up close to the hips.
      b. Arch the back slightly.
      c. Lean slightly forward and keep the head up.
      d. Move fairly rapidly to maintain the balance more easily.

15. **Seal Slap**—Fall to a front leaning support as for the "Seal Crawl," but this time propel the body forward by moving both hands simultaneously and slapping them against the chest before replacing them on the floor. Continue forward with rhythmic hops.
   Hints: a. Keep the head up.
      b. Allow the elbows to "give" a little and then push up vigorously with the arms.
      c. In the same motion, whip the hands up to the chest and immediately replace them on the floor.
      d. As the hand are replaced, allow the elbows to bend again as before.
      e. The body must remain straight.

Partner Stunts with Forward Motion

(Excellent for Use in Relay Races)

Partners should be about equal in height and weight. A fast way of approximating this equality is to line the class up according to height and have them count off by twos. Adjustments will have to be made in a few cases, but this usually matches partners quite well.

In the descriptions and hints for the partner stunts, the top man is indicated as T and the bottom man as B. Some stunts do not call for one of the partners to be in a top position and the other on the bottom, but the same means of differentiating between the two men is used. When three men are in the stunt, the third is indicated as M for middle.

1. **Wheelbarrow**—(Two people). B assumes a front leaning support position with legs spread while T stands between B's legs, grasps them at the knees, and lifts them upward. B then walks forward on his hands while T walks behind, supporting the legs. (A more advanced method is to have T grasp B's ankles instead of his knees.)

    Hints: a. Keep the hands shoulder width apart.
    b. The head must be up—look forward.
    c. Take short, quick steps.
    d. Do not sag at the hips. Keep the body straight.
    e. T must not push B by walking too fast. B sets the pace and T follows it.

2. **Tandem**—(Two people). B assumes a position on all fours with hips flexed. T sits astride B's back and bends forward to place his hands on the mat or floor in front of B's hands. T bends knees and places his feet on B's hips. The couple proceed forward in this position.

    Hints: a. Both move their left hands forward at the same time and B steps forward with the left foot also.
    b. T clamps thighs tightly against B's sides.
    c. Do not try to move too fast.
    d. The stronger of the two should be on the bottom.

3. **Centipede**—(Three to six people). This stunt is the same as the "Tandem" except that more participants are used. B and T assume the same position as for the "Tandem" and then the third one sits astride T's back and puts the hands on the floor. The fourth sits on the third's back, etc. All walk forward in this position.

    Hints: a. The hints for the "Tandem" apply here.
    b. Take very short steps to avoid a sideward swaying motion which would upset the performers.
    c. Bunch the children together as much as possible.
    d. All must clamp tightly with their legs.

4. **Scooter**—(Two persons). T sits on B's feet and places the feet so that B can sit on them. B's legs are between T's. Both have their knees flexed and they grasp each others shoulders. T then leans backward and raises his feet off the mat, which causes B to rise to a semistanding position. As T lifts his feet he partially extends his legs and lowers them again, with B still sitting on them. B now lean backward, raises his feet, and draws them in close to him before replacing them on the mat. T is still on the feet. They continue to scoot across the mat in this manner.

    Hints: a. As T raises his/her feet he/she also pulls upward and toward him/her on B's shoulders.
    b. B assists T by placing some weight on own feet and pulling the body forward by the grasp on T's shoulders.
    c. T must not fully extend legs for then B could not be let down easily.
    d. T always extends the legs (partially) when they are raised and B always flexes them as they are raised.

5. **Jumping Wheelbarrow**—(Two pupils). The starting position is the same as for the regular "Wheelbarrow." However, the bottom pupil moves forward by pushing off from both hands at the same time. To add to the difficulty, the hands may be either clapped together or slapped against the chest before being returned to the floor. The top person may support either at the knees or at the ankles.

    Hints: a. The bottom one should lean slightly forward (shoulders in front of the hands).
    b. Keep the head up—look straight forward.
    c. Bend the arms slightly and then straighten them vigorously to produce the hop.
    d. The hops should be short, rapid, and rhythmic.
    e. T must not push. Simply support the legs and walk forward at the pace set by the bottom performer.

Self Testing Stunts

Use these stunts in a testing program. Grade on the number of stunts correctly executed on the first trial (2 points) on the second trial (1 point) or failed on both trials (0 points). They can also be used in the middle of calisthenic exercises as a challenge and relief of monotony.

1. **Human Ball**—Sit on the mat, place the arms between the legs and reach around to the outside of the ankles with the hands. Draw the feet in close to the buttocks and tip over onto the left knee and shoulder. Next, roll across the back (knees in the air) to the right shoulder and leg; from there roll up to a sitting position. Continue rolling several more times. Stop, then, and roll to the other side.

   Hints: a. Keep the knees well spread and the feet in close.
   b. Be sure to roll to the side first. Momentum will be lost if you roll to the back first.
   c. Roll in a smooth, continuous motion.
   d. To return to a sitting position, push hard with the knee and tilt the head upward.

2. **Knee Spring**—From a kneeling position with the knees and hips fully flexed and the toes extended backward, swing the arms backward, then vigorously forward and spring upward, bringing the feet in under the body to a stand.

   Hints: a. A fast, partial extension of the knee and hip joints must accompany the vigorous forward and upward arm swing.
   b. Lean slightly forward.
   c. Keep the head up—look forward.
   d. As the spring is made, quickly draw the feet under the body.

3. **Double Heel Click**—From a stride stand (feet apart) jump upward, click the heels together twice, and land with the feet apart. Repeat several times in rhythm. As soon as you land from one, rebound immediately for the next.

   Hints: a. Keep the legs straight but relaxed. Don't tense up.
   b. Click the heels together as soon as the feet leave the floor. Allow them to separate as the body travels upward.
   c. Click again as soon as the body starts to descend and let them separate on the way down.
   d. Don't try to click them too fast.

   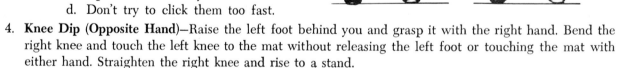

4. **Knee Dip (Opposite Hand)**—Raise the left foot behind you and grasp it with the right hand. Bend the right knee and touch the left knee to the mat without releasing the left foot or touching the mat with either hand. Straighten the right knee and rise to a stand.

   Hints: a. Use a mat when learning the stunt.
   b. Keep the weight directly above the supporting leg.
   c. Bend at the waist slightly and hold the free arm forward for balance.
   d. The left knee should land opposite the middle of the right foot.
   e. Rise as soon as the knee touches. Don't put any weight on the knee. Keep the tension in the supporting leg.

5. **Knee Dip (Same Hand)**—This is the same as the "Knee Dip" except that the left hand grasps the left foot behind the body instead of the right hand grasping it. This is more difficult than the other way.

   Hints: a. The same hints apply as in No. 14 except for the hint "d."
   b. The left knee should touch the floor a little further forward—about even with the toes of the right foot.

6. **Single Squat**—Stand on the left foot and extend the right leg forward. Bend the left knee to a full squat position and straighten again to a stand. Neither the hands nor the right foot may touch the floor.
   Hints: a. Extend the arms sideward or forward for balance.
   b. Lean forward slightly from the hips.
   c. The hips must go straight downward and be directly above the left foot.
   d. The right leg should be parallel to the floor.
   e. Straighten as soon as the full squat has been reached. Keep the supporting tension in the left leg.
   f. A partner may lightly hold the performer's hand or hands as an aid in learning.

7. **Mule Kick**—Leap from the feet onto the hands and raise the flexed hips overhead into an inverted position. Then extend the legs upward and at the same time push vigorously with both hands. From the push-off from the hands, land on the feet and immediately leap onto the hands again. Repeat several times in rhythm. The hands must not reach the floor until after the feet have left it, and when the hands push off, the feet must not touch the floor until the hands have left it.
   Hints: a. Keep the head up.
   b. Leap from both feet.
   c. Pretend to dive over a waist-high obstacle directly in front of you and place the hands close to where the feet had been.
   d. Keep the hips flexed while leaping onto the hands.
   e. The arms should be slightly flexed when the hands land so that they can shove off immediately.
   f. The push should come from the shoulders as well as the arms.
   g. Coordinate the arm push and the leg extension.
   h. The leg extension is followed immediately by a hip flexion.
   i. Imagine that the body again passes over the obstacle mentioned above.
   j. Let the knees give a little as the feet land so that the next leap can begin immediately.
   k. The landing spots for the hands and feet should be only about 24 inches apart.

8. **Jump Through**—Stand on the left foot and grasp the right toe in front of the body with the left hand. Jump over the right foot with the left one without letting go of the right toe. Land on the left foot without losing balance and with the right toe still grasped in the left hand.
   Hints: a. Grasp the tip of the toe with the *fingertips*.
   b. Hold the right foot about 6 inches in front of the left knee.
   c. As the jump is made, draw the left knee to the chest and *extend the left arm downward*. Try to pass the left hand *under* the left foot instead of trying to bring the foot over the hand.
   d. Lean forward as the jump is made.

9. **Extension Push-Up**—Lie face downward with the arms extended forward and the toes curled under. Press downward with the hands and raise the entire body off the floor. Only the hands and feet are on the floor. The trunk should be at least 4 inches from the floor.
   Hints: a. Tense the abdominal and gluteal (buttocks) muscles.
   b. Be sure that the toes are tucked well under.
   c. Keep the hands shoulder width apart.
   d. Surge forward slightly by pushing with the toes when pressing downward and backward with the arms.
   e. Keep the head up.
   f. Warm up the pectoral (chest) muscles and abdominal muscles before trying the stunt.

Floor Exercise Stunts and Transitions

The following moves fit admirably into beginning floor exercise routines. Some, though relatively easy, are found in top notch routines. Remember, each should be done as perfectly as possible.

1. **The Top**—Jump into the air, make a full revolution (whole turn) and land on both feet at the same time, approximately in the same spot from which the jump was made. The balance must be maintained. Repeat the stunt but turn in the other direction.
   Hints: a. Start with the feet about a foot apart.
         b. For a turn to the right, flex the hips and knees slightly and swing the arms backward.
         c. Spring upward with an equal push from both feet.
         d. At the same time whip the left arm to the right and reach across the right shoulder. Bring the right hand over the shoulder too.
         e. The head must twist sharply to the right as the turn is made.
         f. Keep the body straight and erect.
         g. Flex the knees slightly when landing to aid in keeping the balance.

2. **Dead Man's Fall**—Stand with the body straight and stiff and the arms at the sides. Fall forward to a lying position. Just as the body passes the halfway mark on the way down, extend the arms forward to break the fall. The body must not bend at the hips.
   Hints: a. Before trying this stunt loosen up the wrists by shaking and rotating them.
         b. Let the arms give slowly as the hands contact the floor. Do not keep the arms stiff.
         c. Practice on a mat.
   Note: This can be done while raising one leg backward as the drop is made. The body is momentarily supported by both hands and one foot. The chest is close to the floor and the raised leg is kept straight and lifted as high as possible. This is frequently performed in competitive floor exercise and is called a "Swedish Fall." The position is held only momentarily.

3. **Arabesque (Scale)**—Stand on the right leg and raise the left leg backward to a position at *least* parallel to the floor. Bend forward at the waist so that the trunk is also parallel to the floor and the back and left leg form a curved line. Extend the arms sideward. Both legs must be straight. With a hop bring the right leg to the floor and raise the left one backward. Continue to alternate the positions of the legs rhythmically. There must be a period of flight (neither foot on the floor) while the change is being made. Both legs must remain straight.
   Hints: a. Keep the head up and the back arched if possible.
         b. Push off strongly from the left foot.
         c. Make the change as rapidly as possible.
         d. Bring the right foot directly under the right hip.

4. **Tuck Jump**—Jump upward and as the body ascends, draw the knees to the chest and grasp the shins with the hands. As the body decends, release and lower the legs, coming to a stand. Try several jumps in quick succession.
   Hints: a. Swing arms up hard to shoulder height when jumping.
         b. Stop arm lift sharply and quickly grasp shins.
         c. Start drawing knees upward as soon as you leave the floor.
         d. Release and lower the legs right after grasping them.
         e. Try several jumps in quick succession.

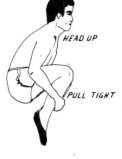

HEAD UP

PULL TIGHT

5. **Pike Jump**—Extend the hands forward, jump upward, and bring the feet to the hands by flexing the hips. Immediately drop the legs and return to a stand. Repeat a number of times *in rhythm.* Try it first with legs spread.

   Hints: a. Lean slightly forward when jumping.

         b. Keep the head up.

         c. Keep the legs straight.

         d. Avoid reaching downward with the hands. Bring the feet up.

   Spot: Stand behind the performer and support him under the armpits the first few times he jumps.

6. **"L" Lever**—Sit on the floor with the hands on the floor beside the hips. Straighten the arms and raise the body from the floor, keeping the legs parallel to the floor. Only the hands are in contact with the floor.

   Hints: a. Tighten the abdominal muscles.

         b. Take the weight on the fingertips. The fingers are spread and pointing forward.

         c. Lean backward slightly with the head and chest.

   Note: This can also be done with the legs spread and the hands between the legs.

7. **"V" Lever**—Start from an "L" Lever (#6) and simply increase the flexion at the hip joint till the body and legs form a "V" instead of an "L."

   Hints: a. Develop hip joint flexibility and abdominal strength first.

         b. Lean back a little more as the flexion increases.

         c. Keep the head slightly forward.

8. **Splits**—No *skill* is involved, but flexibility is demanded. An individual's anatomical structure may not be conducive to executing this move but everyone can, with practice, get closer to success. Simply stand with one foot forward of the other and continue to slide the foot further and further forward till the buttocks touches the floor.

   Hints: a. Turn the rear foot outward.

         b. Start *slowly.* When you feel a real stretch, pause for several seconds, then try to go a little further.

         c. Place the hands on the floor on either side of the body to give some support.

         d. Maintain the weight on the arms till completely down.

         e. Keep both legs straight.

         f. Few can learn this during one session. For most, several days (or longer) is needed to develop the required flexibility.

9. **"Y" Scale**—From a stand, lift the right foot upward with the knee outward and grasp the instep with the right hand. Now, extend the right leg sideward and upward. The knee should be straightened and the left arm raised left sideward and upward.

   Hints: a. Work on flexibility first. Do a lot of stretching.

         b. Get a firm hold on the instep and push against your hand.

         c. Use the left arm for balance.

10. **Needle Scale**—Like the "Y" Scale, this is a balance on one leg. As extreme flexibility is required, this is usually done by girls, but some boys can master it. Stand on the left leg, raise the right leg backward and upward while leaning forward with the trunk. Continue raising and leaning till the right leg is straight up and down and the chest rests against the left leg.

    Hints: a. Move slowly but steadily. Fight for balance as you move.
            b. Keep the eyes focused on a spot on the floor.
            c. Keep the head up as long as possible.
            d. Grasp the left leg near the ankle with both hands and pull the chest to the leg.
            e. Use the support from the hands to help maintain balance.

11. **Jump Turn (Tour Jeté)**—Step sideward with the left foot with a ¼ turn left and swing the right leg forward (past the left leg) and upward. Immediately push off from the left leg, execute a half turn left and land on the right leg with the left leg raised behind. The legs "scissors" in the air. In all, a ¾ turn is made from the starting position (¼ + ½ = ¾).

    Hints: a. Do not separate the parts. Make it one continuous, flowing movement. Step, turn and spring as one movement.
            b. Keep the legs straight and close together.
            c. Swing the right leg hard and high.
            d. Lean slightly backward as the leg swings forward and upward.
            e. Land in good balance with the left leg high.

12. **Jump Foot**—Place the right foot against a wall about 12 inches from the floor. Jump over the right foot with the left without removing the right from the wall. Finish facing away from the wall.

Hints: a. Start facing the wall.
      b. A good lift from the shoulders is needed.
      c. Don't place any weight on the right foot.
      d. Push hard on the floor with the left foot and then quickly draw the foot up. Be sure to bend the left knee.
      e. Pivot on the right foot as the jump is made so that the back is toward the wall when landing on the left foot.
      f. Try the stunt without using the wall. Simply extend the right leg and hop over it with the left foot with a half turn right. Do not bend or lower the right leg.

13. **Flank Around**—From a front leaning support with the hands shoulder width apart, swing both legs in a half-circle to the left under the left arm and finish in a rear support. The feet must not touch the floor as they swing in the half circle.

LEAN ON RIGHT

PUSH FROM LEFT

Hints: a. Lean forward slightly (shoulders ahead of the hands).
      b. Sag at the waist, then whip the hips upward and push off from the toes.
      c. With the push from the toes, push with the left hand and lean way over on the straight right arm.
      d. Flex the hips slightly as the legs whip around.
      e. Arch the back and lean backward on the right arm just before the heels hit and the left hand is replaced.

Note: The Flank Around can be done to an "L" Lever (#6) by replacing the hand very quickly and keeping the hips flexed.

14. **Squat Through**—From a front leaning support, bring the legs forward between the arms and finish in a rear leaning support. (The body is supported by the hands and the heels with the back toward the floor and arched.)

TOES UNDER   SAG   LEAN FORW.   WHIP HIPS UP   HUNCH BACK   KNEES FORW.   HEAD UP   LEAN BACKW.   TURN HANDS

Hints: a. Lean slightly forward, hands a *little* more than shoulder width apart, arms straight.
      b. Sag at the waist then whip the hips upward.
      c. At the same time, push off from the toes and draw the knees toward the chest.
      d. Be sure to keep the head up at this point.
      e. Hunch the back as the legs swing through.
      f. Continue the forward momentum of the legs and extend them to a rear support.
      g. Shift the body lean from forward to backward as the legs pass through.
      h. As the legs pass through, allow the hands to rotate so the fingers point outward and backward.

Note: This too can be done to an "L" Lever (#6). As the legs pass between the arms, straighten the knees but keep the hips flexed and tighten the abdominal muscles.

15. **Stoop Through**—This is the same as the Squat Through except that the knees are kept straight.
    Hints: a. The hints are the same except for the bending of the knees. The hips must be raised very high and a high degree of flexibility is required.

16. **Leg Circling**—Bend the knees, place the hands on the floor with the right knee between the arms and extend the left leg sideward. Move the left leg forward under both hands (raise, then replace the hands) and continue to circle the leg to the right, then backward under the right foot and return it to the starting position. Continue to circle the leg without pausing or touching the left foot to the floor. Keep the left leg straight. The body does not turn as the leg circles.

    Hints: a. Keep the weight on the right foot as the hands are raised to pass the right leg under them.
            b. As soon as the leg passes under, replace the hands and lean forward on them to bring the right foot off the floor so the left leg can pass under.
            c. Lean well forward and bend the arms slightly as the right foot is raised.
            d. Keep the right knee bent and the right foot close to the buttocks.
            e. Replace the right foot in its original spot and push from the hands to throw the weight back on the foot.
            f. Keep the left leg straight and make the circles smooth.

17. **Elbow Lever**—From a front support position move the right hand back and place it on the mat beneath the right hip. Bring the right elbow under the right hip and rest the hip on it. Raise the legs from the mat and maintain a horizontal position of the body with only the hands touching the mat.
    Hints: a. Turn the right hand so that the fingers point backward.
            b. Move the left hand forward and to the left of the left shoulder.
            c. Place the right elbow almost to the center of the abdomen.
            d. Keep the head up.
            e. The weight rests along the entire right upper arm.
            f. Lean forward slightly, keep the chest high, and arch the back to bring the toes off the floor. Don't push off from the toes.
            g. When this is mastered try lifting the left hand off the floor and balance on the right hand only.

18. **Alligator Walk**—Assume an "Elbow Lever" position on the right elbow but keep the knees well spread and the legs bent. Then shift the body over to the left elbow and move the right hand forward. Return the body to the right elbow and move the left hand forward. Continue walking forward in this manner.

Hints: a. All of the hints for the "Elbow Lever" apply here except the last one. The back should not be arched.

b. Lean well forward and take the weight on the hands when transferring the weight from elbow to elbow.

c. Have both elbows turn inward to facilitate sliding the body from one to the other.

d. Slide the body over as far as possible on each elbow.

e. Take small steps.

f. Move the right hand forward as the body is being shifted from the left elbow.

16

Tumbling Stunts

Tumbling stunts are those activities performed on a mat, or mat substitute, which require the performer to turn over, make a complete revolution, and return to his starting position. A stunt described as moving to the left should be practiced moving to the right as well. Several of these stunts can be done safely by first graders.

Individual Stunts

1. **Log Roll**—From a prone lying position with the arms stretched overhead, roll sideward to the left. Continue to roll to the end of the mat. The body must be straight and the performer must not roll off the side of the mat.
   Hints: a. Raise the head slightly, twist it to the right and raise the right shoulder.
   b. Obtain momentum by extending the toes to the right and bearing down on them.
   c. Arch the back when rolling onto it.
   d. Adjust your position on the mat (to prevent rolling off the side) by rolling the hips and not the shoulders or vice versa as the need arises.

2. **Stump Log Roll**—Some logs do not have all branches cut off when they roll downhill. Here, two stumps remain. Start in a front leaning rest (push-up) position, body and arms stiff and straight. Raise the right arm sideward, pivot a half turn on the left arm and replace the right hand under you. (back to mat). Now raise the left arm, pivot a half turn on the right and replace the left hand (facing mat again). Continue rolling.
   Hints: a. Do not sag at the hips (Log's don't bend)
   b. Keep the legs together.
   c. When replacing hands, place them fairly close together.

3. **Sideward Roll**—From a position on the hands and knees roll sideward onto and across the back and come up to a similar position again. The performer must come smoothly to the knees without losing his balance.

 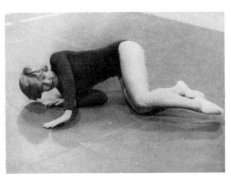 

Hints: a. Bend the left arm (bring the elbow under the body), twist the head to the right and lower the weight onto the left shoulder and left hip.

b. As this is done, raise the right knee from the mat and fall left sideward.

c. As the weight comes onto the back (shoulders and hips both touching mat), bend the right arm and bring the elbow in close to the body.

d. Continue the roll and return to the starting position by pushing on the right elbow, forearm, and knee.

e. The knees and hips remain flexed during the entire stunt.

4. **Forward Roll**—From a squat stand, place the hands on the mat shoulder width apart. Tuck the head toward the chest and bend the arms so that the *back* of the head touches the mat slightly in front of the hands. Push off with the legs and roll forward to a stand. The roll must be in a straight line, and the hands should not be used to assist in getting to the feet. The roll must be smooth and continuous.
Hints: a. Raise the hips as the tucked head is lowered to the mat.

b. Place the BACK (not the top) of the head on the mat and push from the toes as the hips move forward.

c. Push from the hands as the shoulders strike the mat.

d. As the hands push off, reach for the shins and pull them in close to the body so the heels will be close to the buttocks.

e. Keep the knees close to the chest, the back rounded, and keep leaning forward with the head and shoulders.

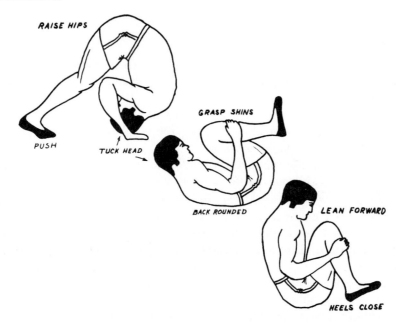

Spot: a. Kneel to right of performer, place right hand on back of his/her *head* (not the neck) and left hand under the right upper leg.

b. Lift with left hand, tuck the student's head with right hand, then push forward on back of the head as he/she comes to a stand.

5. **Variations of Forward Roll**—(I) Raise the right foot backward, bend the left knee and place the hands on the mat. Tuck the head and roll forward as in the regular "Forward Roll," but keep the right foot from touching the mat. Do not use the hands to aid in coming to a stand on the left foot.
Hints: a. Keep the left knee close to the chest and the left foot close to the buttocks.

b. Lean well forward and reach forward with the arms when coming up on the left foot.

c. The right leg is extended forward when finishing the roll.

d. Don't pause—make the rise to a stand part of the roll.

(II) Raise the arms sideward, squat, tuck the head to the mat, and roll forward without allowing the hands or arms to touch the mat.

Hints: a. Spread the knees when squatting.
   b. Raise the hips and place the back of the head on the mat as close to the feet as possible.
   c. Keep the back rounded and the knees close to the chest.
   d. Lean forward and reach forward with the arms when coming to the feet.

Spot: a. Kneel just behind the performer's outstretched right arm, reach under it to place the right hand on the back of his head. Left hand is placed as in stunt No. 4.
   b. Support performer's head to prevent dropping onto it instead of lowering onto it.
   c. Lift with left hand as in stunt No. 4, then finish with a push with the right hand on the back of the head to help him/her up.

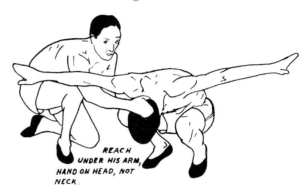

REACH UNDER HIS ARM, HAND ON HEAD, NOT NECK.

(III) Squat and grasp the ankles, tuck the head forward and roll forward, and come to the feet without releasing the ankles.

Hint: All the hints for variation II pertain here except that the arms can't be extended forward when coming to a stand.

Spot: Spot as for the stunt above.

(IV) Do a series of three forward rolls without straightening to a stand at the completion of each roll. Go right into the second and third rolls from the squat position.

Hint: At the completion of each roll, remove the hands from the shins and place them on the mat to begin the nevt roll. Emphasize the placing of the hands by *slapping* the mat.

(V) Start as for a forward roll, but keep the legs *straight* and widely *spread* when the weight comes onto the shoulders. Briefly extend the legs upward to gain momentum, then quickly pike deeply, place the hands on the mat between the legs and push downward to come to a stand without bending the knees.

Hint: Lean well forward when coming up and get as much speed as possible. The greater the speed and the spread of the legs, the easier the roll.

6. **Shoulder Roll**—From a standing position with the left foot forward, lean forward onto the hands (left hand leading) and allow the arms to bend until the left shoulder lands on the mat. Raise the hips and roll on the left shoulder, across the back to the right hip and onto the feet again.
 Hints: a. Raise the right foot backward when leaning forward onto the hands.
    b. Turn the left elbow inward as it bends.
    c. Twist the head to the right and tuck the chin to the chest.
    d. Keep the knees close to the chest and the back rounded.
    e. Lean into the roll. Get a little momentum.
    f. After it is learned, try it from a slight run and a one-foot takeoff.

7. **Backward Roll**—From a squat stand, lean slightly forward and then rock backward onto the buttocks and roll backward across the back to a stand. The roll must be in a straight line, and the knees must not contact the mat.
 Hints: a. The hands strike the mat first to break the fall. The fingers must point forward.
    b. Keep the head tucked, the back rounded, and the knees close to the chest during the entire stunt.
    c. Use the backward momentum gained by dropping to the hips. Don't hesitate.
    d. Reach back with the hands IMMEDIATELY when the hips hit the mat.

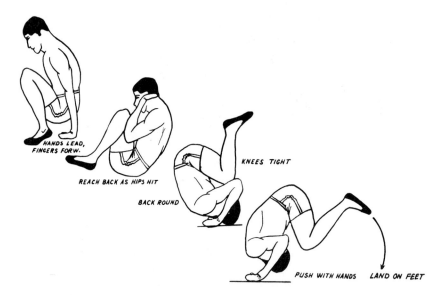

e. Keep the elbows in close to the body and place the hands close to the shoulders, palms down, fingers toward the shoulders.

f. Push with the arms as the feet pass over the head to take the body weight off the neck.

g. Bring the feet to the mat close to the hands as the arms take the weight.

Spot: a. Kneel to the left of and behind the spot the pupil's left hand will first contact the mat. As he/she leans back, place the right hand behind the left shoulder (fingers pointing upward) and the left hand on the small of the back.

b. Lift upward on the shoulder with the right hand to take the pressure off the neck and, if needed, push on the back with the left.

c. The push with the left hand should be slightly upward and backward.

8. **Combination Forward and Backward Roll**—The "Forward Roll" is done as described above except that the ankles are crossed just after the roll is begun. As the performer comes to his feet he/she describes a half turn and does a "Backward Roll." The two rolls should be continuous. Go from the forward roll into the backward roll without a pause.

Hints: a. All cues for the forward and backward rolls apply here.

b. In making the turn for the backward roll, turn right (if the left foot is in front) by rising on the balls of the feet (heels off floor) and untwisting the ankles.

c. Stay in a squatting position while making the turn.

d. The momentum of the forward roll should be used to aid in the backward roll.

9. **Dive Roll**—From a short run, take off from both feet, dive over pupils kneeling side by side and go into a forward roll. The body must contact the mat in the following order: hands, back of head, shoulders, back, hips, and feet. The performer must roll up to his feet in one continuous motion and must not touch the kneeling persons in diving over them.

Hints: a. Practice first without a run and without the kneeling students. Stand and take off from both feet. Don't dive too far at first.

b. Raise the flexed hips high when taking off.

c. Tuck the head forward as the hands strike the mat and place the BACK of the head between the hands.

d. Give SLOWLY with the arms when the hands hit so the body will be lowered to the head and shoulders without a jar.

e. Keep the back round and the knees close to the chest as the roll continues.

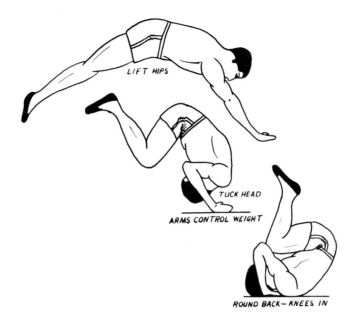

LIFT HIPS

TUCK HEAD

ARMS CONTROL WEIGHT

ROUND BACK—KNEES IN

Spot: a. Kneel on the performer's right, opposite the spot where he/she will land and place the right hand on the back of his/her head *while he/she is in flight* and press downward and forward toward his/her chest to tuck the head.

b. Support the head if he/she doesn't take the weight on his/her own hands.

c. Place the left hand on the abdomen and lift at the same time the right hand is placed if the dive is too flat.

10. **Roll, Dive Roll, Roll**—Begin the stunt by doing a regular "Forward Roll." As you come to the squat position, leap forward from both feet and do a "Dive Roll." When finishing the "Dive Roll," go right into another "Forward Roll."

Hints: a. Do not hesitate after completing the first roll. Use the momentum of the first roll to aid in gaining distance for the "Dive Roll."

b. Be sure to raise the hips high when going into the "Dive Roll."

c. The third roll is just like the third roll in the "Series of Forward Rolls."

Spot: Spot for the "Dive Roll" as described above.

11. **Modified Cartwheel**—Face the mat with the right foot forward and the arms raised upward. Reach back with the arms, bend backward slightly with the body, and shift the weight to the left leg. Then whip the arms forward and downward, bend forward, and shift the weight to the right foot while raising the left one upward. Place the right hand in front of the right foot and as it strikes the mat; push off from the right foot. Place the left hand in front of the right hand, and now both feet should be overhead. As the body continues the motion, lift the right hand, place the left foot in front of the left hand, raise the left hand, and land on the right foot. The arms and legs act as the spokes of a wheel. (Some will prefer going to the other side.)

Hints: a. Draw a chalk line down the center of the mat and start with the right foot at one end, pointing toward the other.

b. Bend the right knee slightly and get a good lift from the straight left leg as the hands whip toward the mat. Momentum and a high left leg are very important.

c. Place the right hand on the chalk line about 18 inches from the right foot with the fingers pointing to the right.

d. Push hard from the bent right leg as soon as the right hand is placed.

e. Place the left hand on the line about 18 inches from the right hand with the fingers pointing in the same direction as the right. This will automatically turn you sideways.

f. Swing the right arm upward as it is brought off the mat.

g. Bring the left foot then the right to the chalk line about two feet apart with the toes pointing in the opposite direction to that of the hands.

h. Keep the arms and legs straight (except for the bent right leg for the push-off).

i. Keep the head neutral and the back straight during the stunt. Focus the eyes on the mat between the hands.

Spot: a. Stand to the performer's right opposite the spot the hands will land.

b. Cross your right arm over the left and reach for his/her hips as he/she pushes off with the right foot. Place your right hand on his/her left hip and left hand on the right hip (palm turned left).

c. Support the hips and guard against his/her falling toward you when both of the hands are on the mat.

12. **Cartwheel**—This is the same as the "Modified Cartwheel" except that the left side is toward the mat and the arms are held sideward to start. The left hand whips sideward and downward to the mat followed by the right hand. The legs are swung up as before, and the landing is the same. This is more difficult because it is harder to bend sideward than it is to bend forward and also, the right leg can be swung higher when it goes backward than when it goes sideward. Some will find it easier to start right sideward.

Hints: a. Sway right sideward, then lean vigorously to the left and whip the left hand to the mat with the fingers pointing backward.

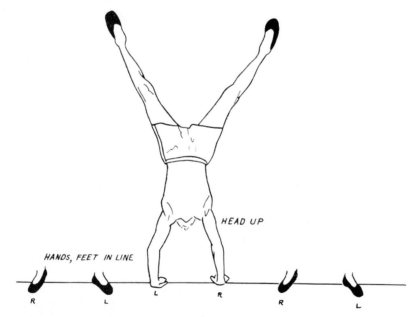

b. At the same time, swing the right arm over the head and downward in an arc as the right leg is lifted sideward and upward.

c. All other hints are the same.

Spot: Same as for the "Modified Cartwheel" except that you start by standing directly behind the performer and move along as he/she goes.

13. **Cartwheel with Heel Click**—Start the regular "Cartwheel" but click the heels together and spread them again while the feet are overhead. Finish as in the regular "Cartwheel."

Hints: a. Start to bring the feet together as soon as the second foot leaves the floor.

b. The heel click should occur directly over the head. Keep the legs straight.

c. Spread the legs again immediately.

Spot: Same as for the regular "Cartwheel."

14. **Skip Step**—(The Skip Step is not a *stunt* in the true sense of the word. Rather, it is a preparatory move used to start many of the following stunts. Its use permits a change in the forward momentum produced by the run and enables the body to adapt more quickly to a new position. It can be done with either foot, but here it will be described on the left.)—From a short run, take off from the left foot, throw the arms upward, and at the same time, swing the right leg forward and upward. Land on the left foot again and then step on the right foot. In other words, take off left, land left, then right.

Hints: a. Practice with just a few running steps first.
   b. Don't make the hop too long or too high.
   c. Lean slightly forward when taking the hop.
   d. Swing the arms upward as the hop is made.
   e. Keep the right leg loose and relaxed. The knee should bend.
   f. Whip the hands downward to the mat as the right foot contacts the floor.

15. **Round Off**—From a short run and "Skip Step" starting on the right foot, whip the hands to the mat as soon as the left foot strikes, crossing the right hand over in front of the left. As the hands strike the mat, kick the legs upward and twist the trunk to the left. Push off with the arms and shoulders as the legs come overhead and snap the legs downward. Land facing the starting point. There must be a period of flight between the time the hands leave the mat and the feet contact it. (Students should try this to both sides, then stick to the side that seems easiest for them.)

Hints: a. Learn the "Skip Step" first, then practice the "Mule Kick" (Stunt No. 7, pages 00-00).
   b. As the left foot lands in the "Skip Step," whip the hands straight downward in front of the body, not off to the side.
   c. Place the left hand in front of and fairly close to the left foot with the fingers pointing slightly to the left.
   d. Just after the left hand is placed, cross the right hand over the left with the fingers pointing backward. The arms may be slightly bent.
   e. Swing the right leg upward hard as the hands go downward.
   f. Push off from the left foot as the hands land and bring the feet together overhead. Legs and hips must pass directly over the head, not off to the side.
   g. The twist occurs automatically, due to the crossed arms.
   h. Push off hard from both hands as the twist is made. (Feet are still overhead.) Much of the push comes from the shoulders.

    i. Snap the legs downward as the push is made. Bend the hips to bring the feet close to where the hands had been.

    j. Keep the head up during the entire stunt.

    k. Go through it slowly at first. Without a run, place hands properly, kick up through a handstand position, twist, and land without a push-off. When "feel" of stunt has been acquired, run and whip through it hard.

Spot: Stand to the left of where the hands will land and place your left hand under his/her right shoulder as the right hand is placed. Lift as he/she pushes from the arms.

16. **Round Off into Backward Roll**—Do a "Round Off" and go into a "Backward Roll" as soon as you land from the "Round Off." Go into the roll with straight legs.

    Hints: a. Bend the knees slightly and flex the hips backward as soon as you land from the "Round Off."

           b. As the hips flex, lean well forward and hold hands below the hips to break the fall.

           c. The fingers *must* be pointing *forward.*

           d. Finish the roll as in an ordinary "Backward Roll."

           e. Avoid hesitating when landing from the "Round Off."

    Spot: Spot as for No. 15.

17. **Chest Roll**—Place the hands on the mat and swing up into a momentary "Hand Balance." Bend the arms till the chest touches the mat and roll backward on the chest, abdomen, and thighs, in that order. As the knees strike the mat, push from the hands, flex the hips to bring the feet under the body and come to a stand.

    Hints:

           a. Keep head up and back fully arched when lowering to the chest.

           b. Bend the arms *slowly.* Control the lowering of the body.

           c. Maintain the balance when lowering by increasing the arch slightly. Keep the legs overhead till the chest hits the mat.

           d. The chest should strike the mat slightly in front of the hands.

           e. Keep the back arched. Don't flex the hips till the knees hit and the push-off from the hands is made.

    Spot: a. Stand beside the performer and guard against an overbalance forward.

           b. Prevent dropping by grasping the legs if the back is not fully arched when the chest strikes the mat.

LEGS STILL UP

BACK STILL ARCHED

BEND ARMS SLOWLY

CHIN ON MAT

CHEST AHEAD OF HANDS

18. **Cartwheel Flip**—From a short run and "Skip Step" on the right foot, whip both hands to the mat when stepping on the left foot. Place the hands on the mat with the right hand in front of the left. Swing the feet overhead, pivot around the right arm while the feet are in the air and make a whole turn to the left. Push off from the hands and land on the feet, facing forward. The feet must pass over the head and there must be a period of flight between the time the hands leave the mat and the feet contact it.

    Hints: a. Practice first from a stand. Place the hands in position (left hand in front of left foot, right hand directly in front of left hand with fingers pointing to left) and walk around right arm by stepping to the right with the right foot and crossing the left foot over the right while raising the left arm as the head turns to look over the left shoulder. Keep the right hand in place.

LOOK TO LEFT

DRAW FEET UNDER

LIFT LEFT
AND
PUSH FROM RIGHT

b. Try again from a stand with the hands in place, but this time kick the legs upward and pivot on the right arm. Again keep the right hand in place.

c. Now try the stunt from a run—whip the hands to the mat directly in front of the body after the "Skip Step."

d. Swing the right leg upward *as* the hands go to the mat.

e. Push from the left foot *as* the hands strike the mat.

f. As the feet join each other overhead, turn the head sharply to the left (look over the left shoulder) lift the left hand from the mat and push off hard from the right.

g. With the push, draw the feet toward the body so that they will land close to where the hands had been.

19. **Snap Up**—From a lying position on the back, flex and raise the hips till the knees are above the face, and place the plams flat on the mat beside the head, fingers pointing toward the shoulders. Extend the legs vigorously upward and forward and arch the back. At the same time, push hard on the mat with the hands. Bring the feet under the body and come to a stand.

PAUSE-

SPOTTER
SUPPORTS BACK,
LIFTS SHOULDER

KEEP HIPS
HIGH

PUSH HARD

Hints: a. Don't start the snap till the backward momentum obtained from raising the hips has been lost. Pause before snapping.

b. The body weight should be on the head and shoulders, not the back. Keep the hips high. A very slight *forward* movement of the hips as the snap occurs may help.

c. Push directly downward with the arms. Do not let the hands slip backward.

d. Extend the arms completely.

e. Arch the abdomen upward. Don't lower the hips.

f. Bring the feet as close as possible to the starting position of the hands. Spreading and bending the knees will help.

Spot: a. Kneel on the performer's left, place your left hand under the small of the back and your right hand under the left shoulder.

b. At the snap, support the back with your left hand (don't let the hips drop toward the mat) and lift upward with the right hand.

Note: If the performer has trouble in getting an arch, the spotter can brace his/her hips with a knee while the performer slowly brings his feet to the mat by arching. The shoulders remain on the mat as the feet are brought down. This will allow the "feel" of arching.

20. **Rolling Snap Up**—Squat and place the hands on the mat. Tuck the head as for a "Forward Roll" and roll slowly forward. As the weight comes onto the neck and shoulders, execute the "Snap Up."

Hints: a. Place the hands well in advance of the feet and place the back of the head on the mat close to the feet. This will place the shoulders in the proper position in relation to the hands as the roll is made.

DRAG LEGS

SNAP AS SHOULDERS HIT

b. Let the legs drag behind when beginning the roll. Keep the legs straight and the hips tightly flexed. The feet should remain on or near the floor till the shoulders hit.

c. Snap into the stunt the moment the weight comes onto the neck and shoulders. Don't hesitate. Make use of the momentum from the roll.

d. All other hints are the same as for the regular "Snap up."

Spot: Same as for the "Snap Up."

21. **Snap Up with Arms Free**—Assume the starting position for the "Snap Up" but remove the hands from the mat. Complete the "Snap Up" without the aid of the arm push.

Hints: a. The regular "Snap Up" should be mastered first.

b. When learning this stunt, place the hands on the thighs and shove against them when extending the legs and arching the back.

c. The back snap must be more vigorous and more downward pressure with the head must be exerted than for the regular "Snap Up."

Spot: Same as for the regular "Snap Up."

22. **Snap Up with Half Twist**—This stunt is the same as the regular "Snap Up" (using the arms to push) except that a twist is added while the body is in the air. Land facing the starting spot.

Hints: a. All of the hints for the regular "Snap Up" pertain here.

b. The extension of the legs is more nearly upward instead of upward and forward as for the regular "Snap Up."

c. In addition, just as the arms are pushing downward, twist the body by lowering one shoulder and raising the other and twisting the head in the direction of the turn.

d. Flex the hips slightly as the twist is completed to come to a stand.

Spot: For a twist left, kneel at the right side, reach under the back with your right hand to grasp his/her left hip, and place your left hand under the right shoulder. At the snap, pull toward you with your right arm and lift with the left.

23. **Handspring on Rolled Mat**—From a run and "Skip Step," place the hands on a rolled mat (or on the back of a pupil kneeling on all fours) and swing the legs upward, over the head, and down on the other side. Only the hands should contact the rolled mat and the performer should come directly to the feet.

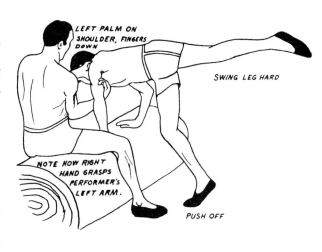

Hints: a. As the forward foot strikes the floor, swing the rear leg upward and whip the hands toward the mat.

b. The shoulders will be slightly ahead of the hands as the hands hit and the arms should be slightly bent.

c. As the hands hit, push off hard from the forward foot and swing it upward to the other foot.

d. This leg continues forward without a pause and as it reaches the vertical, the hips are snapped into an arch which drives both legs toward the mat.

e. A vigorous arm push occurs at the same instant as the hip snap.

f. The push comes from the shoulders as well as the arms.

g. The head is kept up throughout the entire stunt.

h. The feet should land close to the rolled mat. A good arch is needed to accomplish this.

Spot: a. Straddle the rolled mat with the legs to keep it from moving as the performer places his hands.

b. As the student's hands are placed, put your left hand under the left shoulder and rotate the right hand to the right (thumb down) to grasp the left upper arm from the inside. Use your wrist as well as the hand. The thumb remains alongside the fingers.

c. Lift upward with the left hand as he/she snaps into the arch and maintain the grip with the right hand (move forward if necessary by coming up on the left foot) to keep him/her from falling forward when landing.

d. A spotter can be used on both sides. The right side spotter should reverse the directions for the left and right hands.

e. Be careful not to lift too high with the hand on the shoulder. Merely *support* the shoulder and prevent it from dropping. If the spotters lift, the performer can't push.

f. If there isn't enough momentum from the leg swing and push-off, place your right hand on the abdomen and push upward and forward.

24. **Handspring**—From a short run and "Skip Step," whip the hands to the mat, swing the legs upward and over the head, and push off from the hands to land on the feet. Only the hands and the feet are to contact the mat and there must be a period of flight between the time the hands leave the mat and the feet contact it.

Hints: a. After the "Skip Step," whip the hands to the mat *close* to the forward foot.
      b. At the same time, swing the rear leg upward.
      c. As the hands strike the mat, push off from the forward foot and bring both legs together over the head.
      d. The arms should be *slightly* bent and the shoulders *slightly* in front of the hands. (Advanced performers will have shoulders slightly *behind* hands to achieve "blocking" affect.)
      e. Do not allow the shoulders to move forward once the hands have been placed.
      f. Keep the head up.
      g. As the hips come overhead, snap the back into a vigorous arch. Speed is important.
      h. At the same time, push hard from the hands.
      i. Bring the feet in as close to where the hands had been as possible. Spreading the feet somewhat will facilitate this.
      j. The stunt is done in one vigorous, forceful movement.
Spot: Kneel on the knee closest to the performer at the spot the hands will land and spot as for the "Handspring from Rolled Mat."

25. **Headspring**—This is like the "Handspring" except that the arms are bent enough to allow the head to touch the mat as the legs pass over the head.

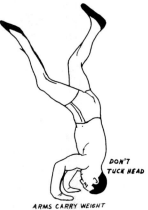

ARMS CARRY WEIGHT

DON'T TUCK HEAD

  Hints: a. Bend the arms slowly (carry the weight on the arms) till the head touches.
      b. Control the weight with the arms. Very little weight comes onto the head.
      c. Place the top of the forehead slightly ahead of the hands. Do not tuck the head when placing it on the mat.
      d. Coordinate a strong push from the hands and a vigorous snap of the back into an arch.
      e. The "Handspring" hints pertain to the "Headspring" also.
  Spot: Spot as for the "Handspring."

26. **Series of Continuous Headsprings**—This is the same as the "Headspring" except that a second one is started immediately after landing from the first.
  Hints: a. Follow the hints found under "Headspring."
      b. Take off from both feet for the second one.
      c. Be sure to keep the hips well flexed and delay the snap until the hips have passed over the head.
      d. Bring the feet well under you when landing so the body will lean forward for the next one.
  Spot: Spot as for the "Headspring," but move along with the performer as each one is completed.

27. **Headspring from Headbalance** — Assume a "Headbalance" position, Flex the hips and lose the balance forward (legs drop backward, knees straight). As the balance is lost, extend the hips into an arch, push with the arms, and come to a stand.

MOVE HIPS FORWARD

FLEX HIPS

SNAP AS BALANCE IS LOST

WEIGHT ON TOP OF FOREHEAD

ROLL TO TOP OF HEAD
MOVE HANDS • PUSH

  Hints: a. Move the hips as they are flexed. The balance should still be maintained.
      b. Keep the legs straight.
      c. Keep leaning forward till balance is lost, then move hands up even with head. Weight moves to top of head.

      d. As soon as the hands are moved, push hard with the arms and shoot the legs upward and forward, arching the back.

Spot: Kneel beside the performer's head and place both hands under his upper back. Lift upward as he snaps his hips.

28. **Handspring wih Half Twist**—This is the same as the "Handspring" except that a half twist is executed with the snap of the hips. Practice the "Snap Up with Half Twist" first.

    Hints: a. Follow the hints for the "Handspring" up to the point where the push-off is made.

        b. With the push, twist the hips to the right, look over the right shoulder, and bring the left arm over the body and the right arm under. Lift the left shoulder.

        c. Flex the hips slightly after the twist is made to facilitate the landing.

    Spot: Spot on the side away from the twist (left). Place your left arm under the back as his/her legs pass over the head and grasp the right hip. The right hand goes under the left shoulder and lifts as the right one pulls toward you.

29. **One Arm Cartwheel (Near Hand)**—Stand with the left side toward the mat, the left arm raised, and the right hand on the hip. Lean to the right, then quickly back to the left and place the left hand on the mat while swinging the legs overhead as in the regular "Cartwheel." The right hand stays on the hip.

    Hints: a. Do a regular cartwheel immediately before trying the One Arm. If still hesitant, try another but put very little weight on the right arm.

        b. Place the left hand with the fingers pointing backward.

        c. Keep the arm straight (elbow locked).

        d. Keep the head up and the back arched.

        e. Swing the right leg upward forcefully as the left hand goes to the mat.

        f. Push from the left leg as soon as the left hand hits. Lots of momentum is needed.

        g. Keep the legs well spread.

    Spot: Spot as for the "Cartwheel."

30. **One Arm Cartwheel (Far Hand)**—Stand with the left side toward the mat, the right arm extended upward, and the left hand on the hip. Sway right sideward, then throw the weight vigorously left sideward onto the right hand. Continue as in the regular "Cartwheel."

    Hints: a. First learn the regular "Cartwheel" well, then practice for the "One Arm Cartwheel" by gradually decreasing the amount of weight placed on the left hand. Try four or five in a row rather than waiting for rest of squad after first try. Soon the left hand will not need to be used.

        b. A great deal of speed (momentum) is needed.

        c. As the right arm goes to the mat, lift the right leg high and tip sideward on the left.

        d. Push hard from the left foot as soon as the right hand hits.

        e. The fingers of the right hand point backward.

        f. Keep the head up, the back arched, and the legs well spread.

    Spot: Spot as for the regular "Cartwheel."

31. **One Arm Handspring**—This is the same as the "Handspring" except that only one arm is used for the push. Place the other hand on the hip. Master the "Handspring" from both arms before trying this.

    Hints: a. Keep the supporting arm straight, elbow locked.

        b. Place the hand fairly close to the forward foot.

        c. Be sure the head is kept up.

        d. Guard against letting the shoulder move forward as the push-off from the foot is made.

        e. The whip, or snap, is very fast.

        f. A very vigorous push is needed from the lead foot.

        g. Practice with both hands on the mat at first, then gradually reduce the weight on one arm.

    Spot: Kneel on the side of the supporting arm and lift on that shoulder with both hands.

32. **Leap to a Handspring**—This is like the regular "Handspring" except that the takeoff is from both feet instead of one. Leap onto the hands from both feet (period of flight) and continue on over to the feet (period of flight).

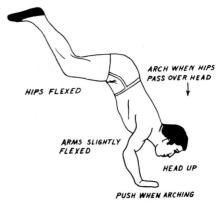

Hints: a. Place the hands close to the feet (18 inches) and keep the arms slightly flexed.

b. Keep the hips well flexed until they pass forward of the shoulders.

c. Just after the hips pass over the shoulders, snap into an arch and immediately push downward with the arms.

d. The snap comes just a little later than for the regular "Handspring."

e. Keep the head up.

Spot: Kneel beside the spot the hands will hit, place both hands under the closest shoulder, and lift.

33. **Backward Roll to a Handbalance**—Start as for the "Backward Roll." As the hips come overhead and the weight comes onto the shoulders, extend the legs and hips upward, press downward with the arms, and pass through a momentary handbalance position. From there, flex the hips, push from the hands, come to a stand.

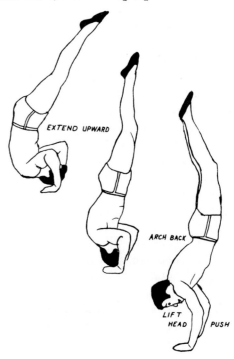

Hints: a. Practice the "Lift and Toss" (stunt No. 9, page 94) first.

b. As the weight comes to the rounded back, place the hands palms downward on the mat beside the head with fingers pointing to shoulders.

c. Immediately thrust the legs upward (arch the back) in an explosive movement. This must not be done slowly. The extension is *part* of the role.

d. At the same time, push vigorously with the arms.

e. The direction of the leg extension is slightly backward. A good arch of the back is needed to bring the feet overhead.

f. With the arm push, snap the head up.

g. Timing is important. A too early extension will result in a fall on the back; too late will cause the legs to go backward instead of upward.

Spot: Stand opposite the performer's starting position and grasp his/her legs immediately if he/she extends too soon and starts to fall forward. It isn't necessary to spot if extension is late.

34. **Backward Roll to a Headbalance**—This is the same as above (to a handbalance) except that the stunt finishes in a headbalance. Roll backward as before and extend, but not quite so vigorously. Also do not push as hard with the arms. From the headbalance, tuck the head and roll forward to a stand. This is more difficult than going to a handbalance because the amount of extension and arm push must be controlled.

Hints: a. Place the hands as before.

b. Extend the body fast, but not as forcefully.

c. At the same time, push with the hands only enough to take some of the weight off the head. The head also pushes but is not lifted off the mat.

d. With the hip extension and arm push, roll across the head to the top of the forehead.

e. At the same time, shift the hands backward so the head and hands form a triangle with the head as the point. The shift of the hands is part of the push and must be done quickly.

f. Brace hard with the hands as soon as they have been moved back.

Spot: Grasp the ankles and lift straight upward as the performer extends upward.

35. **Tinsica**—This stunt is like the "Cartwheel," but it is done forward instead of sideward. Start with the right foot forward and place the right hand on the mat in front of it. Raise the left leg backward, place the left hand ahead of the right and push off from the right foot. The legs pass over the head (remaining spread) and land first on the left foot then the right.

    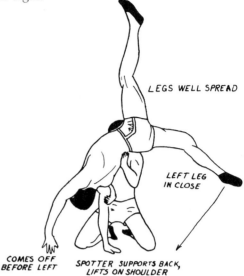

    LEGS WELL SPREAD

    LEFT LEG IN CLOSE

    COMES OFF BEFORE LEFT

    SPOTTER SUPPORTS BACK, LIFTS ON SHOULDER

    Hints: a. Use a "Skip Step" and whip the hands downward.
    - b. Kick the left leg up vigorously and, as the right hand contacts the mat, push off hard from the right foot.
    - c. Arch the back well. Bring the left leg as close as possible to the spot where the hands had been.
    - d. Keep the arms straight and the left shoulder directly over the left hand.
    - e. The legs should remain straight.
    - f. Push off from the left hand, using the shoulder for the push.

    Spot: Kneel beside the spot where the hands will hit, support the back of the performer with one hand and place the other under his shoulder and lift.

36. **Forward Walkover**—Usually done by girls but flexible boys can do it also. Place the hands on the mat parallel to each other, slightly ahead of the right foot while raising the left foot backward and upward as high as possible. As the hands hit, push from the right foot. The left leg continues over to land close to the hands. Push from the shoulders to bring the body upright. There is no period of flight. The hands remain in contact till the left foot lands. The legs remain straight and well spread.

    Hints: a. Keep shoulders directly above hands as left leg swings upward.
    - b. Raise left leg high as possible before pushing from right.
    - c. The left leg moves in a continuous, stretched arc.
    - d. Good shoulder and upper back flexibility is required.
    - e. Reach forward with the right foot as the left lands.
    - f. Push from (extend) the shoulders and the fingers.
    - g. The shoulders are still over the hands.

    Spot: a. Kneel by performer's right hand and place left hand on his/her right shoulder while placing the right in the small of the back as he/she arches.
    - b. Support with the right hand and lift with the left.

37. **Back Flip**—From a stand, spring upward, turn over backward (feet pass over the head) and land on both feet, slightly behind the takeoff spot. First learn the "Sitting Foot-Pitch Back Flip" (No. 23, page 96).

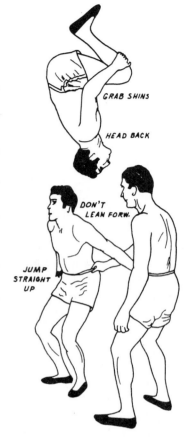

GRAB SHINS

HEAD BACK

DON'T LEAN FORW.

JUMP STRAIGHT UP

Hints:
  a. Bend the knees and swing the arms backward to obtain momentum for the spring, but *do not* lean forward with the shoulders. They should be over the hips.
  b. Spring hard and swing the arms forward and upward. They should be slightly bent.
  c. Just before the height of the jump is reached, snap the head back and draw the knees to the chest.
  d. Grasp the shins with the hands over the head. Bring the knees *up* to the hands, don't reach down to the knees.
  e. Hold a tight tuck (pull the knees in tight) till you see the ground, then open up for the landing. Keep the eyes open.
  f. The jump should be almost straight up. Do not lean too far backward when springing.

Spot:
  a. If a safety belt is used, the spotters grasp the ropes close to the swivel. The performer's arms are in front of the ropes. The spotters lift upward as the performer jumps.
  b. Two towels may serve as a safety belt, one in front and the other behind the performer. A spotter at each side grasps the towels and holds them together, close to the performer's waist.
  c. Two spotters may grasp the waistband of the performer's trunks (getting a handful of the shirt and supporter too). The one on the left uses the right hand, the other one the left. This hand lifts and supports, while the free hand can be used under the performer's thigh to help to turn him over.
  d. As the performer learns the stunt, the assistance can be reduced to an upward push on the hips as he/she turns over, and finally it can be done alone.

38. **Back Handspring**—From a standing position, sit backward as into a chair. As the balance is lost, extend the legs and swing the arms vigorously upward and backward. Push off from the heels, arch the back, reach for the mat with the hands and land in an inverted position. As the hands hit, push off and snap the legs down to a stand.

Hints:
  a. Keep the back upright (shoulders directly over hips) as you sit backward and swing the arms backward. Be *off* balance at this point.
  b. Whip the arms forward, upward, backward, and downward, in a hard, circular motion, keeping the arms fairly straight.
  c. At the same time, arch the back by throwing the abdomen upward.
  d. As the arms go back, snap the head back and *keep* it back.
  e. Drag the legs. Don't jump for height. Simply snap the abdomen upward.
  f. Bring the hands as close to where the feet had been as possible and keep the arms straight.
  g. As the hands hit, push off and flex the hips with a snap.
  h. There must be a period of flight between the time the feet leave the mat and the hands hit and also after the hands leave the mat before the feet hit.

Note: This is frequently learned on a trampoline to give the performer more confidence and because the spring of the bed makes it easier to get your hips overhead.

Spot:
  a. To start, two spotters should "carry" the performer through the stunt. The spotter on the performer's left uses his right hand to hold his partner's left, just behind and above the performer's hips. The free hands are placed on the back of the performer's thighs. The per-

former then arches back over the clasped hands of the spotters and they lift him up and over onto his hands so he gets the feel of the stunt.

b. After several trials, the performer can throw for the stunt. Spotting is as above, but not so much lifting and carrying.

c. A spotting belt may be used if available. Spotters must support, rather than lift as when spotting for the "Back Flip."

d. If only one spotter is used, kneel on the right knee, slightly behind and to the left of the performer and place the right hand in the small of his/her back, fingers pointing upward. As he/she springs, lift upward on the back and support it till the hands hit. The left hand can lift on the performer's left upper leg to help him/her over. Use one spotter only after he/she has tried it several times with two.

39. **Front Flip**—From a run, spring off from both feet, turn over forward in the air (hips and feet over head) and land on both feet in front of the takeoff spot.

Hints: a. Lift with the arms as the jump is made. The hands reach upward from a position in front of the chest and not from below the hips.

b. Lean *slightly* forward. Height is important. Imagine you are flipping over a wall at head height.

c. At the height of the spring, tuck the head forward, raise the hips and draw the knees to the chest. The hips should pass higher than the head. Tuck tightly.

d. Swing the arms downward and backward. Grasp the shins with the hands.

e. Open the tuck and raise the head to land.

Spot: a. If a safety belt is used, the spotters must run along beside the performer as the run is begun. At the takeoff, they lift upward on the ropes (one hand close to the swivel) to support the performer.

b. A short mat may be held about 18 inches from the floor by six students and the performer may try his "Front Flip" into the mat. (Ropes passing through the handles and under the mat will save the handles from ripping off.) As the performer gains proficiency the mat may be dropped. A strong piece of canvas or a spotting net may be used instead of the mat.

c. If enough mats are available, pile the mats to a thickness of about three feet and have the performer do the flip from the floor to the piled mats. He can start with a high "Dive Roll" and gradually work into the flip. Even if he/she lands on the back, no harm will result as the drop will be minimal.

d. An indoor high jump pit made of sponge rubber or a layer of inflated old automobile inner tubes covered by a mat make excellent places to practice the "Front Flip."

e. A single spotter may stand to the right of the performer's takeoff spot and place his right hand on the back of the performer's head as he/she jumps upward. The hand can be used to flip the performer over by pressing downward, backward, and upward in an arc. Place the left hand on the abdomen and lift upward as the right hand presses downward.

40. **Flying Front Flip**—This stunt is fundamentally the same as the "Front Flip." However, it is begun with a swan dive. Jump upward so that the body is parallel to the floor, back arched, head up, and arms stretched sideward before tucking into the flip.

Hints: a. A fast run is needed.

b. Take off from both feet.

c. Get as much height as possible, carrying the legs very high.

d. Hold the "Swan" position (head up, back arched, arms sideward) momentarily only.

e. Tuck the head forward and flex the hips, pulling them overhead and forward as vigorously as possible.

f. At the same time, bring the arms vigorously downward to grasp the shins and pull them in tight to the body.

g. Tuck up very tightly.

h. Open by extending the legs downward and lifting the head.

41. **Russian Front Flip**—This flip has an entirely different technique, and for most people it is a little more difficult. From a run and a two-foot takeoff, throw the arms backward and upward, tuck the head forward, flex and raise the hips over the head, turn over and land again on the feet. It is wise to practice this first from a takeoff from a Reuther Board (semi-springboard used in vaulting).

Hints: a. Raise the arms overhead on the "hurdle" (last step before landing on both feet) for the takeoff.

b. The feet should be slightly ahead of the hips.

c. Swing the arms vigorously downward, backward and upward. The emphasis is on the upward thrust.

d. Resist the tendency to bend forward at the waist as the arms drive upward as far as they can go behind you.

e. Keep the arms fairly close together—don't spread them sideward.

f. Tuck the head well (chin on chest), but don't bring the head and shoulders down.

g. Flex the hips and bring them up between the raised arms and over the head.

h. Extend the legs downward and look forward as the rotation is completed.

Spot: a. Stand to the right of his takeoff spot, place the right hand on his upper back and support him as he turns over.

42. **Combinations**—Many combinations of stunts are possible. For example:
    a. Cartwheel right (½ turn), Cartwheel left, Round Off, Backward Roll to Handstand.
    b. "Forward Roll," "Rolling Snap Up," "Headspring," "Walkover," "Cartwheel Flip."
    c. "Round Off, "Back Flip."
    d. "Round Off," "Back Handspring," "Back Flip."
    e. "Front Handspring," "Forward Roll," "Front Flip."

Partner Stunts

For most of the partner stunts the partners should be of approximately equal height and weight. When this is not so, it will be mentioned in the stunt's description.

1. **Forward Double Roll**—B (bottom student) lies on back with feet raised. T (top student) straddles B's head and grasps the raised ankles. B grasps T's ankles and T tucks and does a "Forward Roll." B is pulled to his feet by the grasp on T's ankles and he/she also does a "Forward Roll." This brings T up again and the performance is repeated. The rolls should be smooth and continuous.

Hints: a. As T starts the roll, he/she takes a *slight* forward leap, lifts the hips upward and *places B's feet* on the mat close to the hips.
   b. T bends the arms and places the back of his/her tucked head on the mat between B's feet.
   c. T controls his/her weight with the arms, bending them fairly slowly to avoid dropping on the head.
   d. B raises head and shoulders and leans forward as T leaps.
   e. Both stay well tucked. They keep their knees bent as they roll across their backs so their feet can be placed close to their buttocks.
   f. Each must place his/her partner's feet on the mat before the head lands.
   g. *Exaggerate* the lowering of the body when first learning the stunt.

Spot: a. Stand to the right of the performers and place the right hand on the shoulder of the one going into the roll. Give a little support as he/she lowers if he doesn't take his weight on the arms.
   b. Grasp the bottom person's right upper arm with the left hand and lift if he/she has difficulty in getting up.

2. **Triple Over and Under Rolls**—L (one on left), C (one in center), and R (one on right) kneel on hands and knees, side by side, about 18 inches apart. C rolls sideward to left toward L while L does a leap over C and rolls right. R leaps over L and rolls to his left. C has come to hands and knees by this time (following the roll) and leaps right sideward over R who is rolling toward him/her. This leaping and rolling continues. As each one comes to the outside, he/she always leaps toward the center over the one rolling toward him/her.
   Hints: a. Start the leap as soon as a person starts rolling toward you.
      b. For the leap, push back from the hands to put the weight momentarily on the feet and off the knees. Immediately push off from the toes, reach over the one rolling toward you and spring over.
      c. The hands land first, then the toes. The body must be extended.

d. Roll as soon as you land. Try to make it one motion.

e. Finish the roll by coming directly to the hands and knees and be prepared to leap in the opposite direction.

f. Keep the legs straight while rolling so as not to interfere with the person leaping over you.

3. **Backward Double Roll**—B lies on back (hips at end of mat) with the legs in the air. T straddles the head and grasps the upraised ankles. B grasps T's ankles. T squats and does a backward roll, pulling B's feet to the mat on either side of his/her head. At the same time B rolls to the feet. The ankle grasps must be maintained. When coming up from the bottom position each must land squarely on the feet and the knees must not touch the mat or the bottom person.

Hints: a. T pulls upward and backward on the legs of B, then bends knees for the backward roll.

b. He/she sits down as close to his/her own heels as possible.

c. When rolling onto the back, lift the legs upward (keeping knees flexed) to raise B's chest upward and aid in getting B to his feet.

d. B pushes downward on T's ankles to aid coming to his/her feet.

e. The hips of both should remain flexed.

f. Each one does the roll as close to the partner as possible and they both stay well tucked.

Spot: Move along beside the couple and lift on the bottom person's shoulder if help is needed.

4. **Back-to-Back Pull Over**—B faces T and they clasp hands. They turn back to back, retaining the grasp (hands are swung sideward and overhead). B leans forward and pulls T upward and over his back. T rolls across B's back and down to a stand facing him. They again turn and now T pulls B over.

Hints:

KEEP LEGS STRAIGHT, HIPS FLEXED

HIPS HIGH

a. B must have hips just below T's hips.

b. Both partner's arms should be straight.

c. As B leans forward, he pulls on T's arms and T lies backward and flexes the hips to bring the feet over the head.

d. B's bending must occur at the waist. The knees should be kept fairly straight.

e. T *must wait* until B starts to *lean forward* before he leans backward and flexes his hips.

f. T keeps hips flexed all the way.

g. B must be careful not to step backward while throwing T.

h. The pair should be about the same height and weight.

Spot: a. Stand at B's right side with the right hand on T's left shoulder from in front of his arm.

b. The left hand is placed under T's back to lift upward if necessary.

c. Support T's shoulder as he rolls backward over B.

5. **Bobbin Backward**—B stands behind T and bends forward to place his head between T's legs and grasps T's ankles. T leans backward as B straightens up to a standing position. T places his hands on the mat behind B and B releases T's ankles to allow him to turn over to his feet. T then places his head between B's legs and the positions are reversed.

Hints: a. As T leans backward he must reach backward with his arms and look backward at the same time.

b. B does *not* start to straighten *until* T has started to lean backward.

c. B's legs must remain fairly straight. The hips must be high.

d. B straightens slowly, without a jerk or snap. He maintains his grip on T's ankles until T is inverted and his hands touch the mat.

e. T places his hands close to B's heels. The arms are stiff, the *head up*.

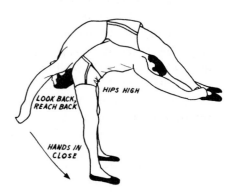

LOOK BACK, REACH BACK

HIPS HIGH

HANDS IN CLOSE

Spot: a. Stand at B's left and place the right hand on T's left shoulder by reaching in front of the raised left arm as he leans back. This support is to prevent his falling on his head if the arms fail to support him.

   b. Place the left hand under T's lower back to aid in lifting him over if he needs help.

6. **Bobbin Forward**—T stands behind B and does a handbalance with his hands about a foot from B's heels. He drops his legs over B's shoulders. B grasps T's ankles and bends forward which pulls T up and over B's back. B then places T's feet on the mat in front and T comes to a stand in front of B. Then B does a handstand behind T and the positions are reversed.

   Hints: a. Partners should be about equal in height and weight.

   b. The handbalancer must keep the arms straight and the head up.

   c. The knee joints must strike the bottom person's shoulders.

   d. B must be well braced and *must bend* forward from the waist *before* T removes his hands from the mat.

   e. The top person flexes at the hips *after* the partner has started to bend forward.

   f. B must not fail to put the partner's feet on the mat. If he/she continues to hold the ankles, the partner will fall forward on his/her face.

   Spot: a. Aid in placing T's legs over B's shoulders.

   b. Place one arm under the handbalancer's back to lift in case the bottom person is dragged backwards by the handbalancer's weight.

   c. The other hand grasps the performer's nearest arm as he/she is lifted to prevent falling forward when landing.

7. **Knee-Shoulder Spring**—B lies on back with feet apart, close to buttocks. The knees too are spread and the arms are extended upward. T takes a short run and skip step, places his/her hands on B's knees and shoulders in B's hands and swings the legs upward and over, coming to a stand beyond B's head.

   Hints: a. The "Skip Step" should be close enough so that the forward foot lands close to B's buttocks.

   b. As the forward foot lands, place the hands on B's knees (fingers forward) and start the rear leg swinging upward. A high leg swing is very important.

   c. Lean well forward as this is done so that the shoulders are over B's shoulders.

   d. Push off hard from the supporting foot as the shoulders contact B's hands.

   e. As the feet swing overhead, snap the back into an arch, lay the head back, and push from the hands.

   f. B must push upward on T's shoulders as T snaps into an arch.

   Spot: a. Kneel on the left knee to the left of B's head, place the right hand under T's right shoulder, and hook his right arm above the elbow with the left hand and wrist (palm upward).

   b. As T snaps into an arch, lift up on the shoulder and keep the grip on his/her right arm to prevent a fall forward.

   c. Come up on the right leg if necessary to move forward with T.

8. **Triple Jump and Roll**—R and C face each other and L stands behind C. They stand about four feet apart. C does a forward roll toward R who does a straddle jump over the rolling C. As R lands he goes into a forward roll toward L who leaps over and also goes into a forward roll as soon as he/she lands from the jump. By this time, C has regained his/her feet, turned around, and is ready to straddle-jump over L who is now rolling toward him/her. Continue six or eight times.

Hints: a. Be sure to stay tucked up in a ball when rolling. Stay as compact as possible.

b. Start to leap over the person rolling toward you as the roll begins. Let him/her roll under you.

c. The leap should not be very far forward. Height is more important.

d. Straddle the legs well while leaping. Swing the arms upward and keep the trunk erect. *Don't lean forward or look downward.*

e. Go into the roll as soon as you land from the jump.

f. Come to your feet and turn around as soon as you finish the roll so as to be ready to straddle over the one rolling toward you.

g. Start rather slowly then gradually speed up.

h. Once you start your roll, don't hesitate. Go right on into it.

9. **Lift and Toss**—T assumes a lying position on the upper back with his legs upward and hips raised from the mat. The palms are placed on the mat beside the head with the fingers pointing toward the shoulders. B stands behind T's buttocks with his right foot under the raised buttocks and the left foot close to T's right armpit. B grasps T's ankles and lifts upward and forward on them, flipping T off the mat and over onto his feet. As B lifts, T extends his hips and pushes with his hands to help get the body into the air. He then flexes the hips and brings the feet down to a stand.

Hints: a. T must be loose and relaxed. B lifts and lowers T's legs in a pumping motion to test for relaxation.

b. At a prearranged signal, B lifts and T snaps into an arch.

c. With the snap, T throws his head up and pushes hard with the hands.

d. B shifts his weight to his forward foot as he lifts to insure an upward and forward lift.

e. He releases T's ankles at the height of the lift.

Spot: Stand behind the spot where T will land and be prepared to brace the back in case he/she loses the balance backward.

Note: This can be done with two throwers—one on each ankle.

10. **Handspring from High Back**—B assumes a bent position with hands on knees, and legs well spread. T runs from behind B, places his/her hands on B's back, and, with a jump, does a "Handspring" over B.

Hints: a. B must have his/her back flat and firm and have one leg forward as a brace to prevent being pushed forward by T.

b. T takes off from *both* feet and raises the hips overhead, keeping them flexed. The head should be forward.

c. The arms bear the weight and are slightly flexed, with the shoulders somewhat in front of the hands.

d. As the hips pass beyond the head, T snaps the back into an arch, pushes from the arms, lets the head drop back, and lands on the feet.

e. The arm push should be straight downward.

Spot: a. Stand in front of B and brace his/her right shoulder with your right hip. The left foot is well forward and the right knee partly bent.

b. As T does the handspring, place the right hand on his/her right shoulder (fingers pointing downward) and hook the right arm with your left hand and wrist, just above his elbow. Grasp the arm from below.

c. Support his/her shoulder with the right hand and maintain the grip with the left hand to prevent falling forward when landing.

11. **Front Flip from Shoulders**—T mounts to a stand on B's shoulders with the assistance of the spotter. B reaches upward to grasp T's hands. T then jumps into a front flip from B's shoulders and lands with his/her back toward B. Their hands remain grasped.

   Hints: a. T must not just *fall* forward, but jumps and raises the flexed hips upward over the head and tucks the head and knees to the chest.
   b. B must present a firm base. He/she must not step back.
   c. B's arms must be firm so that T can derive partial support from them.

   Spot: Stand to the right of B and reach up to support T's upper back as he/she flips over.

12. **Double Cartwheel**—B and T face each other and B bends left sideward, placing the right arm around T from the left and left arm around T from the right. B grasps hands behind T's back and straightens up, uncrossing the arms, and in so doing, lifts T up to an inverted position. T then grasps B around the waist and spreads his/her legs. B bends left sideward till T's left foot strikes the mat followed by the right. This brings B into an inverted position. T bends right sideward until B's right foot hits the mat followed by the left. Again the positions are reversed. Continue, rolling as a wheel rolls.

   Hints: a. A lot of speed and momentum is needed in the sideward bending.
   b. The feet must be very widespread.
   c. Rock slightly to the right to gain momentum for the left sideward bending.
   d. Keep the legs braced because as soon as the legs hit, you must lift your partner.

   Spot: Two spotters are needed. One stands behind each person to prevent collapsing backward. They can also help in the lifting if needed.

13. **Rear Foot-to-Pelvis Back Flip**—B lies on his/her back and T straddles B's shoulders, facing his/her head. B brings the feet under T's buttocks and T springs into a back flip assisted by a push from B's feet. T's feet go over his/her head and he/she comes down to a stand facing B.

Hints: a. B must time the push with T's spring.

   b. The direction of the push is upward and forward, away from him/her.

   c. As T springs upward and is pushed by B, he flings the arms upward, snaps the head backward, and tucks the knees quickly to the chest to gain "spin."

   d. Open up to land.

Spot: a. Stand behind and to the left of T and place the left hand on his/her lower back and the right hand on his/her left shoulder from in front of the arm. The left hand pushes upward to create spin and the right hand maintains its grip to prevent T's falling backward.

   b. A safety belt should be used if it is available. Two spotters are then used.

14. **Sitting Foot-Pitch Back Flip**—B sits on the mat with legs spread and the back of his/her hands on the mat between the legs. T steps onto B's hands and springs into a "Back Flip" (complete revolution in the air) assisted by a lift from B's hands.

Hints: a. T steps on B's hands with the balls of the feet.

   b. He swings both arms backward and bends the knees somewhat, being careful to keep back and head erect, and springs upward, swinging the arms vigorously overhead.

   c. As he/she does, B lifts straight upward and rolls backward, legs spread, to get out of the way.

   d. As T reaches the height of the spring, he/she snaps the head backward and quickly draws knees to the chest and wraps arms around the shins.

   e. Open just before landing.

   f. T must be careful not to lean backward as he/she springs.

Spot: a. If a belt is used, a spotter stands on each side of T and grasps the rope close to the swivel. They lift upward as he/she jumps.

   b. If one spotter is used, stand at T's left and grasp his/her belt with the right hand. Lift upward with this hand as the jump is made and push upward on T's thigh or buttocks with the left hand to increase the spin.

   c. The left hand must be shifted to the back of T's left shoulder as he/she lands to prevent his/her losing balance backward.

15. **Toe-Pitch Back Flip**—B stands with legs well spread, the right foot slightly behind the left and both knees well bent. He/she places the back of the left hand in the right and grasps the left thumb, with the fingers of the left hand extended across the right wrist. The forearms are pressed tightly against the front of the pelvis. T steps on to B's left hand with the right foot and places the hands on B's shoulders. Now he/she springs up off of the left foot, presses downward against B's hands with the right foot and goes into a "Back Flip." B assists by lifting upward against the downward pressure of T's leg.

Hints: a. B's body and head are erect, shoulders directly over the hips. Much of the lift comes from the legs.

   b. T hops on the left foot as he places his/her right foot into B's hand.

   c. Most of the drive comes from the right leg.

   d. The spring is straight upward. T must stay close to B on the way up.

   e. B lifts straight upward, following T's foot as far as possible.

   f. Only at the height of the lift does T throw arms upward, snap the head back and tuck.

   g. B *must not* step back.

   h. Practice the lift without the flip a few times to get correct timing. When doing this, T must be sure to keep his head forward.

Spot: a. When practicing the lift alone, stand directly behind T and place a hand against the back to prevent loss of balance backward.

   b. When spotting for the flip, a spotter should stand at either side and be prepared to support T's shoulders as he/she turns and comes down. Also be prepared to brace the back in case of an overspin.

   c. A safety belt should be used if it is available.

16. **Ankle-Pitch Front Flip**—B stands behind T who bends the right knee to lift the foot backward. B grasps the ankle and lifts upward on it as T springs off his/her left foot and turns over forward, doing a "Front Flip" to a stand.

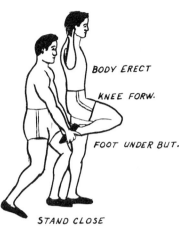

BODY ERECT

KNEE FORW.

FOOT UNDER BUT.

STAND CLOSE

    Hints: a. T brings the right knee forward and right foot directly under the buttocks. The upper leg is almost parallel to the floor.

         b. Dip downward on the left knee and spring upward (not forward), getting added lift by throwing the arms upward.

         c. As height is gained, whip arms downward and under, grasping the shins.

         d. At the same time, tuck the head and raise the hips overhead, bringing the knees to the chest.

         e. B dips (bends knees) at the same time T does.

         f. As T jumps, B lifts straight upward on the left foot and helps T to get height and gain spin.

         g. T straightens out as the feet come downward to land.

    Spot: a. Stand at T's right, and as he/she does the flip, place the right hand on the back of his/her neck and push downward, backward, and upward in an arc.

         b. Be ready to reach up and grasp the right upper arm in case of an overspin.

         c. If a safety belt is used, two spotters hold the ropes close to the swivels and lift as the flip is done.

17. **Back-Pitch Back Flip**—B stands with legs well braced, hands on knees, and body bent forward at the waist. T starts a run from behind B, jumps to B's back and does a "Back Flip" off the back as B straightens up with a snap. T lands on his feet behind B.

    Hints: a. T takes off from one foot and jumps just high enough to clear B's back. B should be fairly low.

         b. T lands with feet fairly close together on B's upper back.

         c. B is prepared to spring as *soon* as he lands. The knees are partially bent, the arms are back, the head is looking straight ahead.

         d. B straightens with a snap as soon as he feels T's feet.

         e. B must *not* move forward.

         f. As B straightens, T swings his arms up over his head, pushes from his legs, and throws his head backward.

         g. They should practice the jump to the back a number of times before trying the flip. This will help them get used to the timing.

THROW ARMS UP, HEAD BACK

SPOTTER'S HAND ON BELT

SPOTTER PUSH ON THIGH TO AID SPIN

BACK FAIRLY FLAT

HEAD UP

THROW WITH LEGS AND BACK

    Spot: a. One man stands in front of B and braces his/her shoulder to prevent his/her moving forward.

         b. Two other men spot T with a safety belt. They run along with T as he/she runs for the jump to the back. They hold the ropes close to the swivel.

         c. One person may spot by grasping T's belt with the left hand and pushing up on T's hips with the right hand as T springs.

17

Static Balance Stunts

Balance stunts are often used in both tumbling and simple stunt programs, and are often considered to be part of these activities. Though they are never used in tumbling *competition,* they constitute an important part of competitive floor exercise routines. These stunts are characterized by a single position (relatively difficult to hold) that is obtained and *maintained* for a number of seconds before it is discontinued. The various "scales" and "levers" found in the Simple Stunts chapter under the heading of "Floor Exercise Stunts and Transitions" also meet this criteria but these balances are separated because they involve balance on body parts other than the feet and are primarily in an inverted position.

Students should practice till the various balances can be held without wavering for over five seconds. Good form (stretched body, legs straight and together, toes pointed) actually aids in the performance of the balances. This is so because the number of variables are reduced. A loose, wavering body with the legs bent and waving about is bound to throw the balance off.

Several mechanical principles should be considered and followed when teaching balance stunts. (1) The broader the base, the easier to achieve stability. This can easily be illustrated by trying to balance a cone on its tip and then turning it over to balance it on the opposite end. (2) The closer the center of gravity is to the base of support, the greater the stability. Establish this fact by having the pupils try a "tucked" head balance and then an extended one. (3) If balance is "lost," begin to make the needed adjustments *immediately.* If one waits too long, too much momentum is gained by the body, and it cannot be restored to balance. Demonstrate this principle to the clas by balancing a ruler on your hand. Show how you can move the base under the center of gravity to balance the ruler, but if you wait too long to move it, it cannot be done.

The individual balance stunts can usually be done by half of the squad at one time while the other half does the spotting. After the first group has tried the stunt several times, its members change places with the spotters. The performers should line up along the edge of the mat and work across, rather than down the length of the mat.

In spotting balances, do not grasp, lift and *hold* the person in the position of balance. Release the performer as much as possible so he can learn to make his own adjustments and keep his balance. However, keep your hands very close and ready to regrasp if he starts to fall. Only in extreme cases of need should the spotter *lift* the performer's legs into position. The performer should kick up and then the spotter steadies the body.

If a student has tried a number of times and failed to kick high enough (perhaps through fear of kicking too hard, overbalancing, and landing on the back), the following device is often successful: place him/her in the proper position to kick into the balance, then hold your hand in a relatively low position behind and above him and tell him/her to kick your hand with a foot. When he/she does this, raise your hand a few inches and have him/her repeat. Keep increasing the height slightly each time, and before long he/she will be kicking up to where he/she should be. This is the result of concentrating on a new objective—simply that of reaching your hand. In this way confidence in ones own abilities can be developed.

However, if this fails, the spotter is justified in reaching down, grasping the legs, and lifting them into position. Once one "feels" where the position is, he/she may become more successful in future attempts. Don't keep performers in the inverted position too long—8 to 10 seconds is enough at one time.

Individual Stunts

All of these stunts can be used in the construction of pyramids. (See Chapter 18.)

1. **Tip-Up**—Squat and place the hands on the mat about shoulder width apart with the arms between the knees. Rest the knees on the upper arms just above the elbows and lean forward. Raise the toes from the mat and balance on the hands.
   Hints: a. Keep the head up and the hips and knees well flexed.
   b. The elbows are bent slightly backward and sideward.
   c. The fingers point forward and the hand is cupped (palm raised slightly from the mat).
   d. If the weight is too far forward, press downward with the fingertips and raise the head. If it is too far backward, press downward with the heels of the hands and lower the head.
   e. If the balance is *lost* forward, tuck the head and go into a forward roll.

2. **Head Balance**—Place the hands on the mat, shoulder width apart and the head just as far in front of the hands as they are apart from each other. Raise the feet overhead so that the balance is maintained on the head and hands with the body in an inverted position.

   Hints: a. Place the top of the *forehead* (at the hairline) on the mat, not the top of the *head*.
   b. Bring the feet in close to the hands so as to raise the hips.
   c. Raise the feet slowly by pressing downward with the hands.
   d. Keep most of the weight on the hands and arms until the hips are directly above the head.
   e. Keep the knees bent until the hips are above the head.

   f. Straighten the legs upward slowly and arch the back. Keep the balance all the way up, not just at the peak.
   g. If the balance is *lost* forward, immediately press with the hands to take the weight off the neck, tuck the head and hips, and roll forward. Flex the hips and come to the feet if the balance is *lost* backward.

   Spot: Stand behind the performer and catch and steady him/her at the hips. Don't assist too much. Let loose as soon as possible but be prepared to grab again.

   Note: This is frequently taught by having the performer kick up one leg at a time. (See hints *b* and *c* for Stunt No. 3, below.) However, a beginner will be apt to do one of two things: not kick hard enough because of the *fear* of going over, or kick too hard and *go* over. The method suggested above allows them to gain balance in a tucked position (which is relatively easy) and then keep it as they extend upward.

3. **Head-Forearm Balance**—Place the forearms on the mat with the elbows shoulder width apart and the hands together. Place the top of the forehead in the hands. Raise one leg and push off from the other to an inverted position.

   Hints: a. Do not interlock fingers. Place the back of one hand on the other palm.

   b. Bring one foot forward as far as possible and keep the other one extended.

   c. Swing the rear leg upward (keeping it straight) and push from the forward foot. Do not push too hard.

   d. Use pressure on the elbows to help raise the hips.

   e. Bring the feet together overhead and stretch the body upward (back arched).

   f. If no spotter is present and the balance is lost forward, tuck the head, flex the hips and go into a forward roll.

   Spot: Same as for the "Head Balance."

   Note: The method for raising the legs in the "Head Balance" is not used here because it is too difficult to get the hips high enough with the elbows on the mat and the elbows can't produce the pressure that the arms can. Also, after having learned the "Head Balance," they have a better idea of keeping the balance.

4. **Handbalance**—From a standing start with one foot forward, whip the hands toward the mat and swing the rear leg upward. As the hands contact the mat, push off from the forward foot and raise it to join the other foot overhead. This inverted position on the hands must be maintained.

   Hints: a. Place the hands on the mat shoulder width apart, *close* to the forward foot, pointing forward.

   b. *Keep the head up* throughout. Focus the eyes on a spot a few inches ahead of the hands.

   c. Keep the legs and the back stretched when swinging up.

   d. The shoulders should be *slightly* in front of the hands and should *not* be moved forward as the legs swing upward.

   e. Keep the arms straight.

   f. If you feel the balance being lost forward, press on the fingers and lift hard with the head *immediately.*

   g. If you feel the balance being lost backward, bend the arms slightly and pull the elbows inward while pressing down hard on the heels of the hands and lowering the head a little.

   h. It is extremely important to start these adjustments at once. The fingers, hands, and arms work almost continuously to keep the balance.

   i. If no spotter is used, move one hand forward and pivot on the other if the balance is lost forward. At the same time, bend at the hips and bring the legs down.

   Spot: Stand in front of the spot where the hands will land and brace the left shoulder with your right leg. Keep your left leg behind the right. Catch his/her legs as they come up and do not allow the shoulders to move forward.

5. **Pivot Handstand (Pirouette)**—Swing up to a handstand as before. After a good, steady handstand has been achieved, shift the weight to the right arm, lift the left hand from the mat, pivot a half turn on the right arm and place the left hand on the mat on the other side of the right hand. Then turn the right hand so its fingers point in the same direction as the left.

Hints: a. Get really steady before starting the turn.
   b. Stretch (extend the body) by pushing on the right arm.
   c. At the same time, lean to the right.
   d. Turn the head and look to the right of the right hand.
   e. Bend the left arm just slightly as it is moved.
   f. Replace the left hand as soon as possible.
   g. Slightly shift the weight to the left hand as it lands so that the right hand can be turned.

Spot: Steady the performer's legs as he/she turns. Walk around with him/her.

Note: This pivot can also be done at the time the legs kick up. Turn the right hand to the right and place it close to the right foot as the left leg swings upward. Start the pivot as soon as the right foot pushes off. Since the right hand is already turned, it will not be necessary to turn it after the left is placed.

6. **Forearm Balance**—Kneel and place the forearms on the mat with the elbows slightly further apart than the hands. Swing the legs upward one at a time and maintain the inverted position, supported by the forearms and hands only.

Hints: a. The shoulders should be *slightly* in advance of the elbows.
   b. Raise the hips as high as possible by bringing one foot in close to the elbows before kicking upward.
   c. Swing the straight rear leg upward and push from the forward foot at the same time. The higher the swing, the easier to get up.
   d. Do not move the shoulders further forward as the legs go upward. Keep them high.
   e. Keep the head up and the back arched.
   f. If the balance is too far forward, raise the head and press downward with the fingers.
   g. If the weight is too far backward, lower the head, bear down on the elbows, and flex the hips slightly.

HEAD UP

SHOULDERS HIGH

Spot: Stand close to the performer and catch the legs as they swing upward. Release the hold as the balance point is found.

7. **Head Balance Change to Head-Forearm Balance**—Assume a "Head Balance" and, while in the inverted position, move the hands to a "Head-Forearm Balance" and return again to the "Head Balance." This may be done by changing the hands one at a time or both together.

Hints: a. Be sure that both the "Head Balance" and the "Head-Forearm Balance" are well learned before trying the shift.
   b. When changing one hand at a time, lean slightly forward (overbalance) and to the right and quickly place the left forearm on the mat.
   c. The right hand bears much of the weight at this point.
   d. Now lean slightly to the left and forward and place the right forearm on the mat.
   e. The left elbow bears much of the weight as the change is made.
   f. In returning, lean slightly to the left when placing the right hand on the mat and to the right when replacing the left hand.
   g. When moving both together, increase the arch *very slightly,* taking all the weight on the head momentarily, and *quickly* shift the hands forward to the head and drop the elbows to the mat.
   h. The weight immediately comes to the elbows, so bear down hard on them.
   i. When changing back, again increase the arch and move the hands back to place.

Spot: The same as for the "Head Balance."

8. **Pike Press to Head Balance**—Assume a prone position and place the hands under the shoulders with the fingers pointing forward. Raise the hips and drag the feet up toward the head, keeping the knees straight. When the hips are overhead, raise the legs upward into a "Head Balance." Maintain the balance and then lower to a prone position again by reversing the procedure. Keep the legs straight at all times.

Hints: a. In the prone position, put the chin on the chest and the top of the forehead on the mat.
b. Use a downward and slightly backward pressure of the hands to raise the hips and drag the feet forward.
c. The toes are extended backward.
d. Keep the weight on the top of the forehead.
e. Don't lift the feet from the mat till the hips are as high as possible. If you *can't* lift the *straight* legs, bend the knees slightly.
f. Press with the hands and bring the feet off the mat but keep them low (hips still well flexed) till the hips are moved well forward.
g. Then raise the legs, and, as they approach the vertical, move the hips back into an arch.
h. To return, flex the hips slowly and let the hips move forward again as the legs come down.
i. Keep the hips high until the toes touch the mat and then slide the feet backward and lower the hips.

Spot: Stand behind the performer and, if he/she has difficulty in getting the feet off the mat, grasp the hips and pull toward you. As the legs are lowered, grasp the hips again and keep them forward of the head until the toes touch.

9. **Rolling Straight Body Press to Head Balance**—Arch the back and hold the hands close to the chest, palms forward. Drop to the knees, roll across the thighs, abdomen, and chest and as the weight comes on the chest and hands, bear downward with the hands to bring the legs overhead into a "Head Balance."

Hints: a. Lean well backward (arch the back) when dropping to the knees.
      b. Maintain a big arch throughout the stunt.
      c. Get lots of momentum to aid the hands in inverting the body.
      d. As the hands press downward to lift the body, increase the arch, if possible.
      e. Place the head far enough in front of the hands.
Spot: Stand beside the legs and lift upward on them if help is needed.

10. **Squat Press to Handstand**—Start from a "Tip Up" position (stunt #1). Slowly elevate the hips and legs till a "Handstand" position is achieved.
    Hints: a. Keep the head up.
          b. Hunch the upper back and shoulders and bear down on the arms to raise the hips.
          c. Also, allow the shoulders to move forward slightly as the hips are raised.
          d. Keep the hips, knees, and arms well flexed till the hips are directly above the head.
          e. Slowly extend the hips, knees, and arms.
          f. Fight for balance throughout the extension.
    Spot: a. Stand in front of the performer, grasp hips and pull gently toward you as he/she presses.

11. **Pike Press to Handstand** (Stiff-Stiff)—From a straddle stand, place the hands on the mat shoulder width apart and as close to the feet as possible. Slowly raise the hips and legs to a handstand position. Do not bend either the arms or the legs. Hip joint flexibility is important.
    Hints: a. Turn the hands slightly outward and keep the head up.
          b. Lean forward with the shoulders and raise the heels from the mat (toes support the weight).
          c. Press downward with the arms and draw the hips upward. Keep the hips well flexed.
          d. As the hips come directly above the shoulders, start to extend the hips. The legs remain well spread.
          e. As the legs pass the horizontal and continue upward, gradually reduce the forward lean of the shoulders.
          f. Bring the legs together when they are vertical.
          g. It may be necessary to slightly flex the arms and legs when learning.
    Spot: a. Spot as for the "Squat Press"
          b. This may be practiced by placing the hands about 10″ from a wall, lowering the head to place the upper back against the wall for support and then beginning the press.

Partner Stunts

These stunts, too, can be used as parts of pyramids. (See Chapter 18.)

In all stunts where one person stands on another person, the "Top" should either wear soft-soled, flexible gymnastics shoes or work barefooted.

1. **Thigh Stand** (First Method)—B stands behind T and bends forward to place his/her head between T's legs. He/she then straightens to a stand with T seated on the shoulders. Now B squats slightly and T places the feet on B's thighs. B grasps T's legs just above the knee and T straightens the legs to stand on B's thighs. He/she leans forward with the back arched and arms extended sideward. At the same time B ducks his/her head from between T's legs and leans backward.
    Hints: a. B has a firm position with the legs spread and bent rather deeply and the toes pointing slightly outward.
          b. T places the feet on B's thighs with the toes at the knees.
          c. He/she keeps the head up and back arched as he/she straightens the legs. The hips are thrust forward.
          d. B straightens arms as he/she leans backward.
          e. If T begins to fall forward, B releases the hold on T's legs.
(Second Method)—B stands behind T with legs spread and grasps T's waist. T reaches back and holds on to B's wrists. Both squat slightly and T springs upward, assisted by a lift from B, and places his/her feet on B's thighs. B shifts hands to T's knees and leans backward, arms straight. As this goes on, T straightens the knees, extends arms sideward and leans forward slightly, arching the back.

Hints: a. They stand very close to each other.
b. As T jumps upward he/she arches the back and leans backward.
c. B maintains a squat position and supports T as he/she places feet.
d. B slides one hand down to the thighs at a time.
e. He must have an almost right angle flex at the knees and hips while shifting hands.

Spot: Stand in front of T and grasp one upper arm with both hands as he/she mounts and be prepared to support him/her should he/she fall forward.

2. **Chest Balance**—B assumes a position on hands and knees and T stands at B's side. T bends forward to place chest and upper arms across B's back and reaches under B's body with the hands from the near side. T then swings legs overhead, one at a time and maintains the balance position.

Hints: a. B's hands and knees should be spread fairly wide to assure a steady base.
b. T's shoulders should be just past B's far side.
c. T should bring one foot in close to B, raise the hips as high as possible, and extend the other leg back. He/she swings the extended leg as high as possible and pushes off from the forward foot.
d. Keep the back arched and the head up.
e. If T overbalances forward, he/she must raise the head and tighten the grip (pull) on B's body.
f. If T can't keep from losing balance backward, he/she must shift shoulders further over B's body.

Spot: Stand at B's far side ready to prevent T's overbalancing forward.

3. **Advanced Chest Balance**—Two bottom people assume a position on their hands and knees, side by side. A center person assumes a hands and knees position on their backs at right angles to them. T then steps on the bottom pupil's hips and pushes up to a "Chest Balance" on the center one.

Hints: a. Learn the stunt well the simple way first.
b. The three bases must be firm and steady. The bottom two should spread knees and arms fairly wide and brace each other.
c. T's starting position is a little further forward than for the stunt above.
d. He/she presses downward with the arms to raise the hips. Lower the head slightly if needed.
e. The hips and legs remain flexed till they are overhead, then they are extended upward.

Spot: Two can be used. One to aid T in getting the legs up and the other at T's back to prevent an overbalance.

4. **Knee-Shoulder Balance**—B lies on his/her back with feet close to buttocks and spread. The knees too are spread and the arms are extended upward. T places hands on B's knees and shoulders in B's hands and swings the legs overhead to an inverted balance.

Hints: a. T must step in close to B's buttocks with the forward foot.
b. He/she leans forward to place the shoulders into B's cupped hands.
c. He/she then straightens the arms so that B's arms will be perpendicular to the floor.
d. Now he/she swings the rear foot upward and pushes from the forward foot at the same time.
e. At the same time T presses downward with the hands to aid in inverting the body.
f. Keep the head up and the back arched. Stretch upward with the toes, legs, and body.
g. Look directly into B's eyes.
h. B moves his arms forward or backward as needed to help in the balancing.

Spot: a. Stand at B's head and steady T's legs if help is needed.
b. Don't let him/her lose balance forward.
c. Don't help too much. Gradually decrease the assistance.

5. **Shoulder Balance** (Two bottom persons)—The bases kneel side by side on their hands and knees, and T stands behind them. He/she leans forward to place the head between their bodies and the arms around their waists. He/she then swings legs upward and maintains the inverted balance, supported by shoulders and upper arms.

Hints: a. T keeps the head up as it is placed between the bases' shoulders.

  b. He/she squeezes their hips tightly with the arms.

  c. The hands should be on their abdomens and *not* directly under his/her shoulders.

  d. Bring one leg as far forward as possible and swing the other leg upward. At the same time, push from the forward leg.

  e. The back remains arched.

  f. Pull up with the hands (on the bottom person's abdomens) if the balance is too far forward. If it is too far backward, press downward on their backs with the upper arms and slightly flex the hips. Begin this adjustment the *moment* the balance is lost.

Spot: Stand at the side to prevent T's overbalancing forward.

6. **Shoulder Balance on Partner's Thighs**—B places his hands on the mat behind him and raises the hips high. The knees are bent and spread medium wide. T stands in front of B's knees, places his/her head between the legs and his/her shoulders on the thighs and kicks up to an inverted position, grasping B's shins (thumbs down) from the front.

OVERBALANCED- SHOULD PULL ON HANDS TO CORRECT

HIPS HIGH

  Hints: a. B must keep his/her feet directly under the knees and the thighs must be parallel to the floor (hips raised knee high).

  b. T keeps the head up and pushes from both feet.

  c. His/her hips should remain flexed until they are directly above the shoulders.

  d. T's back must be arched as the legs are extended upward.

  e. He/she maintains balance by the grasp on B's shins. Pull on the shins if the balance is too far forward, and push on them if it is too far backward.

Spot: Stand at B's side to prevent T's overbalancing.

7. **Head Balance on Partner's Abdomen**—B places hands on the mat behind him/her and assumes a position with arms perpendicular to the floor, the body from the knees to the head in a straight line, and the knees bent, spread, and directly over the feet. T places hands on B's knees, head on B's abdomen, and kicks to a "Head Balance."

  Hints: a. The regular "Head Balance" must be mastered first.

  b. B must be a firm, unmoving base.

  c. T keeps one foot close to B's feet as he/she places the head. Put pressure on the head before kicking up so that B will be accustomed to the weight.

  d. Keep the rear leg straight and swing it upward while pushing from the forward foot. At the same time, push with the arms.

  e. The weight must be on the top of the forehead, the back must be arched.

  f. Keep much of the weight on the hands.

Spot: Stand at B's side to prevent T's overbalancing.

8. **High Chest Balance**—Two bases face each other and place their hands on the other's shoulders. They then flex their knees, keeping their backs straight. T steps onto their thighs (close to the hips) and leans forward across their arms. He/she holds to their near arms and places his/her shoulders just over the far arms. T then springs off their thighs and raises his/her legs overhead to an inverted position. T dismounts by flexing the hips and dropping back to the floor.

  Hints: a. The "Advanced Chest Balance" should be learned first (Stunt No. 3, page 105).

  b. The bases must have their feet well spread for balance, and their shoulders directly over their hips. (They must not lean forward.)

  c. T keeps his/her arms bent and raises the hips by pushing downward on the bases arms with the hands.

    d. Knees and hips remain flexed till they are over the head. Then they are straightened upward. The head is kept up throughout the stunt.
    e. The bases straighten their legs as T extends upward.
Spot: a. One spotter stands on the far side of the bases and braces T's hips to prevent an overbalance.
    b. Another spotter stands on the near side to push up on T's legs if help is needed in getting inverted.

9. **Shoulder Balance on Partners' Arms**—Two bottom persons face each other and grasp each other's shoulders. T mounts to one's shoulders from behind, places the hands on their arms, leans forward to place shoulders on their arms (head goes between the arms) and raises the hips and legs overhead to a "Shoulder Balance."

    Hints: a. A spotter helps T get to a kneeling position on a base's shoulders.
    b. T's hands are placed close to the shoulders of the person he is kneeling on and raises his/her hips as he/she puts the shoulders on their arms.
    c. Push downward with the hands to raise the hips.
    d. Keep the head up.
    e. The hips and legs remain flexed till they are overhead.
    f. As the hips come overhead, extend the legs upward and arch the back.
    g. The hand grip helps to keep the balance.
    h. Flex the hips and knees and place the knees on the bases' shoulders when coming down.
    i. The two bottom students must stand straight (don't lean forward) and have a good, wide base. Their heads should remain up.

    Spot: Two spotters should be used; one on either side. They must be alert to catch T if he/she loses balance. One aids T to mount by clasping hands and letting T step up on the hands.

10. **Knee Stand Balance**—B lies on the back with knees apart and bent and hands extended upward. T straddles B's head and grasps the upraised hands. T then raises his/her legs forward, supporting the entire weight on B's straight arms and places the feet on B's knees and leans forward, pulling B to his/her feet. B leans backward (still holding T's hands) to counteract T's forward lean.

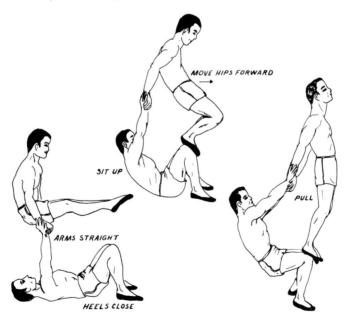

Hints: a. B's feet must be *close* to his/her buttocks, and the knees and feet should be the same distance apart.

b. Both person's arms must be stiff and straight.

c. T places the toes just over B's knees.

d. T moves the hips forward, bringing them ahead of the hands. The knees bend as the hips thrust forward.

e. B partially sits up to allow T to do so.

f. T then straightens the legs while continuing to lean forward which pulls B to his/her feet.

g. T keeps the back arched as the legs straighten. The head is kept up.

h. B keeps his/her head forward and leans forward as much as possible to get the hips off the mat. He/she then leans back to counteract T's forward lean.

Spot: a. Stand at T's side and support his/her arm as he/she places the feet on B's knees.

b. Then move behind B and lift from under the arms if he/she can't get up alone.

11. **Shoulder Balance on Partner's Feet**—B assumes a lying position on the back with knees against the chest and elbows on the mat with the hands extended upward. T straddles B's head and grasps the upraised hands, leans forward to place shoulders on the upraised feet, and kicks upward to an inverted position on them. B then straightens his/her legs upward. To dismount, B flexes the knees and T bends at the hips.

Hints: a. B keeps hands firm to give T a point of resistance to press against.

b. B's hips must be on the floor to keep them as steady as possible.

c. T starts with the feet close to B's head.

d. He/she swings one leg up at a time and keeps the head up.

e. B keeps knees bent till T gains balance.

f. T uses the grasp on B's hands to help get balanced. If he/she goes too far forward, pull on the hands, and if he/she starts to fall backward, press against them.

Spot: Stand at T's shoulder to catch his/her legs and help to get balanced. If T falls forward, grasp the nearest arm close to the shoulder and lift upward which will set him/her on the feet.

12. **The Level**—B assumes a front support position and T sits astraddle the shoulders facing the feet. T then hooks toes under B's thighs and leans backward. This weight should bring B's feet from the floor so that he/she will be in a horizontal position supported only by the hands. Thus both are lying in a horizontal plane, B facing downward and T facing upward, supported by B's hands.

Hints: a. B must keep the weight well forward. (Shoulders in advance of the hands.) The arms are straight and locked in position with the hands rotated outward slightly.

b. As T leans backward he/she must lift upward with the legs.

c. If T's weight is insufficient to raise B's legs, throw the arms overhead.

d. If this is yet not enough, B must shift the shoulders even further forward.

Spot: Kneel by T's head as he/she leans backward to prevent the banging of the head on the mat if B's arms collapse.

13. **Low Arm-to-Arm Balance**—B lies on the back with the legs spread and arms extended upward. T straddles B's chest and leans forward, reaching down to grasp B's upper arms at the deltoid muscles. B grasps T's arms also. T then swings legs upward and overhead and maintains the inverted balance position, supported by B's arms.

    Hints: a. B's shoulders are squarely on the mat.
    b. T's arms are outside B's.
    c. His/her feet must be close to B's armpits as he/she springs up.
    d. Push off from both feet simultaneously and keep hips flexed (but head up) till the hips are overhead. Then extend the legs upward and arch the back.
    e. Press with the arms to help get the hips up as you push off from the feet.
    f. Do not push the shoulders forward as you push off from the feet.
    g. B does the balancing—shifting the arms forward or backward as needed.
    h. If T overbalances, B turns him/her sideways and he/she comes down to the side.

    Spot: Stand beside B's head and catch T's feet to aid in finding the balance point.

    A second method of getting into position is for B and T to assume a "Knee-Shoulder Balance" (Stunt No. 4, page 105. T then transfers one hand at a time from B's knees to the upper arms.

    Hints: a. B's arms must be vertical before T starts to transfer the hands.
    b. T overbalances slightly and leans to the left when moving the right hand forward.
    c. Place the arm outside of B's and grasp B's arm just below the deltoid muscle.
    d. Overbalance forward and to the right when moving the left hand forward.
    e. The movements must be smooth and slow.
    f. After moving the first hand, the balance must be well secured before moving the second one.
    g. Help to maintain balance by adjusting the head position, arch, and by pressure on B's arms.

    Spot: Same as above.

    A third method of getting into position is with a "Foot-to-Pelvis Assist." B lies on his/her back with his/her feet against T's pelvis and T leans forward to secure the "arm-to-arm" grip. T then lifts the legs slightly and B straightens his/her legs a little so that T is supported by B's feet. Then B flexes his/her legs and immediately pushes upward with the feet to bring T to the inverted position. With the push from B's feet, T snaps the legs into an arch.

    Hints: a. B brings the hips off the mat when originally supporting T.
    b. T's shoulders should be directly over B's shoulders with the legs slightly elevated.
    c. As B dips the knees, T lowers his legs and then both whip their legs upward at the same time.
    d. B's leg thrust is upward and slightly backward toward the head.
    e. T must keep the head up.

    Spot: Same as above.

14. **Snap to Low Arm-to-Arm Balance**—B and T lie on their backs with their heads against each others shoulder (left ear against left ear) and their arms grasped in an arm-to-arm grip. T then rolls backward flexing his/her hips and, as his weight comes onto the upper back and shoulders, forcibly extends the legs upward and snaps into a "Low Arm-to-Arm Balance" assisted by a lift from B's arms. After holding the position, B moves the arms backward, T places his/her head on the mat and rolls down to a lying position as at the start of the stunt.

Hints: a. B's shoulders are squarely on the mat with the feet spread to give a firm base.

    b. The direction of T's extension is *slightly* backward. Much speed and force is required.

    c. T must arch as he/she extends which will bring the legs directly overhead.

    d. Snap the head back as soon as it is raised from the mat.

    e. B must coordinate the arm lift with T's snap-extension.

    f. B's arm lift come entirely from the shoulder joints. The arms remain straight.

    g. If the snap is too late or the direction of extension is backward, T should flex his hips, spread his legs and land astride B's hips.

    h. When rolling down to a lying position, T tucks his/her head and flexes the hips as he/she is lowered backward by B.

Spot: Stand by B's shoulder and aid T in getting balanced. A quick grasp and upward lift on the legs may be needed at first. If T snaps too soon, catch him at the waist to prevent his falling on the back.

15. **High Arm-to-Arm Balance**—B and T face each other with the arm-to-arm grasp. T springs upward and straddles B's hips with his legs and B bends forward from the waist at the same time. B then straightens upward with a snap and lifts T overhead to an "Arm-to-Arm Balance." To dismount, T flexes his hips and drops to his feet.

    Hints: a. B stands with feet spread and one foot slightly in front of the other for balance.

        b. He bends the knees as well as the hips when bending forward to get a swing for the lift. Use a smooth "rocking chair" motion for the bending and lifting.

        c. T straddles B as high on the body as possible.

        d. Press against B's sides with the legs until the throw is made, but don't lock the legs around B's back.

    e. As the performer is thrown upward, he/she relaxes the leg grip, *flexes and raises the hips* and keeps the feet close to B on the way up. He/she pushes downward on B's arms to help.

    f. As the hips come overhead, extend the legs upward into an arch.

    g. Keep the head back throughout the stunt and use it to aid the balance.

    h. B maintains the balance by moving backward or forward as required.

Spot: a. Stand behind and to the left of B and support T's shoulder with the right hand and grasp the arm with the left in case of an overbalance.

    b. Allow the feet to continue downward to the mat and maintain your grip to prevent his falling forward on his/her face in landing.

16. **Handbalance on Two Partner's Thighs**—Two bottom students face each other while kneeling on one knee. T stands behind their raised knees, places his/her hands on their thighs, and swings to a "Handbalance." The bases support T's hips with their hands.

Hints: a. The raised knees should be close to each other and be directly over the feet.

    b. T places the hands close to the bases' hips.

    c. T has one foot close to the kneeling students and the other stretched backward. T swings the back leg upward and pushes from the forward foot.

    d. T's head must be up, the back arched, and the arms straight.

Spot: The bottom performers can spot T.

17. **Knee-Shoulder Lever**—B faces T who leans forward and places his/her head between B's thighs and rests the shoulders against them. T raises his/her hands backward and upward and B grasps the wrists. B now leans backward, pulls on T's arms, and T raises the legs from the floor so that his/her body is arched and parallel to the floor.

Hints: a. B flexes at the knees and hips.

    b. T moves his/her feet backward as far as possible, keeping them on the floor.

    c. B leans backward as this is done.

    d. T tightens the chest, back, and shoulder muscles and arches the back to bring the legs off the floor.

    e. B leans even further backward to counterbalance the weight.

Spot: Grasp B from behind to prevent loss of balance either forward or backward.

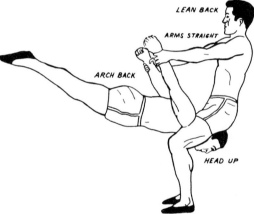

18

Pyramids

Pyramid building is stimulating to any program of tumbling or gymnastics. It can be adapted to the beginner and to the expert. It is a group enterprise and successful performance requires the cooperation and teamwork of every one in the pyramid. It allows and stimulates creative expression since there are no set patterns and innumerable combinations may be developed. Pyramid building utilizes all the available boys and girls. The heavy ones form the bases, the medium students form the middle layers, and the light ones form the top pieces.

To develop the group thinking and cooperative planning that is so highly recommended by educators today, the class can be divided into groups and each group can plan, practice, and present its own pyramid. The class as a whole can then evaluate the pyramids and indicate first, second, and third places. This should be done only after the instructor has taught several pyramids and explained the fundamentals of pyramid building to the class.

Care must be taken in the selection of individuals for various positions in the pyramid. Each must be capable of performing the assigned part or the entire pyramid will suffer. Each participant must also be sure of the order in which the pyramid is built up and broken down. Preliminary combinations in two's three's, and four's should be mastered first before attempting complete, large pyramids.

There are various types of pyramids. They usually have a high center point but may be high on the ends and low in the middle. They may have a number of high points. They may be in a straight line, a semicircle or a full circle. Two pyramids may cross each other. They may be in one plane, or several. They may be done without apparatus or be built on a parallel bar, horse, ladders, or any other piece of equipment. They may be ambulatory and be moved forward, backward, or in a circle. They may use fifty people or three. In short, the limitations of the instructor's or the class' imagination are the limitations to the possible types of pyramids.

The secret of good pyramid building lies in the ability of everyone to work together, work smoothly, and work on command. Each pyramid should start with the performers in a straight line. At the first signal the bottom pieces should step out and take their places quickly. On the next signal the middle ones assume their positions. Then the top mounters assume their positions. The pyramid is held momentarily and then at another signal the group breaks up, quickly and efficiently forming a straight line again.

All of the individual and partner balance stunts found in the preceding pages may be used as parts of a pyramid. Other possibilities will be shown in diagram form. These are only meant to be suggestive. Each instructor and most participants may devise many more.

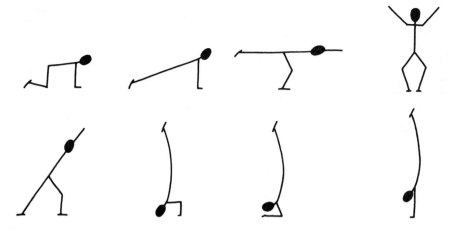

Single Balances and Poses for End Pieces

Doubles Balances and Poses for End Pieces

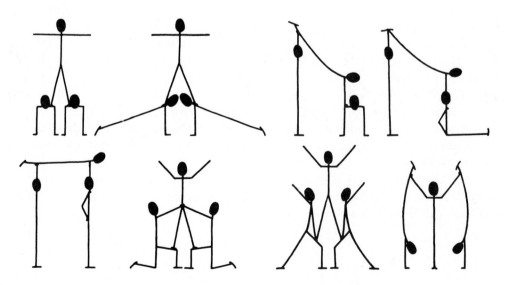

Three Person Balances for End Pieces or Centers

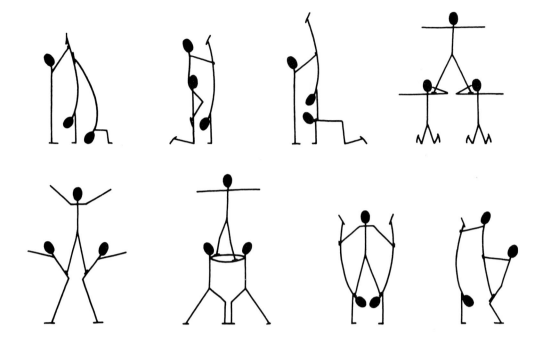

Three Person Balances for End Pieces or Centers

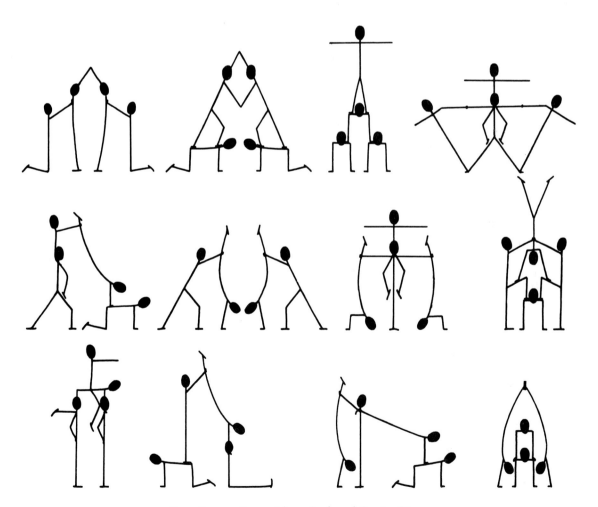

Four Person Pyramids or End and Center Pieces

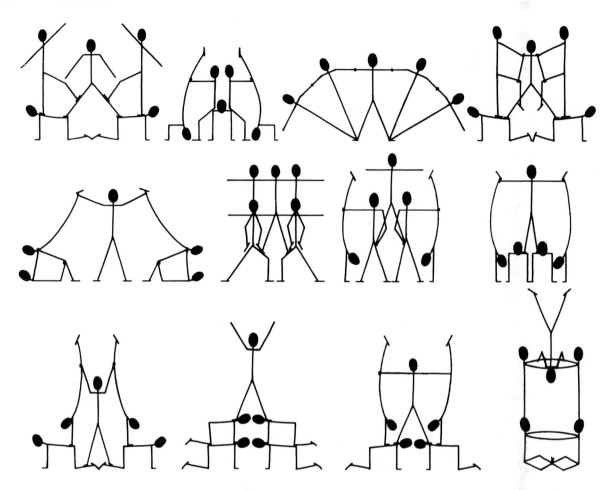

Five Person Pyramids or End and Center Pieces

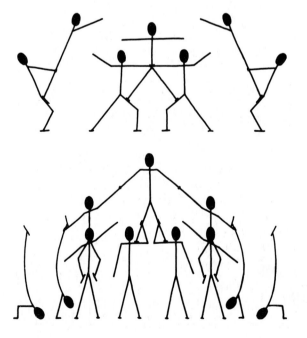

Complete Pyramids of Seven or more People

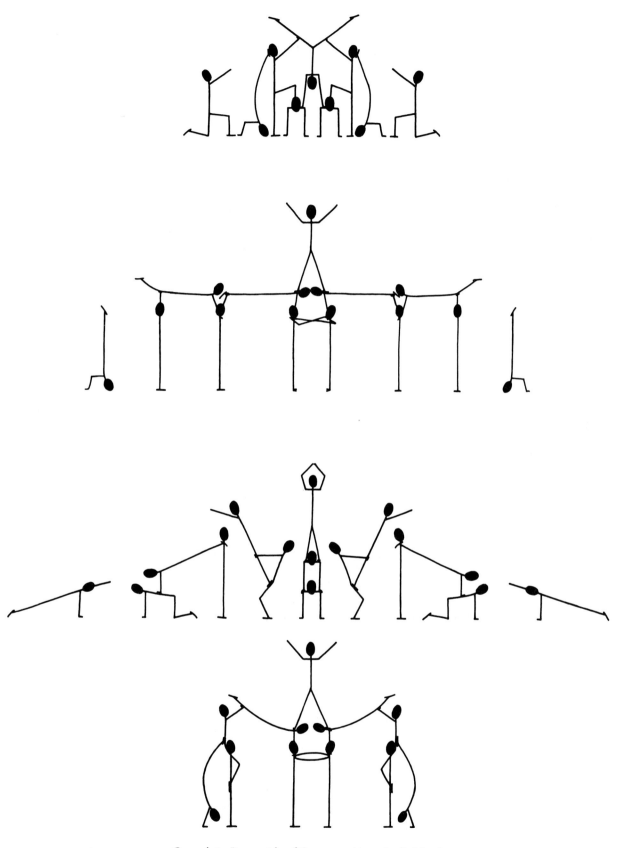

Complete Pyramids of Seven or More Individuals

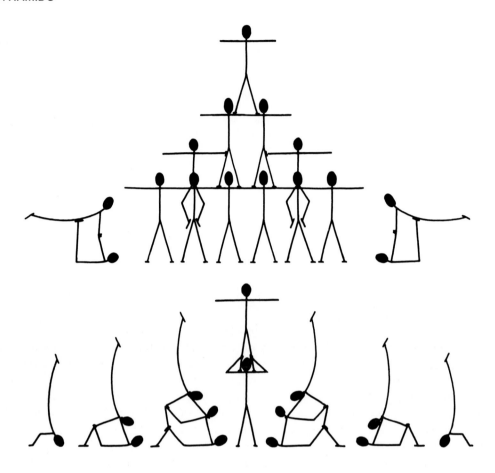

A good climax to a demonstration or exhibition which includes pyramid building is the type of pyramid commonly called a "squash pyramid." The diagram below will illustrate its construction which is simple. The surprise comes in the way the pyramid collapses. At a signal, each individual in the pyramid quickly extends arms forward and legs backward and the pyramid simply falls in a heap. It is not at all dangerous and much simpler than it looks. Every one must "extend" at the same time.

19
Floor Exercise

Floor exercise is one of the older and yet one of the newest of the competitive gymnastics events. This event took the place of tumbling in the recent history of gymnastics. It is an event that is included in both men's and women's competition, and it is similar but yet quite different for the sexes.

Basically the floor exercise event is composed of simple stunts, balances, and tumbling skills (found in chapter 15). In addition, men must display strength type skills, and women use dance as well as tumbling to connect the various moves which comprise the routine. Floor exercise involves more creativity in developing routines than any other event. It is the longest of the men's events, lasting approximately a minute and a half, and women have the additional task of choreographing their routines to music. The tendency for beginners is to do a series of single tricks. This is somewhat true in all the events, but is more apt to cause difficulty on the floor because so many moves end on the feet—inviting a pause. In other events the moves end with a swing of some sort which is more readily transferred to the following skill.

How can this continuity, so important to successful performance, be encouraged? First of all, the problem must be recognized. A coach who is unaware of it will not do anything about it. Second, it must be attacked right from the beginning—with basic moves. For example, to combine a forward roll with a cartwheel, learn to come up on one foot from the roll and step onto the other to go into the cartwheel. No pause, hesitation, or extra foot movement should be made. If a person comes up on the right foot with the left foot held forward for the step into the cartwheel yet finds it easier to do a cartwheel with the right side leading, he/she must learn to rise on the left foot and step onto the right. This would be an easier change to make than attempting to change the direction of the cartwheel.

In trying to join a forward roll and a dive roll, many novices hesitate after the roll because they finish it too low—in a deep squat position. Try finishing the roll in a semisquat position with the shoulders forward and hips directly over the feet. It will be impossible to stop if the correct position is achieved, and a step forward will have to be taken in order to prevent a fall forward. The head should be up and the arms reaching forward. When this can be done smoothly, simply spring into the dive roll instead of stepping forward to prevent the fall.

Another problem frequently encountered by "would be" floor exercisers is the expectation that flexibility will be demonstrated. Flexibility is no longer specified as a composition requirement for men's floor exercise, yet most judges anticipate that flexibility will be shown. It need not, of course, be demonstrated in a specific stunt such as the splits, but it can, for example, be revealed in a series of good back handsprings. Unfortunately, there is no easy way to acquire joint suppleness. Yes, some are naturally more flexible than others, yet even the "naturals" must work at the job. (See Chapter 6 on training and conditioning for gymnastics.) Also, flexibility is frequently specific in locale. One may be fairly "loose" in the hips but relatively rigid in the shoulders, or vice versa. In general, women tend to be more flexible than their male counterparts and are concerned less with this component.

There has been a trend in recent years for women to incorporate more dance and fewer acrobatic skills into their floor routines. The female gymnast who does not have a good background in dance will be increasingly handicapped as she rises to higher caliber competition. Training in classical ballet is particularly helpful in this regard. Men too, can benefit from dance training, and it is not unusual to see some dance elements in high level men's competition. In fact, several dance elements have been included in Olympic compulsory routines.

Another important requirement of a complete men's floor exercise routine is the performance of a skill requiring considerable strength. This element is depicted in the various presses to handstands, the holding of a planche, or a wide-arm handstand. It is true that all stunts require some degree of strength, but an exceptional display must be shown to satisfy this requirement. Interestingly enough, strength is *not* a requirement for the women. In fact, women must work in such a way that they do not have to use strength to complete their movements, i.e. they must look effortless.

Although it may seem paradoxical, good flexibility can actually reduce the amount of strength required to perform, for example, a straight-arm, straight-leg press to a handstand. Even for a planche, flexibility is an aid. Adequate wrist flexibility permits the shoulders to come far enough forward to properly balance the weight.

In this event, a final requirement is the proper use of the entire 40' x 40' area. A typical pattern is to start in one corner, proceed at a diagonal across the mat to the opposite corner, and then move along near the edge of the four sides. (See diagram below.) This postulation frequently causes problems for the novices, who get stuck in a corner and have difficulty moving out and around. Tumbling, of course, is the easiest way for the gymnast to travel—if he/she can tumble well.

If strip floor exercise is used instead of the regulation area, the "space" problem is reduced, but another difficulty arises—that of making a 180° turn in a graceful and unusual manner when reaching the end of the mat. This turn should not be (as it so often is) a simple turn by use of the feet. The turn ought to be incorporated in either a stunt or transitional move.

To help in constructing floor exercise routines, a few samples are given below which with slight modifications are appropriate for both boys and girls. The numbers in parenthesis refer to where the descriptions of the named stunts can be found. Also, stick figures of the sequence moves are pictured below the verbal descriptions.

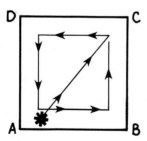

Beginners' Routine

From a stand in one corner (corner A in the above diagram) facing the diagonal corner (corner C), start with a "Tuck Jump" (jump upward, bring knees to chest, wrap arms around shins, and straighten to a stand), to a Dive Roll (No. 9, page 76), to a Forward Roll with legs spread (No. 5, V, page 75), to a stand with body bent forward at waist, back flat, head up, arms sideward. Place hands and head on mat, keeping legs straight and Pike Press to Head Balance (No. 8, page 103). Hold two seconds then tuck the head, flex the hips and knees, and roll forward, coming up on the right foot and stepping forward on the left foot to start a Modified Cartwheel (No. 11, page 77) with the left hand leading. Land first on the right foot, then step sideward on the left with a half turn left and do a Cartwheel (No. 12, page 78) with the right side leading. Land on the left foot with a quarter turn right (face toward corner C), step on the right foot into an Arabesque (No. 3, page 66) and hold for two seconds. Pivot on right foot (still in Arabesque position) and face toward corner D. Hold one second and drop to a Swedish Fall (No. 2, page 66, see "Note"). Now tuck the head, raise the hips (drag right foot forward) and go into a forward

A TOWARD C →

TUCK JUMP   DIVE ROLL   FORW. ROLL LEGS STRAIGHT   PIKE-PRESS HOLD   RISE ON RIGHT LEG

A TOWARD C →

MODIFIED CARTWHEEL TO LEFT   TURN LEFT ON LEFT FOOT   CARTWHEEL TO RIGHT   ¼ TURN RIGHT ON LEFT FOOT   ARABESQUE

D ← C

1⅛ TURN LEFT   FRONT HANDSPRING   RUN   PIKE JUMP   TUCK TO FORW. ROLL   SWEDISH FALL   ARABESQUE

D TOWARD B →

KICK TO HAND BALANCE   HOLD   TUCK TO ROLL   ROUND OFF   BACKWARD ROLL TO HAND BALANCE   SNAP DOWN

Roll (No. 4, page 74), and finish the roll with a Pike Jump (No. 5, page 67). Run two or three steps (toward corner D) and execute a Front Handspring (No. 24, page 83). Jump into a one-and-an-eighth turn (land facing corner B). Kick up to a Handbalance (No. 4, page 101), hold for two seconds, then bend the arms, tuck the head, and roll forward to a stand. Run, Round Off (No. 15, page 79) to a Backward Roll to a Handbalance (No. 33, page 86), and snap down to a stand. NOTE: Directions (left and right) can be reversed if desired.

Intermediates' Routine

Start in corner A, facing corner C. Run, Front Handspring (No. 24, page 83) to a Dive Roll (No. 9, page 76), come up on one foot, Cartwheel (No. 12 page 78) to a Round Off (No. 15, page 79), to a Backward Roll to Handbalance (No. 33, page 86). From the Handstand, pivot on one arm and do a Cartwheel down to a stand facing B. Kick into a Hand Balance, hold two seconds, then pirouette a half turn (two ¼ turns on hands), hold one second and lower legs *slowly* to a stand (face C). Drop backwards to a Backward Roll and come to a squat stand on one foot with the other leg extended sideways. Do two Single Leg Circles (No. 16, page 70) and Squat Through (No. 14, page 69) to a rear-lying support. Execute a half turn to a front lying support, lower to a prone position and Pike Press to a Head Balance (No. 8, page 103). Now do a Headspring from a Headbalance (No. 27, page 84) and go immediately into a Rolling Snap-Up (No. 20, page 82) to a Snap-Up with Half Twist (No. 22, page 82) to land facing C. Cartwheel left (toward A), half turn, and One-Arm Cartwheel right (No. 29, page 85), quarter turn (face A) and Dive Roll to a stand (No. 9, page 76, jump upward with a 1½ spin right to land facing D. Run toward D and execute a Round Off (No. 15, page 79) to a Backward Handspring (No. 38, page 88) to a Back Flip (No. 37, page 88).

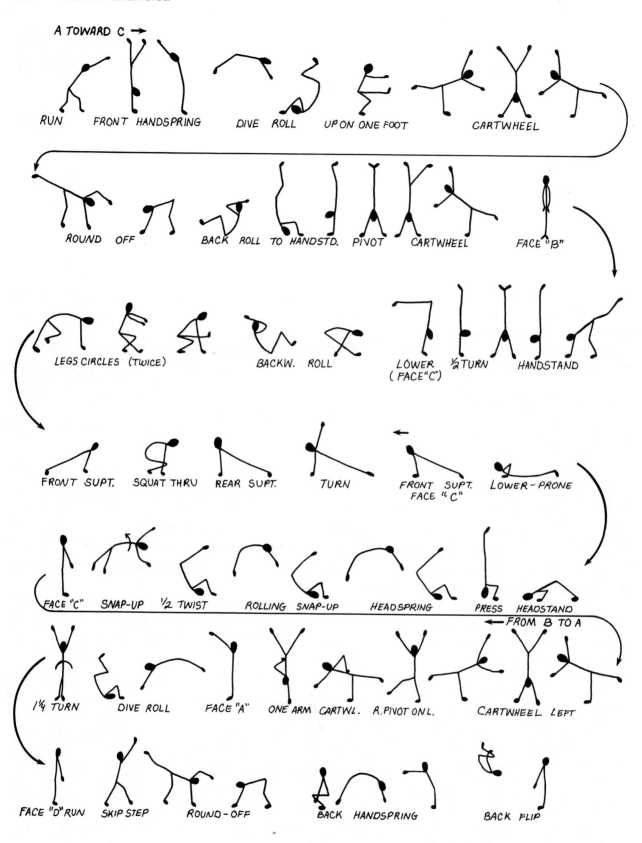

A TOWARD C →

RUN · FRONT HANDSPRING · DIVE ROLL · UP ON ONE FOOT · CARTWHEEL

ROUND OFF · BACK ROLL TO HANDSTD. · PIVOT · CARTWHEEL · FACE "B"

LEGS CIRCLES (TWICE) · BACKW. ROLL · LOWER (FACE "C") · ½ TURN · HANDSTAND

FRONT SUPT. · SQUAT THRU · REAR SUPT. · TURN · FRONT SUPT. FACE "C" · LOWER-PRONE

FACE "C" · SNAP-UP · ½ TWIST · ROLLING SNAP-UP · HEADSPRING · PRESS · HEADSTAND

← FROM B TO A

1¼ TURN · DIVE ROLL · FACE "A" · ONE ARM CARTWL. · R. PIVOT ONL. · CARTWHEEL LEFT

FACE "D" RUN · SKIP STEP · ROUND-OFF · BACK HANDSPRING · BACK FLIP

20

Pommel Horse

The pommel horse (formerly called side horse) is considered by many to be the most difficult of the men's apparatus to work. Women do not perform on this piece except to vault over it when the pommels are removed. (See Chapter 22). For beginning classes for both boys and girls the pommels should be left on for the vaulting which makes it easier for the children. No vaulting will be covered here because it is included in the chapter on vaulting.

A very fine sense of dynamic balance is required (and developed) in this event. Probably the highest incidence of broken routines occur here both in practice and in meets. It is not a particularly spectacular event in the eyes of an uninformed spectator (except for the "Flair" recently developed by Kurt Thomas) and there is certainly less danger of physical harm to the performer, but it takes a maximum amount of ability and perseverance to work it well.

As stated in Chapter 2, the concept of complete routines of at least eleven moves combined into one smooth-flowing exercise is the goal for competitive gymnastics. Even when team gymnastics is not contemplated, combining several stunts into sequences is beneficial. Greater organic stimulation is derived than when performing one trick at a time. Also, more skill is required (and developed) because a more exacting performance of the first skill is required in order to be able to go immediately into the next one. These small combinations should be started as soon as possible.

Refer to the chapter on nomenclature (Chapter 13) for aid in interpreting the terminology used in describing the various positions on the apparatus.

The top of the horse should be about waist high. For competition the height is designated as 45¼".

A skill that can be performed to both sides (left and right) will be described to one side only, however, it should be practiced to both sides. Most students have a "better" side. (Some perform more easily to the right, others to the left.) Often, a beginner is unaware of this phenomenon. Trying the stunt to both sides will reveal his preference. Also, advanced performers are sometimes required to do "compulsory" routines which may be constructed to their nonpreferred side. Learning these simple moves to both sides will develop a degree of ambidexterity which is beneficial for the advanced gymnast.

Sometimes a teacher is unable to give an actual demonstration of much of the support work on the horse. This should not deter him from picturing the stunts for the class because he can stand behind the horse and use his arms to represent the movements of the legs. This demonstration method should be used frequently even if the teacher is an able performer because the arms can be held in any position indefinitely while needed explanations are being made, and they can be moved much more slowly (and thus their movements will be easier to follow) than the legs in an actual demonstration.

Wearing long pants will facilitate the leg movements in support work. If loose sweat pants are worn, keep them close to the thighs with tape or a rubber band.

Painful forearms are sometimes experienced by beginners (and even by experts when they overdo practice periods) similar to the "shin splints" acquired by track men from running on a hard track. Rest and icing down the tender area are both effective in alleviating the pain, but if it isn't too bad, relief while working can be effected by taping the flexors of the forearm. Tape tightly three-fourths of the way around the arm from the wrist to just below the elbow.

1. **Flank Mount to Rear Support**—From a side stand frontways, hands on pommels, jump and swing both legs left sideward and over the neck of the horse, releasing the left hand as the legs pass over. Replace the left hand on the left pommel and maintain the rear support.

   Hints: a. Push off hard with the left hand as the jump starts.
   b. At the same time, lean heavily on the straight right arm. The right shoulder is to the right of the right hand.
   c. Straighten the body (arch slightly) as it passes over the horse.
   d. Replace the left hand *immediately,* keeping the arm straight.
   e. Resist the tendency to bend at the waist as the left hand regrasps. Keep extended.
   f. Lean slightly backward with the right shoulder as the body passes over the horse.

   Spot: a. Stand on the *near* side of the horse beside his right arm and support it above the elbow with both hands.
   b. Start a gentle, backward pull on his right arm as his body passes over the horse.

2. **Rear Mount to Rear Support**—From a cross stand frontways at the croup, place both hands on the croup. With a slight jump, bring the legs up on the left side and over the horse. Release the left hand as this is done and pivot a one-fourth turn on the right arm. Place the left hand on the nearest pommel and finish in a rear support with the right hand on the croup and the left hand on the pommel.

   Hints: a. Stand slightly to the right and well behind the croup to start. Lean toward the horse.
   b. With the jump, push from the left hand and place the weight on the right arm. Don't jump too high.
   c. Bend at the hips as the legs swing left and pivot on the straight right arm.
   d. Place the left hand on the pommel as soon as possible.
   e. Try to extend the hips a little as the left hand grasps the pommel.
   f. Lean backward with the shoulders at the same time.

   Spot: a. Grasp his hips from behind and lift slightly (support him) as his feet leave the floor.
   b. Walk around behind him as he pivots and maintain the support until he replaces his left hand.

3. **Flank Mount Left with Half Twist Left to Front Support**—From a side stand frontways with left hand on neck, right hand on left pommel, jump and swing both legs left sideward over the neck (under the left hand) and at the same time push off with the right arm, execute a half twist left and finish in a front support with the right hand on the neck and the left hand on the right (formerly left) pommel. This can also be done from a stand in front of the saddle to a front support in the saddle.

   Hints: a. This is executed much like the "Rear Vault with Half Twist" except that a fourth *less* twist is made.
   b. Though the shoulders lean forward at the start, they are brought back as the body passes over the horse.
   c. The hands must be replaced very quickly.

4. **Flank Dismount from Single Feint**—From a front support, swing the right leg over the croup to a feint position (weight on right arm, body facing left end of horse, one leg on each side of horse). Swing the right leg back, join it to the left leg and swing both legs over the neck to a side stand rearways.

   Hints: a. *Keep* the right shoulder over the right hand and the right elbow locked throughout the stunt.
   b. Pivot on the right arm as the right leg swings back in a circular path to pick up the left leg and then both legs circle to the left. The swing of the right leg is continuous.
   c. Push off hard from the left hand just before the legs pass over the neck.
   d. The hips as well as the legs swing left sideward and upward.
   e. Arch the back (stretch) as the legs pass over, and release the right hand.
   f. Land directly in front of the saddle. This can be done if the right shoulder stays over the right hand.

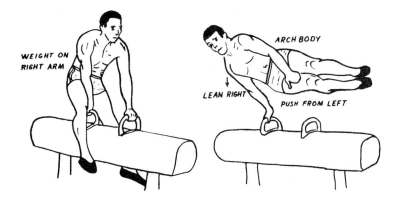

Spot: a. Stand beside the saddle, between the horse and the performer's right leg as he feints, and grasp his right arm with the right hand above his elbow and the left hand on his right wrist.

b. As he swings his right leg back over the croup, move beside the croup by pivoting to the right (left side toward croup) and lift on his right arm and pull toward you to resist the tendency for him to lean to his left.

5. **Front Scissors from Cross Riding Seat**—From a riding seat on the croup facing the pommels, grasp the near pommel with both hands in an over grasp and lean backward, allowing the legs to swing forward. Then lean forward, take the weight on the hands and swing the legs backward and upward, crossing one leg over the other to execute a half twist and land in a cross riding seat on the croup facing away from the pommels.

Hints: a. Sit close to the pommels.

b. Keep the legs straight throughout the stunt.

c. Raise the body from the horse (take the weight on the hands) as the legs swing backward and upward.

d. Don't flex the hips. The body swings as a unit, with the fulcrum at the waist.

e. Use the momentum of a good leg swing and carry the shoulders well forward of the hands.

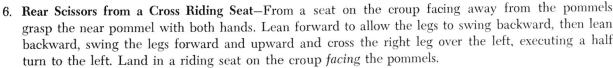

Spot: No spotting needed.

6. **Rear Scissors from a Cross Riding Seat**—From a seat on the croup facing away from the pommels grasp the near pommel with both hands. Lean forward to allow the legs to swing backward, then lean backward, swing the legs forward and upward and cross the right leg over the left, executing a half turn to the left. Land in a riding seat on the croup *facing* the pommels.

Hints: a. Sit close to the pommels.

b. Straighten the arms when leaning forward and keep them straight for the backward lean.

c. This raises the hips off the horse and the arms support the body. The buttocks rests against the hands.

d. Obtain a good, free swing of the body without much flexion at the hips. Keep the legs straight.

e. Release the right hand as the twist is made.

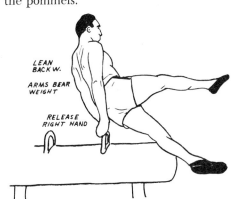

Spot: No spotting needed.

Practice Device to Develop "Swing." (First phase) This is not a pommel horse "stunt" but working on it will enable one to do the real skills better. Jump to a front support at the neck (left hand on neck, right hand on left pommel) and "walk" around the horse in a counter-clockwise direction by moving one hand at a time. After going entirely around the horse, start at the croup and do the same thing, moving in a clockwise direction.

Hints: a. Start with the right hand on the front half of the pommel so there will be room for the left hand when it transfers.

b. Lean on the straight right arm and move the left hand to the left pommel (both hands on same pommel).

c. Shift weight to left arm and move right hand to right pommel.

d. Shift weight to right arm and move left hand to right pommel.

e. Continue working your way around the croup and back to the neck on the other side of the horse.

f. The body hangs straight down as this is done.

Second Phase: Jump to a straight arm support in the saddle (one hand on each pommel) spread the legs wide and sway the legs and hips from side to side. The legs remain straight and spread.

Hints: a. The movement comes from the shoulders, not just at the hip joint. The entire body should move from side to side.

b. Keep the legs spread throughout and the arms straight.

c. As the legs swing left, the center of the hips should be at *least* even with the left pommel.

d. The center should be at or past the right pommel when legs go right.

e. Continue, but now try to push off with the left hand (lean on the right arm) as the legs move left, and reverse when they move to the right.

f. Work for as much height as possible on the swings.

Spot: No spotting needed for either phase.

REMEMBER: THE SECRET TO GOOD POMMEL HORSE PERFORMANCE IS AN EXCELLENT SENSE OF BALANCE AND THE KEYWORD IS "SWING" (from the shoulders) WITH *NO* PAUSES OR EVEN HESITATIONS.

7. **Single Leg One-half Circle and Return**—Jump to a front support and circle the left leg forward under the left hand and regrasp with the left hand. Then return the leg to the near side of the horse by again passing it under the left hand and regrasping. Repeat twice more in rhythm, alternating the left and right legs.

Hints: a. Practice by swinging both legs left then right sideward, keeping them together and on the near side of the horse.

b. As the legs swing left sideward, lean on the right arm and push off from the left hand.

c. Regrasp with the left hand and lean on the left arm as the legs swing right sideward and push off from the right hand.

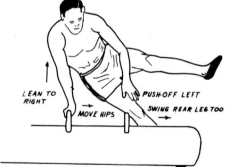

d. After practicing this several times, cut the left leg forward as the left hand is released (the right leg moves in the same direction as the left but stays on the near side).

e. Regrasp with the left hand and shift the weight to both arms as both legs swing right sideward (left leg on far side, right leg on near side of horse).

f. Swing both legs left sideward, shift the weight to the right arm, push with the left hand and cut the left leg back to join the right.

g. Regrasp as soon as the leg passes over the neck and shift the weight to the left arm.

h. Reverse the procedure using the right leg and hand.

i. Swing from the shoulders and not the hip joints. The hips move left and right like a pendulum as the legs are swung. Both legs move in the same direction at all times even though one is on either side of the horse.

j. Keep the head up and the legs straight. Don't flex the hips.

Spot: No spotting is needed.

8. **Single Leg One-half Circle—Alternate—and Return**—Jump to a front support and swing the left leg forward under the left hand and regrasp with the left hand. Then swing the right leg forward under the right hand and regrasp (to a rear support). Now return the left leg to the near side of the horse under the left hand and regrasp and likewise return the right leg, finishing in a front support. Repeat twice more.

Hints: a. Practice the stunt above until it is fairly well mastered.

       b. Swing both legs to the left and cut the left leg forward while shifting the weight to the right arm and pushing off from the left.

       c. As the left hand regrasps, swing both legs to the right (one on either side of the horse) and shift the weight to the left arm while pushing off from the right hand to allow the forward movement of the right leg.

       d. Extend the hips as the right leg moves forward.

       e. Lean slightly backward (shoulders behind the hands) as the right hand regrasps.

       f. Swing both legs left sideward (on the far side of the horse) and lean on the right arm while pushing off from the left hand to allow passage of the left leg backward.

       g. Regrasp and swing both legs right sideward and lean on the left arm while cutting the right leg backward.

       h. Swing from the shoulders. Both legs move in the same direction all the time. Neither leg hangs still.

Spot: No spotting is required.

9. **Single Leg Circles Forward**—Jump to a front support and swing the right leg to the left, in front of the left leg, and over the neck of the horse, passing it under the left hand. Continue to circle the right leg by swinging it right sideward under the right hand and over the croup and return it to the near side of the horse. Repeat three additional times. The left leg remains on the near side but swings left and right sideward as the right leg does in making its continuous circles in a clockwise direction. Repeat the stunt, circling the left leg to the right.

Hints: a. From the front support swing both legs to the right to gain momentum for the circling to the left.

       b. Swing both legs left sideward, lean on the right arm, push off from the left hand and raise the left leg backward slightly to allow the right leg to pass between it and the horse.

       c. Twist the hips slightly to the left as this is done.

       d. Regrasp with the left hand as soon as the right leg passes over the horse and immediately shift the weight to the left arm while the legs move right sideward (one on each side).

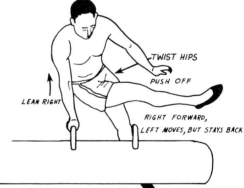

       e. Release the right hand and bring the right leg back to join the left.

       f. This should continue without a break in the rhythm.

       g. Swing from the shoulders. The hips must move sideward as the legs do. The further the hips move, the easier the stunt.

       h. Keep the arms and legs straight.

Note: Beginners can practice this by starting in a front support at the neck (left hand on the neck, right hand on the left pommel) and then following the instructions above. After some proficiency is gained, move to the center. When circling the left leg to the right, start at the croup.

Spot: No spotting is needed.

10. **Single Leg Circles Backward**—Place the hands on the pommels and do a flank mount right to a rear support. Circle the right leg to the left under the left leg and backward over the neck of the horse, passing it under the left hand. Continue the circle of the right leg by swinging it to the right and for-

ward over the croup, passing it under the right hand to join the left on the far side of the horse. Repeat the circling of the right leg twice and dismount. Try the same stunt using the left leg going to the right.

Hints: a. Use the momentum of the flank mount to begin the circling of the right leg.

b. Lean slightly backward as the right leg passes under the raised left leg, and at the same time push off from the left hand and shift the weight to the right arm to allow passage of the right leg.

c. As soon as the left hand regrasps, shift the weight to the left arm and swing the legs to the right, releasing the right hand to allow passage of the right leg.

d. As the right leg joins the left in front, repeat the procedure rhythmically.

e. The left leg remains in front, the right leg circles uninterruptedly.

f. The weight is shifted backward while the legs are in front and directly over the horse while the right leg is behind.

g. Keep the right leg straight and be sure that the hips swing, especially to the left.

Note: As in No. 32, this can be learned at the end of the horse. After getting the idea and the rhythm, move to the center.

Spot: No spotting needed.

11. **Side Scissors (Regular) from Stride Support**—Jump to a front support and swing the right leg forward under the right hand to a stride support and immediately swing both legs left sideward and upward, release the left hand and bring the right leg back over the neck and at the same time cross the left leg over the right to the far side of the horse. The legs swing downward and to the right (one leg on either side of the horse) and the left hand regrasps. Both legs continue to swing to the right and upward, and the legs are again crossed (right over left) as the right hand is released. As the legs come down (right in front, left behind) and begin swinging to the left again, regrasp with the right hand. Repeat twice more to each side. Review the front and rear scissors (stunts #5, 6) before trying this.

Hints: a. The weight must be directly over the center of the horse. Don't lean forward or backward.

b. Keep *both* legs *straight*. A common *fault* is to keep the upper part of the forward leg forward and move only the lower leg backward by bending at the knee.

c. Spread the legs as far as possible.

d. Keep the hips swinging sideward and upward. The higher the better.

e. Lean on the right arm and push off from the left to allow the legs to cross on the left.

f. Roll the left hip forward slightly as the left leg crosses forward and the right hip forward as the right leg comes forward.

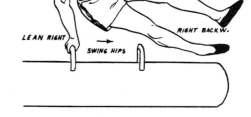

g. Concentrate on swinging whichever leg is in the back higher than the front leg.

h. Regrasp the pommel as soon as possible.

i. Work for a definite, smooth rhythm.

Note: This too can be learned on the end of the horse. It will be easier on one side (left side for scissors to left), but harder on the other side. The scissors to the left can be practiced on the left side, to the right on the right side, and when both have been tried, move to the center to practice continuous scissors.

Spot: No spotting needed.

12. **Side Scissors (Reverse) from Stride Support**—From a front support, swing the right leg to the *left* under the left leg and left hand (see Stunt No. 9), replace the left hand and swing both legs right sideward, crossing the right leg backward over the left leg as it comes forward under the right hand. Cross again on the left side. In the "Regular" Scissors, the rear leg is crossed over the forward leg on each scissors movement. For the "Reverse" Scissors the front leg passes over the rear leg each time.

  Hints: a. In general, the hints are the same.

  b. However, as the legs cross on the *right* side, the right hips rolls *backward* slightly and the left hip goes backward on the left side.

  Note: Practice this on the ends of the horse too.

  Spot: No spotting needed.

13. **Simple Traveling**—Place the left hand on the neck and the right hand on the left pommel and jump to a front support. Swing the left leg forward under the left arm and replace the hand. Swing the right leg forward to a balance support astride the right arm (the right hand is not released). Swing the left leg back under the left arm and shift the left hand to the left pommel. (Both hands are now on the same pommel.) Swing the right leg back and transfer the right hand to the right pommel (both legs on the near side). Swing the left leg forward under the left hand and replace the hand on the left pommel. Swing the right leg forward as before to balance support astride the right arm. Swing the left leg back under the left hand and shift the hand to the right pommel (both hands on the right pommel). Now swing the right leg back and place the right hand on the croup. Swing the left leg forward under the left hand, replace the hand, and swing the right leg forward and dismount to a side stand rearways opposite the croup.

  Hints: a. Place the right hand on the front part of the pommel to make room for the left hand when it is transferred to the same pommel.

  b. Push off from the left arm as the left leg cuts over the neck of the horse.

  c. Replace the left immediately and lean on it as the right leg swings forward.

  d. Push from the left again and swing the left leg back over the neck. With the push, carry all the weight on the straight right arm. Do not pause in the balance support.

  e. As the leg passes over the neck, place the left hand on the left pommel behind the right hand.

  f. Start the left leg back even before the right leg finishes its forward movement.

  g. Shift the weight to the left arm as soon as it grasps the pommel.

  h. Swing the right leg back as soon as the left arm takes the weight.

  i. Shift the right hand to the right pommel as the right leg moves back and immediately lean on the right arm.

  j. Swing the left leg forward under the left hand and continue on to the croup.

  k. Keep the legs and arms straight. Make the movements continuous and uninterrupted.

  Spot: No spotting required.

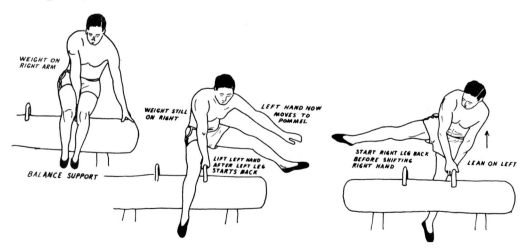

WEIGHT ON RIGHT ARM

BALANCE SUPPORT

WEIGHT STILL ON RIGHT

LEFT HAND NOW MOVES TO POMMEL

LIFT LEFT HAND AFTER LEFT LEG STARTS BACK

START RIGHT LEG BACK BEFORE SHIFTING RIGHT HAND

LEAN ON LEFT

14. **Half Leg Circles to Rear Dismount**—From a side stand frontways at the neck (left hand on neck, right hand on left pommel) jump and swing the left leg over the neck under the left hand, replace the left hand and bring the right leg forward to a balance support. *Immediately* swing the left leg back under the left hand, replace the hand and bring the right leg back, join the left leg to it and swing both legs over the neck with a one-fourth turn left to a cross stand left opposite the neck.

   Hints: a. The first four hints of Stunt No. 13 pertain here.
   b. Now replace the left hand momentarily but keep most of the weight on the straight right arm.
   c. Bring the right leg back (right shoulder over right hand) and whip both legs to the left.
   d. Push off from the left hand (keep hips close to right hand) flex hips and turn left.
   e. Right shoulder is now well over the horse.
   f. Reach back with the left hand and place it on the neck (it doesn't support weight) and release the right hand.

   Note: Review Stunt No. 4. The last part of this is much like it.
   Spot: No spotting required.

15. **Rear Dismount from Balance Support**—From a balance support astride the right arm over the left pommel, swing the right leg back over the horse, pivot on the right arm and turn to place the left hand on the other pommel. (The right leg has passed over both the croup and the neck, and the body is now facing the horse on the opposite side.) The right leg continues its circling movement, picks up the left leg and both legs are swung left sideward over the horse while pushing off with the left hand and executing a quarter turn left. Land in a cross stand left.

   Hints: a. Weight supported by right arm in balance support.
   b. Pivot on right arm as right leg passes backward over horse. The right hand doesn't *need* to turn. It will be in a reverse grasp when the pivot is completed.
   c. However, some like to open the hand and let it ride a half turn on the top of the pommel.
   d. Reach for the other pommel with the left hand as the turn is being executed. The right arm still supports the weight.
   e. Stay close to the right arm with the hips as the left hand is placed and push from the left hand as soon as it lands.
   f. With the push, whip the legs left sideward, flex the hips, and make a quarter turn left to pass over the horse.
   g. Reach back with the left hand and place it (no weight) on the horse.

   Spot: a. Stand on *near* side opposite right arm, beyond reach of right leg.
   b. When the right leg passes, move in quickly to support his right arm and resist his tendency to lean to his left.

16. **Double Rear Vault**—Place the hands on the pommels and spring upward, swinging the legs to the left and over the neck of the horse. Release the left hand, pivot around the right arm with the hips in a flexed position (legs parallel to the floor) and continue on around till the legs pass over the croup to land in a cross stand left. Release the right hand and reach back to the horse with the left just before landing.

   Hints: a. The first few times bring the feet through the saddle and then around to the croup instead of swinging them over the neck. After it has been learned this way, do it as described.
   b. Take off from close to the horse and don't jump too high. Just enough to get the hips over the horse.
   c. All of the weight must be on the right arm.
   d. Keep the hips *close* to the right arm. "Sit" on the wrist.
   e. Push off from the left hand as the spring is made.
   f. The left hand is carried free and aids in keeping the balance.
   g. Turn the head to the right just as the spring is made.

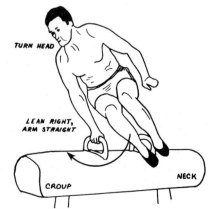

h. Keep the hips flexed. (Think of keeping the feet at the height of the pommels.)

i. *Lean back on the right arm.*

j. Place no weight on the left hand as it touches the horse.

Spot: a. Stand on the *near* side of the horse at the performer's right side.

b. Grasp his right arm above the elbow and lift upward slightly as he jumps and pivots.

c. Move around toward the saddle as he pivots.

d. Keep a gentle pull toward you on his right arm.

e. If he drop his legs, reach over the croup with the right arm and support the legs as he comes around.

17. **Double Rear Mount to Rear Support**—This is the same as the Double Rear Vault except that the left hand is placed on the croup as soon as the legs pass over and weight is placed on the left arm to maintain the support position. The right remains on the pommel in a reverse grasp.

Hints: a. The first 9 hints for stunt #16 pertain here.

b. Add an additional ¼ turn on the right arm.

c. Place the left hand on the croup and lean on it.

d. Drop the legs (from the flexed position) as the left hand is placed.

e. Lean back (shoulders behind hands) as the hand is placed.

f. Finish in a rear support.

Spot: a. Same as for #16 except for a slight push away from you (help him lean backward) as he lands in the support. Give a lot of support on his right arm.

18. **Double Rear Dismount from a Single Feint**—Jump to a front support and swing the right leg over the croup to a feint position. Swing the right leg back, join it to the left leg and pivot on the right arm, swinging both legs over the neck and around to and over the croup, landing in a cross stand left as in the "Double Rear Vault."

Hints: a. The right arm bears the weight. Push off from the left hand when the legs come together.

b. Lean on the right arm. The right shoulder should be to the right of the right hand.

c. Keep the hips low and against the right wrist.

d. The legs should be parallel to the floor. Keep them straight.

e. The momentum is derived from the swing of the right leg.

f. Look over the right shoulder and lead with the feet.

g. The motion should be smooth and continuous once the right leg starts back over the croup.

Spot: a. Stand on the *near* side of the horse but clear of the swinging right leg.

b. As soon as the legs pass, step forward and support the performer's right arm as for the "Double Rear Vault."

19. **Simple Swiss** (Baby Moore)—From a front support with the hands on the front half of the pommels, swing the right leg over the croup as you pivot on the right arm and move the left hand to the rear half of the right pommel (both hands on one pommel). Then reach for the other pommel with the right hand, continue the turn and bring the left leg over the horse to join the right. You are now in a front support on the opposite side of the horse. The turn must be smooth and without stops.

Hints: a. Legs and arms remain straight.

b. Shift the weight to the right arm, start the pivot on the right arm and the leg swing all at the same time while releasing and transfering the left hand.

c. Shift weight to left arm the instant it is placed on the right pommel.

d. Remove and transfer the right hand as soon as the left lands.

e. The legs remain spread till the left joins the right on the far side.

Spot: No spot needed.

20. **Combination Leg Circle Rear Mount Travel to Rear Support**—From a side stand frontways in front of the neck with the left hand on the neck and the right hand in a reverse grip (thumb toward body, knuckles on top) on the left pommel, jump, circle the right leg over the croup and over the neck as the body pivots on the right arm and the left hand is placed on the other pommel. (The legs now

straddle the right arm and the right hand has a normal grip.) Using the momentum of the circling right leg, shift the weight to the left arm and pivot on it as both legs are carried over the croup (right hand is released and placed on the croup) to a rear support on the croup with the right hand on the croup and the left hand on the right pommel.

Hints: a. Think of the entire mount as one smooth, uninterrupted movement.
   b. Push off from the left hand (on neck) as the *straight* right arm bears the weight.
   c. The left leg remains on the near side of the horse at this point.
   d. Shift the weight to the left arm as soon as it is placed on the other pommel.
   e. Lean and pivot on the left arm, push off from the right and at the same time, push off from the left leg (against body of horse).
   f. Flex the hips (bring the legs hip high).
   g. As the legs pass over the croup, place the right hand on the croup.

Spot: a. Stand on the far side of the horse opposite the right pommel but out of the way of his swinging right leg as he starts.
   b. Step in after the leg passes and support (lift up on) his left upper arm as he places his left hand on the right pommel.
   c. If needed, your left hand can reach for his legs to help them over the croup.

Routines:

Small combinations of two or three skills such as a mount to an immediate dismount or a mount, one stunt, and a dismount should be developed soon after support work is begun. Beginners' routines are more difficult to compose on the pommel horse than on other events since there is a scarcity of easy moves on the horse.

In the stunt descriptions, reference to neck and croup, left and right pommels, and near and far side will remain as determined by the original starting position regardless of a turn of the body during the routine. The left pommel will still be called "left" even though it may later be on the performer's right side.

A "Beginning Routine" and an "Intermediate Routine" follow. Work on two or three moves in sequence until they can be done fairly smoothly, then the next few. Put these parts together and continue in this manner till the whole routine can be done without extra swings or pauses.

21. **Beginning Routine**—From a cross stand frontways at the croup, jump and swing the legs left sideward over the croup and pivot on the right arm to a rear support with the left hand on the right pommel and the right hand on the croup (see Stunt No. 2). Continue the movement of the right leg and pass it under the right hand. Regrasp right and swing both legs to the left (one on each side) and bring the left leg back under the left hand. Regrasp left and make a complete leg circle with the left leg (see Stunt No. 9) and return to a front support. Now bring the right leg forward over the croup and place the right hand on the right pommel (both hands momentarily on the same pommel) and the body turns to face the neck. Continue to turn and place the right hand on the other pommel and bring the left leg back over the croup to a front support facing opposite to the original position. Cut the right leg forward under the right hand, swing both legs left sideward (one on each side) then swing them to the right and cut the right leg back again to a front support. Swing the left leg forward under the left hand and start a "Simple Travel" (see Stunt No. 13) to the (original) neck. Bring the left leg forward under the left hand, then the right forward to a balance support on the right arm. Bring the left leg back under the left hand and then the right back, join it to the left, and swing both legs over the horse with a quarter turn to a rear vault (see Stunt No. 14).

22. **Intermediate Routine**—From a stand in front of the neck (left hand on neck, right hand on left pommel), "Double Rear Mount" to a rear support in the saddle (as No. 17). Cut the right leg back, then the left leg back, then the right leg forward to a scissors (No. 11) on the left side to a scissors on the right side. Then cut the left leg forward on the left, bring the right back on the right and do a "Reverse Scissors" (see Stunt 12) on the left side. Now a full leg circle backward (see Stunt No. 10) with

the right leg to a half leg circle backward with the right leg and a half leg circle forward with the left leg. Now bring the right leg forward to a balance support on the right arm and do a "Double Rear Dismount" (see Stunt No. 18).

Note: Both of the above routines can be reversed by starting the mounts in the opposite directions. Some performers will find it easier to do by reversing. Have the stundents try in both directions and stick with the easier one.

21

Parallel Bars

Competitively, girls and women do not work the (even) parallel bars. The difference in strength is usually cited as the reason. However, there is no reason why women/girls can't do the moves in this text. The advanced moves by women on the uneven parallel bars are just as difficult as the stunts done by the men in their event. If an uneven bar is not available, let the girls work with the boys on the even bars.

In order that no time be wasted, the second performer must be ready to proceed as soon as the first one has dismounted. For stunts which require the performer to start at one end of the bar and progress to the other end, the second one can begin when the first has negotiated half of the distance. Be sure that both are spotted. A student should work on each end of the bar on stunts which can be completed at one end. Again both must be spotted.

Stunts described as going to one side (left or right) should be practiced to both sides.

The knees must be bent when landing from all dismounts. This bending action absorbs the shock of landing.

Keep the bars low for straight arm support work as it makes spotting more effective. Be sure adjustment devices for height and width of bars are securely locked.

Unless otherwise directed, the arms should remain straight and stiff (elbows locked) in all supports. The shoulders should be kept back and the head erect. Good body position (posture) should be stressed.

The first four stunts are not truly gymnastics stunts. They are used as strengthening exercises for the arms, ·chest, upper back, and shoulder girdle and can be used along with push-ups, chins, etc., in a developmental program *before* the regular parallel bar work is begun.

1. **Forward Hand Walk**—Jump to a straight arm cross support at the near end of the bars and walk forward in the supported position by moving one hand forward at a time. Walk to the far end of the bars and, with a quarter turn, drop to a side stand between the bars.

    Hints: a. Keep the head and chest up. Don't sag at the shoulders. Look forward.

    b. The arms must be straight (elbows locked).

    c. Take short steps.

    d. Lean on the left arm when moving the right hand forward and on the right arm when moving the left hand forward.

    e. Keep the legs straight and together.

    f. Remove one hand, pivot on the other arm, and drop at the end.

    Spot: Walk beside the performer, grasp his/her closest thigh with both hands and lift upward if he/she shows signs of collapsing.

2. **Forward Hand Walk, Half Turn, and Backward Hand Walk**—Jump to a straight arm support and do the "Forward Hand Walk" to the center of the bars. Execute a half turn by placing the right hand on the left bar with a quarter turn, and with another quarter turn, place the left hand on the other bar. Finish by walking backward to the far end of the bars and drop off to a cross stand.

Hints: a. When making the turn, place all of the weight on the *straight* left arm and place the right hand *close* to the left hand.

b. Lean on the right arm and place the left hand directly across from the right.

c. Shift the weight to the right arm as soon as the right hand is placed so that a smooth, rapid turn can be made. Don't stop after the quarter turn.

d. Keep the head up and the back arched.

Spot: Same as for the "Forward Hand Walk." Spot on the side toward which the performer will turn.

3. **Forward Hand Jump**—This stunt is the same as the "Forward Hand Walk" except that both hands are moved simultaneously.

Hints: a. Keep the head and chest up. Look forward.

b. Take very short (3 inch) jumps. Make them fairly rapid.

c. Lean slightly forward.

d. The momentum is derived from the shoulders. The elbows remain locked. Sag in the shoulders and extend them vigorously upward in a fairly rapid rhythm.

Spot: Same as for the "Forward Hand Walk."

4. **Bent Arm Hand Walk**—Jump to a bent arm cross support at the near end of the bars and walk forward to the far end of the bars while in the bent arm support. Move one hand at a time. At the far end push up to a straight arm support and drop off.

Hints: a. Keep the elbows close to the sides and flexed as much as possible. Bend at the knees if the feet touch.

b. The shoulders are in front of the hands.

c. Shift the weight over to the right arm when moving the left hand forward and to the left arm when moving the right hand.

d. Take *very* short steps in a quick, even rhythm. Don't hesitate after moving one hand.

e. Look forward, not downward.

Spot: Walk beside the performer, grasp the hips, and lift if help is needed.

5. **Hammock Hang**—From a cross stand rearways at the end of the bars, bend the knees, reach upward to grasp the bars, and turn over backward, bringing the feet over the head. Place the instep on top of the bars, slide the feet toward the far end, and arch the back. Return to a stand by reversing the movement.

Hints: a. Keep the arms bent, draw the knees to the chest, and at the same time lean backward to raise the feet overhead.

b. Place the toes on the bars close to the hands and slide them backward till the body is extended.

c. At the same time straighten the arms and raise the head. The back should be arched.

d. To return to a stand, tuck the head forward and flex the hips (draw the feet towards the hands).

e. Flex the arms again when turning forward to a stand and control the landing. Don't just drop the feet.

Spot: a. Stand at the performer's left side and grasp his/her left wrist with your right hand to support him/her if a foot or hand slips.

b. The left hand can aid the turning over by lifting upward on the legs if help is needed.

c. Help to place the feet on top of the bars.

d. Change hands (hold wrist with left hand) and lift on the abdomen with your right if he/she needs help in returning.

6. **Series of Straddle Seats**—Jump to a straight arm cross support at the end of the bars and swing the legs forward and over the bars to a straddle seat in front of the hands. Grasp the bars in front of the thighs and swing the legs backward, bring them together, and swing them forward between the bars to another straddle seat in front of the hands. Repeat the stunt to the far end of the bars and drop to a stand.

Hints: a. Keep the arms straight (elbows locked) while swinging in support.

b. Keep the legs straight when coming to the straddle seat. The inside of the thighs contact the bars. Sit tall, keep the back extended.

c. Lean backward and let the legs move forward.

d. Then lean well forward and swing the legs backward and upward and bring them together to swing forward between the bars.

e. Keep the hands close to the thighs and the arms straight as possible.

f. Keep the head up.

g. Lean *slightly* backward as the legs swing forward to the new straddle seat.

Spot: a. Stand at the performer's right side and grasp his/her right arm just above the elbow with your right hand and place your left on the elbow from behind to prevent the bending of his/her arm.

b. Move along with the student but be careful to keep out of the way of the right leg.

7. **Swing in a Straight Arm Support**—Jump to a straight arm cross support at the end of the bars. Swing the body forward and backward a number of times in an effort to develop a smooth swing. Drop off at the *end* of the backward swing.

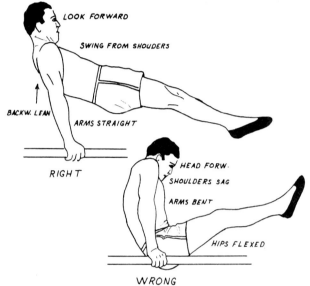

Hints: a. Be sure that the arms are straight. Keep the elbows locked.

b. Swing from the shoulders, not the hips. Keep the body fairly straight.

c. Keep the head up. Look forward.

d. Don't sag in the shoulders.

e. Lean *slightly* forward (shoulders ahead of the hands) as the body swings backward and lean backward slightly as the body swings forward.

f. *All* straight arm support swinging is done this way.

g. Drop off at the "dead point" of the back swing. The body should neither be moving forward nor backward.

Spot: a. Stand at the performer's side and grasp an arm both on the elbow and on the biceps. Help to keep the elbow "locked."

b. Prevent him/her from losing balance either forward or backward by permitting only *slight* forward and backward movement of the shoulders.

c. Use a spotter on *each arm*. One stands in front and the other behind.

8. **Scissors from Cross Support to Straddle Seat**—Jump to a straight arm cross support at the center of the bars and obtain a swing. As the legs swing backward and upward, cross the left leg over the right and execute a half turn to the left, to land in a straddle seat facing in the direction opposite to that of the starting position.

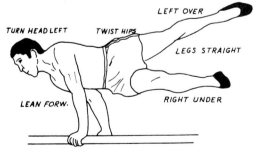

Hints: a. Keep the legs straight and do not try to cross them until they swing higher than the bars on the back swing.

b. Turn the head to the left and twist the hips as the legs cross.

c. Spread the legs wide as the twist is made.

d. The arms bear the weight until the thighs contact the bar.

e. Lean forward with the shoulders while crossing the legs and twisting.

Spot: Support the performer's right arm above his/her elbow, right hand on biceps, left hand on elbow. Stand slightly in front to avoid the legs as they straddle.

9. **Scissors from Straddle Seat to Straddle Seat**—From a straddle seat in front of the hands, swing the right leg in to the middle of the bars, execute a one-forth turn right and place the left hand beside the right on the right bar. The left leg rolls on the left bar and remains extended. Continue the swing of the right leg to the right (between the bars) lean on the left arm, release the right hand, and switch the left leg to the opposite bar. At the same time, swing the right leg over the bar where the left leg had been and transfer the right hand to that same bar, finishing in a straddle seat facing in the opposite direction.

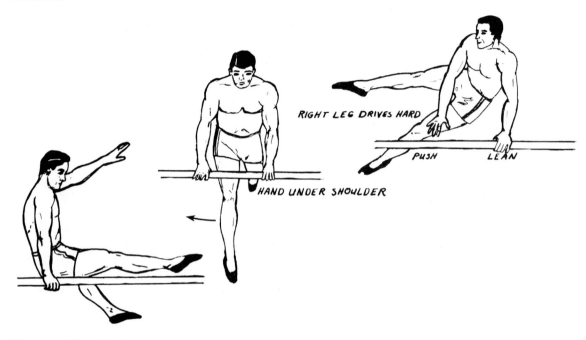

Hints: a. Keep both legs straight throughout the stunt.
  b. Bring the right leg between the bars and roll on the extended left leg as the quarter turn right is made.
  c. Place the left hand about shoulder width from the right (hand directly under shoulder) and shift weight to it at once. The body is now supported by the left leg and both arms.
  d. Start right leg swinging down, up, and to the right in one continuous, driving motion.
  e. Push off from the right arm as soon as the left hand is placed.
  f. Push off from the left leg at the same time and swing it under the right leg to the other bar.
  g. Turn the head to the right.
  h. The right hand and both legs should land at about the same time.
Spot: a. Face the performer, standing beside his/her right arm.
  b. As the right leg swings through the middle of the bars, reach under the bar and place your right hand against his/her left hip and push upward.

10. **Backward Roll Dismount**—From a rear-lying position across both bars (the hips and hands are on one bar and the upper back is on the other bar) flex the hips to bring the legs over the head. Roll back onto the upper back, release the hands and continue rolling on over the bar to a side stand frontways. (Face the bar.)
Hints: a. The shoulders should extend slightly beyond the bar. The arms should be bent, if necessary to achieve this position.
  b. Press downward with the hands to aid in the flexing of the hips.
  c. Drop the head backward (look for the mat) as the hips come over the head.
  d. Keep the hips flexed but don't bend the knees. Reach for the mat with the feet.
  e. Keep the arms extended upward as the hands are released.

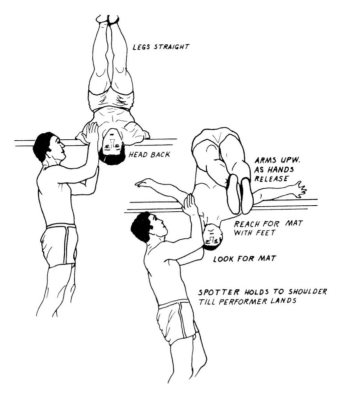

LEGS STRAIGHT

HEAD BACK

ARMS UPW.
AS HANDS
RELEASE

REACH FOR MAT
WITH FEET

LOOK FOR MAT

SPOTTER HOLDS TO SHOULDER
TILL PERFORMER LANDS

Spot: a. Stand at the performer's left and place your right palm (fingers pointing upward) on his/her left shoulder. Push upward on the hips with your left hand *if* he/she needs help in lifting the legs.

b. Transfer left hand to his/her left shoulder (both hands cupping the shoulder) as hands release.

c. Support the shoulder as he/she rolls off and use your grip on the left arm to prevent a backward fall when landing.

11. **Front Dismount from Straight Arm Support**—Jump to a straight arm cross support in the middle of the bars and begin swinging. As the legs swing higher than the bars on the backward swing, lean to the left and swing the body over the left bar to a cross stand right. (Right side toward the bars.)

Hints: a. A free, easy swing (stunt No. 7) should be learned first.

b. Lean over on the left arm while the body is still swinging upward.

c. Also lean slightly forward. The shoulder should be over the left bar, slightly in front of the hand.

d. Transfer the right hand to the left bar just behind the left hand as the weight is shifted to the left arm. The body should be directly above the left bar with the feet at *least* as high as the shoulders.

e. Release the left hand as the right hand grasps the left bar. No weight is put on the right hand, but the grasp is maintained till landing.

f. Keep the head up and the back arched. Do not flex the hips.

Spot: Stand slightly ahead of his/her left arm and grasp the biceps with your left hand and the wrist with the right. Pull him/her over the bar if necessary.

12. **Rear Dismount from Straight Arm Support**—Jump to a straight arm support in the middle of the bars and begin swinging. As the legs swing forward and upward, lean to the left and pass the body over the left bar to a cross stand right.

Hints: a. Lean on the *straight* left arm and push off from the right.

b. Keep the hips in a flexed position but the knees straight while passing over the bar.

c. Lean slightly backward, but keep the head slightly forward.

      d. Grasp the left bar with the right hand before landing.

      e. Advanced performers can grasp the left bar behind the back with the right hand just *before* the left is released.

Spot: Stand slightly behind the performer's left arm and put your right hand above the elbow and your left hand on the wrist. Help him keep the elbow locked.

13. **Flank Dismount from Straight Arm Support**—Jump to a straight arm cross support in the middle of the bars and begin swinging. As the legs swing forward, lean on the left arm, release the right hand, twist the body a quarter turn to the left and pass the body over the left bar to a side stand rearways (back to bar).

Hints: a. As the legs swing forward, pivot on the left arm just as the legs swing higher than the bars.

      b. Keep the left shoulder slightly to the left of the left hand.

      c. Push off with the right hand and swing it upward and to the left.

      d. Keep the head up and extend the hips to get rid of the slight flexion occurring on the forward swing.

      e. The left side must be toward the bar as the body passes over it.

      f. Let go with the left hand immediately after passing over the bar.

Spot: a. Stand slightly to the rear of the performer's left hand and grasp his/her left arm above the elbow with your right hand and the wrist with your left.

      b. Pull the performer toward you and over the bar if necessary.

14. **Inverted Hang Travel**—From a cross stand in the middle of the bars, reach upward, grasp the bars and turn over backward to an inverted hang by drawing the knees to the chest and then extending the legs upward. Travel forward (the direction in which you are facing) by moving one hand at a time while in the inverted position. Return to a stand by lowering the feet forward just before reaching the uprights.

Hints: a. Use the "hook" grasp (thumbs alongside the hands rather than under the bars).

      b. Practice the inverted hang first without walking.

      c. Straighten the arms when the inverted position is gained.

      d. Get the balance while the knees are against the chest (head tucked forward) then slowly extend the legs upward.

      e. Keep the hips slightly flexed and the head forward. The upper back is rounded. (Advanced performers should arch the back and keep the head back.)

      f. Keep the legs between the hands. As the hands move forward, the legs must move forward too. The body remains vertical.

      g. Take short steps. The arms remain straight.

      h. Use the head to help keep the balance.

      i. Be sure you are balanced and steady before moving the hands.

Spot: A spotter on either side walks beside the performer ready to check a loss of balance in either direction. Reach under the bars.

15. **Corkscrew Mount**—From a cross stand right with the left hand in an overgrasp and the right hand in an undergrasp on the near bar, take a slight jump and swing both legs upward and slightly to the left between bars. The left thigh lands on the far bar and at the same time the right leg crosses over the left to the near bar. The chest stays close to the near bar (underneath) and twists as the right leg crosses over. With the twist, release the left hand and place it on the far bar. This results in a lying position on the bars with the right hand and leg on the near bar and the left hand and leg on the far bar. Straighten the arms and push up to a "Straddle Seat."

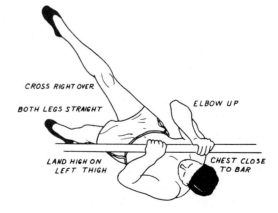

CROSS RIGHT OVER

BOTH LEGS STRAIGHT

ELBOW UP

LAND HIGH ON LEFT THIGH

CHEST CLOSE TO BAR

Hints: a. Keep the chest close to the underside of the bar as the legs swing upward. The arms must remain flexed.

b. Arch the back as the legs swing upward and twist slightly to the left.

c. The outside of the left thigh strikes the top of the far bar *close to the hip.* The right leg is above the left.

d. The right elbow comes above the bars as the twist is made.

e. Roll across the extended left thigh.

f. The entire stunt is done in one continuous, coordinated movement. The twist *actually begins* as the legs shoot upward between the bars.

Spot: Stand between the bars beside the performer's right shoulder. As the legs shoot upward, place your hands under his/her hips and lift them if needed to assure landing high on the left thigh. Switch your right hand to the left thigh to prevent its sliding off the bar as he/she rolls across it.

16. **Knee Circle Dismount**—Jump to a cross support in the middle of the bars and begin swinging. At the end of the backward swing, transfer the left hand to the right bar just in front of the right hand. At the same time, hook the right knee over the right bar, flex the arms, and drop between the bars. The drop causes the body to circle beneath the bar. As the body begins to rise on the other side of the bar, release the right hand and unhook the right leg and land in a cross stand with the left side toward the bars and the left hand still grasping the near bar.

Hints: a. Start in the center of the bars to avoid hitting the head on the front upright or the legs on the rear one.

b. Wait until the *end* of the backward swing before transferring the left hand. Don't swing too high.

c. Lean on the right arm as the transfer is made.

d. The right knee should *hook* the bar at the same time the left hand is transferred. The right knee is bent and the knee joint is on the bar.

e. Keep the chest close to the left bar. (arms must be flexed.)

f. Unhook the knee (straighten the right leg) and swing the right arm sideward just before the upward momentum stops.

Spot: No special spotting is needed. Stand in front of the performer ready to support him/her if necessary.

17. **Front Dismount Right with Half Twist Left**—Jump to a cross support in the middle of the bars and begin swinging. As the body swings backward and upward, lean on the right arm and pass the body over the right bar. At the same time release the left arm and swing it left sideward. The right hand retains its grasp and the body revolves to the left to a cross stand with the right side toward the bars and the right hand grasping the near bar in an undergrasp.

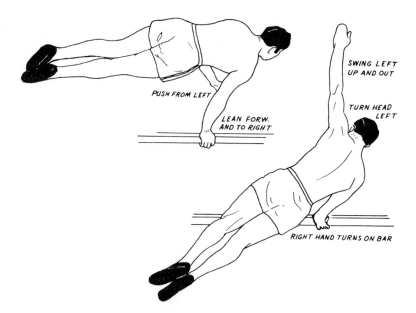

Hints: a. Lean slightly forward as well as to the right.
   b. Pause momentarily with the body in a horizontal plane above the bars before pushing off.
   c. Push off from the left hand and swing it vigorously upward and sideward to cause the body to revolve.
   d. At the same time turn the head to the left.
   e. Don't swing too high.
   f. Keep the head up and the body straight.

Spot: Stand in front of the performer's right arm and support it above the elbow with your left hand and on the wrist with the right hand.

18. **Rear Dismount Right with Half Twist Right**—Jump to a cross support in the middle of the bars and begin swinging. As the body swings forward and upward flex the hips and lean on the right arm. Immediately release the left arm, extend the hips (arch out) and execute a half twist to the right to a cross stand right with the right hand grasping the near bar.

Hints: a. Support the weight with the right arm, leaning slightly backward and to the right. The hips are slightly flexed when finishing the forward swing.
   b. Extend the hips (snap them upward) and twist at the same time.
   c. Push off hard with the left hand and throw it to the right and over the head.
   d. Turn the head to the right as the twist is made.
   e. At the same time, push downward with the right arm and, with either a slight hop or by pivoting, turn the hand to the right and regrasp the bar. If the pivot is used, raise the right thumb so the hand can turn. The "shift" is made at the peak of the twist.

Spot: Same as for the "Rear Dismount from Straight Arm Support."

19. **Front Dismount Right with Half Twist Right**—Jump to a cross support in the middle of the bars and begin to swing. As the body swings backward and upward, transfer the left hand to the right bar in

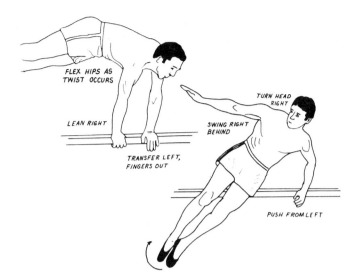

front of the right hand. Release the right hand and twist to the right as the body passes over the right bar and land in a cross stand right. Regrasp the bar with the right hand before landing.

Hints: a. Lean on the right arm when transferring the left hand. Don't *grasp* the bar with the left hand. Simply place it on top of the bar, fingers pointing outward (thumb toward you).

        b. Release the right hand and swing it right sideward (reach behind you) to start the twist to the right.

        c. At the same time, twist the head to the right.

        d. Also, push downward with the left hand to give a little lift to the body.

        e. Hints *b, c,* and *d* occur as soon as the left hand hits the right bar.

        f. Continue reaching around with the right arm and regrasp the near bar.

        g. Flex the hips as the twist is made and bring the feet under you.

Spot: Stand in front of the performer's right arm, but do not hold on. Be prepared to catch under the armpits if necessary.

Note: This can be learned on the floor with everyone practicing it at the same time. Have them get into a front leaning support (push-up position), move the left hand in front of the right with the fingers pointing right sideward. As soon as the left hand lands, push off from it, swing the right arm sideward and upward, turn the head to the right, push off from the toes and turn over (with a period of flight) to a rear support. After working on the floor, have them try it on the bars with the feet behind them on the bars. Move the left hand to the right bar, then bring the left leg under the right and across both bars to the dismount. Then go for the stunt from a swing.

20. **Rear Dismount Right with Half Twist Left**—Jump to a cross support in the middle of the bars and begin to swing. As the body swings forward, flex the hips, lean over on the right arm and push off from the left hand. Then release the right hand, pass over the bar, and twist inward toward the bar, executing a half twist to a cross stand right. Regrasp the near bar with the right hand before landing.

Hints: a. Lean on the right arm while the body is swinging upward.

        b. The body should be directly over the right bar with the hips flexed (legs parallel to the floor) as the push-off is made.

        c. Swing just hard enough to clear the bar.

        d. Release the right hand and swing it around the front of the body and reach for the near bar as the left hand pushes off.

e. At the same time, twist the head to the left and jerk the left elbow back behind you.

f. The right hand should regrasp the near bar and the twist should be completed before landing.

Spot: Stand to the rear of the performer's right arm but do not hold on. Be prepared to catch under the armpits if necessary.

Note: Get the feel of this stunt by first sitting in an "outer cross seat" on the right bar (sit on left thigh, both legs outside of bar) with the left hand on the left bar. Bounce off the right bar, push from the left hand, and reach in front of you with the right hand. Place right hand on bar before landing. Then try as described above.

21. **Forward Straddle Dismount at End of Bars**—From a cross stand facing outward at the end of the bars, jump to a support and begin to swing. As the legs swing higher than the bars in the rear, straddle (spread) them over the bars and push off from the hands to a cross stand rearways.

HEAD UP

LEAN FORW.

SPOTTER LIFTS, PULLS
AND STEPS BACK

Hints: a. The hands must be right at the ends of the bars.

b. Lean slightly forward when straddling the legs.

c. Straddle the legs just before the peak of the rear swing is reached and pike (flex the hips upward) at the same time.

d. Push downward and backward with the arms when releasing the hands and arch out (lift the chest) again.

e. Keep the head up.

f. Don't hesitate once you have started.

g. Beginners may try straddling one leg at a time at first.

Spot: a. Stand directly in front of the performer's right arm.

b. Grasp his/her right arm above the elbow with your right hand and grasp the right wrist with your left hand.

c. Lift upward and pull forward with the right hand as he/she straddles.

d. At the same time, step backward out of the way.

e. If he/she freezes (fails to let go) and falls forward, catch the chest on your right shoulder.

f. A spotter may be used on each arm. The one on the other arm reverses hand positions.

22. **Front Swinging Dips**—Jump to a support at the end of the bars facing inward and begin swinging. Bend the arms (dip) at the end of the backward swing and keep them bent until the end of the forward swing. Straighten the arms as the legs swing upward in front. Swing back in a straight arm support and repeat the dip at the end of the backward swing. Repeat eight to ten times.

Hints: a. Dip only when the legs have reached the "dead point" (end) of the backward swing.

b. Dip completely. Don't just bend the arms slightly.

c. Stay down till the upward swing of the legs at the end of the forward swing helps in the straightening of the arms.

d. Keep the shoulders ahead of the hands when dipping.

e. Keep the head up. Look straight forward.

Spot: a. One spotter stands behind and slightly to the side of the performer. Be ready to step in and catch under the armpits if he/she falls backward.

b. The other spotter stands in front and reaches under the bar to support the performer's chest if he/she falls forward.

23. **Back Swinging Dips**—This stunt is the same as the "Front Swinging Dips" except that the dipping occurs at the end of the forward swing and the straightening occurs at the end of the backward swing.

Hints: a. The preceding hints apply except that they refer to the opposite direction of the swings.

Spot: Same as preceding.

24. **Dip Swing Jump**—Jump to a support and begin swinging. Do a "Front Swinging Dip" but push vigorously with the arms and hop forward with the hands as the legs come up in front and the arms straighten. Regrasp with the hands and swing backward in the straight arm support position.

Hints: a. The "Swinging Dips" must be well learned before the jump is tried.

b. The hints for the "Front Swinging Dips" apply here but the straightening of the arms at the end of the forward swing must be forceful enough to produce the forward jump.

c. Keep the hips flexed as the jump is made, but extend as the hands regrasp.

d. The arms are straight (elbows locked) as the hands regrasp the bar.

Spot: Stand at the performer's side and be ready to support under the thighs if he/she should miss the hand grasp.

25. **Hip Circle to Front Leaning Support**—From a side stand frontways at the middle of the bars reach under the near bar and place the hands on the far bar in an overgrasp. With a slight jump, swing the legs forward and upward over the far bar. At the same time, pull with the arms so that the rest of the body circles over the bar also. Finish in a front leaning support. (Hands on the far bar, arms straight, and thighs on the near bar.)

Hints: a. Start with the upper arms against the near bar and one foot well forward.

b. Swing the rear leg forward and upward and push off from the forward leg.

c. Bear downward with the hands to raise the hips directly toward the far bar. Do not drop the hips.

d. Lean backward and throw the head back as the legs and hips swing upward.

e. Flex the hips as the legs swing over the bar.

f. At the same time, pull with the arms and snap the wrists upward. The wrist snap rotates the hands to a position on top of the bar.

g. The legs continue around and strike the near bar just above the knees. Don't bend the knees at any time.

Spot: a. Stand on the far side of the bars to the left of the performer's hands.

b. Reach under the bar and grasp the left wrist with your right hand in an upper grasp.

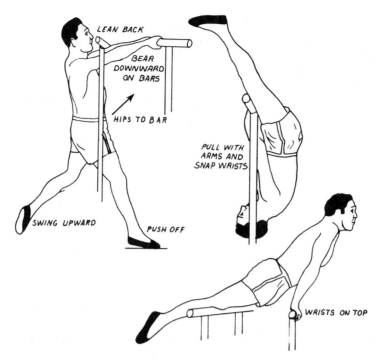

c. As he/she springs and brings the hips toward the far bar, place your left arm under them and lift upward.

d. At the same time, push forward and upward on his/her left wrist to help the snapping of the wrists.

26. **Chest Balance on One Bar**—Assume a front lying position across the bars with the hands and thighs on the near bar and the chest and upper arms on the far bar. Raise the hips and legs upward to an inverted position with the legs directly over the head and maintain the balance. Dismount by tucking the head to the chest, flexing the hips, releasing the grasp on the near bar and falling forward. Grasp the far bar on the way and drop to a side stand rearways.

    Hints: a. The far bar is across the *top* of the chest. If the arms have to be bent to get the bar there, bend them and keep them bent.

    b. Keep the head up.

    c. Press downward with the hands and flex the hips (raise them). Flex the knees too when first learning the stunt.

    d. When the flexed hips are above the head, straighten the legs upward.

    e. Maintain a tight grasp on the near bar and pull with the arms if the balance tends to be lost forward.

    f. Press downward on the bar if the balance tends to be lost backward.

    g. Be sure to flex the head, hips, and legs when dismounting.

    Spot: a. Stand on the far side of the bars to the performer's right and if help is needed, place your left hand on his/her abdomen and push upward.

    b. Place your right hand on the lower back to assist in balancing if needed.

    c. When he/she dismounts, place your right arm across the upper back.

27. **Leg Swing Flank Dismount from Front Leaning Support**—Mount to a front leaning support (hands on the far bar, arms straight, and thighs on the near bar). Lift the right leg sideward, swing it between the bars to the left and then swing it vigorously right sideward and upward, higher than the bars. Join the left leg to it, lean on the left arm, release the right hand and dismount over the bars to a side stand rearways. Release the left hand just before landing.

    Hints: a. Lean well forward in the front leaning support.

    b. Swing the right leg to the left, then right sideward, upward, and *forward*. Guard against the tendency to swing it backwards.

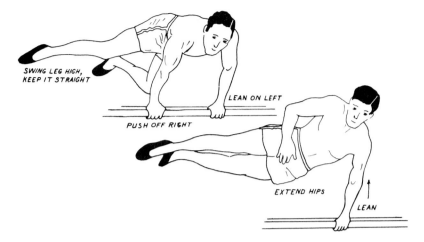

c. Lean on the left arm just before the right leg reaches the height of its swing.

d. Push off from the right hand and from the left leg to bring the left leg up to the right leg as the swing of the right leg lifts the body.

e. With the push from the right hand, arch the back to pass over the bar.

Spot: a. Stand on the far side of the bars at the performer's left side.

b. Grasp his/her left arm close to the shoulder with your left hand and the left wrist with your right hand.

c. Exert a gentle pull toward you with the left hand to cause a lean to the left.

d. If the legs do not clear the bars, turn so that you catch his/her chest on your left shoulder.

e. If the performer has a lot of difficulty, stand in front of the left arm, grasp it above his/her elbow with your right hand and place your left hand under his/her left hip and lift and pull toward you as the right leg swings upward.

28. **Squat Dismount from Front Leaning Support**—Mount to a front leaning support. Squat over both bars with the legs passing between the arms, and land in a side stand rearways.

Hints: a. Lean well forward in the front leaning support.

b. Sag slightly at the waist, then whip the hips upward (flex them) by pressing downward with the thighs.

c. At the same time, draw the knees to the chest.

d. Push downward and backward with the arms as the knees come forward.

e. Keep the head up.

Spot: a. Use two spotters. Both stand on the far side, one in front of each arm.

b. They grasp the performer's arms close to the shoulders with the hand closest to the performer and his/her wrists with the other.

c. As he/she dismounts, the spotters lift upward and step backward out of the way.

d. If the toes catch, the spotters must be sure to support the arms.

e. If only one person spots, proceed as above except that you catch the performer on your own shoulder if the performer's toes catch on the bar.

29. **Rear Dismount from Outer Cross Seat**—Mount to an outer cross seat on the right thigh on the outside of the left bar. The right hand is on the right bar, the left hand is free, and the left leg is straight and points downward. Swing the legs upward and to the right while leaning on the right arm and dismount over both bars to a cross stand with the left side toward the bars.

Hints: a. Lean forward and swing the left arm and leg backward, and then whip the arm and leg forward, upwards, and to the right.

b. At the same time lean far over to the right and place the weight on the *straight* right arm.

c. Push off from the bar with the right thigh.

d. As the body passes over the right bar, reach back with the left hand and grasp the bar before landing.

e. As the left hand grasps the right bar, release the right hand.

Spot: a. Stand to the right of the bars just behind the performer's right arm.
b. Grasp his/her right arm close to the shoulder with your left hand and place your right hand on the wrist.
c. Lift upward and pull toward you on the arm as he/she dismounts.
d. If he has difficulty, shift the right hand to his right hip and lift and pull toward you.

30. **Forward Roll from Straddle Seat to Straddle Seat**—Mount to a straddle seat on the bars and place the hands in front of the thighs. Bend the arms, place the shoulders (upper arms) on the bars, raise the hips, and roll forward across the upper arms to a straddle seat.

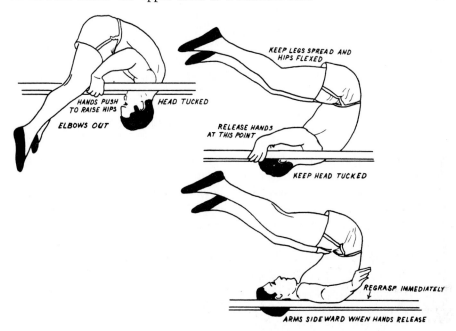

Hints: a. Place the upper arms on the bars as close to the legs as possible.
   b. Keep the elbows out (away from the body). They should be level with the bars.
   c. To do this, the hands are rotated outward on the bars (thumbs on top).
   d. Tuck the head forward and keep the hips well flexed.
   e. Raise the hips and bring them forward by pressing downward with the hands.
   f. Keep the legs straight and well sperad and the hips well flexed. Do not straighten the hips.
   g. Release the hands and roll across the upper arms as the hips pass overhead. The arms remain sideward and serve as an axle around which the body rolls.
   h. Reach forward with the hands while the legs and hips are still over head and grasp the bars at the place where the legs will strike.
   i. Lean forward and push with the hands to come to a seat.

Spot: a. Stand at the performer's right side and place your right hand in the middle of his/her back from beneath the bar as the shoulders are lowered to the bars.
   b. Support the back as he/she rolls and push upward if help is needed in rising to a seat.

31. **Backward Roll from Straddle Seat to Straddle Seat**—Mount to a straddle seat on the bars and place the hands behind the hips. Lower backward till the armpits strike the bars and raise the legs and hips overhead. Release the hands and continue rolling backward (the body is supported by the upper arms) and come to a straddle seat on the bars.

Hints: a. Tuck the head forward.
   b. Raise the legs overhead (flex the hips) when leaning backward by pressing downward with the hands.
   c. The elbows should be slightly flexed so the bars strike the underside of the arms close to the shoulders.
   d. When the hips are overhead (legs well spread, parallel to the floor) release the hands, roll across the upper arms and regrasp the bars behind the shoulders.
   e. The arms must remain sideward as the change is made and act as an axle around which the body rolls.
   f. Keep the legs straight and straddled.
   g. Push with the arms to come to a seat.

Spot: a. Stand at the performer's left side and place your right hand against the upper back from beneath the bar as he/she lowers backward.
   b. Support the back as he/she rolls backward.

c. If needed, place the left hand against the hips and push upward.

d. Be prepared to duck under his/her left arm as it is extended sideward.

32. **Backward Straddle Dismount**—Jump to a support at the end of the bars facing inward and raise the legs forward and upward, flexing the hips. When they are higher than the bars, straddle the legs, push with the hands and pass the legs backward over the bars to land in a cross stand frontways.

Hints: a. Raise the legs as part of the jump.

b. Practice with one leg at a time (release only one hand) before trying it with both legs together.

c. Lean slightly backward as the legs swing forward (shoulders behind the hands).

d. Pause momentarily as the legs reach the height of their swing.

e. Keep the head up. Look forward.

f. Push forward and downward with the hands and straddle the legs at the same time. Much of the push comes from the shoulders.

g. Don't jerk the hips backward to clear the bars; depend on the arm push to get you off.

h. Reach for the bars with the hands as soon as the legs pass under the hands.

i. Bring the feet together before landing.

j. This can also be done from a small swing, but it is a little harder.

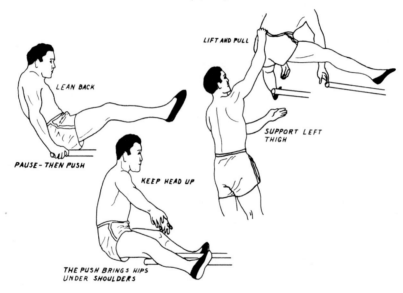

Spot: a. Stand directly behind the performer and grasp the waistband, supporter, and shirt with the right hand.

b. Lift upward slightly and pull backward as he/she dismounts.

c. Support under the left thigh with your left hand to prevent his/her upper body dropping forward as you pull with the right.

d. Be prepared to catch the back on your shoulder if he/she fails to release the hands and starts to fall backward.

e. If done from a swing, spot the same but stand further to the left, out of the way of his/her legs.

33. **Hip Roll**—Mount to a straddle seat in the middle of the bars and place both hands on the left bar with the left hand in front of the right. Lower the trunk forward and twist it to the left to bring the head and shoulders under the left bar. As this is done, bring the left leg over to the right side and at the same time, rotate the body to the left, rolling across the hips on the right bar. The body is extended and parallel to the floor supported at the hips by the right bar. Continue to rotate, and as the weight comes onto the left thigh, cross the right leg over to the other bar and rise to a straddle seat on the bars facing the starting spot.

Hints: a. Keep the chest close to the left bar. The arms remain bent.

b. The weight comes first to the right thigh, then across the hips to the left thigh.

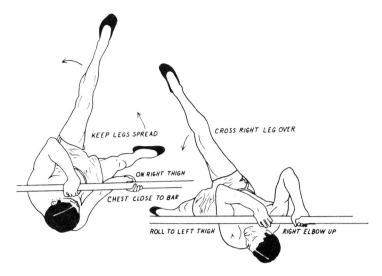

c. As the body rolls on the hips, bring the right elbow above the bars.

d. Keep the legs straight and well spread.

e. With the weight on the left thigh and the right leg crossing over, push downward with the right hand and raise the head and chest. Move the left hand to the other bar.

Spot: Stand between the bars behind the performer and support at the waist as he/she rolls. Duck under the left leg as it is brought over the bars.

34. **Upper Arm Support Swing**—Jump to an upper arm support in the middle of the bars and obtain a swing. This is not a stunt in itself, but a good upper arm swing is important in several advanced stunts.

    Hints: a. The hands are about 12 inches ahead of the shoulders, and a firm grip must be maintained to prevent the upper arms from moving back and forth with the swing.

    b. Keep the elbows at the height of the bar or below. This will prevent sagging at the shoulders.

    c. Press downward with the hands and flex the hips, moving them forward. Then arch out (reach forward with the feet) and swing backward.

    d. Swing from the shoulders, not the hips.

    e. Work for a smooth, easy swing. Relax.

    f. This is sometimes painful the first few times, so foam rubber pads can be taped to the bars under the arms till the performer gets used to the pressure.

    Spot: No spotting needed.

35. **Hip Circle from Upper Arm Support**—Swing in an upper arm support in the middle of the bars. As the legs reach the end of the backward swing, transfer the left hand to the right bar with a one-eighth turn to the right and swing the legs forward and upward around the right bar. The support is maintained by the right upper arm and the left hand. As the body circles over the right bar, come to a position with the body across both bars at right angles to them, facing downward.

    Hints: a. Don't move the left hand till the *end* of the backward swing. Moving it too soon is a common fault.

    b. Shift most of the weight to the right armpit and hook the bar tightly.

    c. Get a good whip from the legs (flex the hips) as the legs swing forward under the right bar.

    d. As the legs come up and over the bar, turn so the body is at right angles to the bar.

    e. Lift the head and chest upward as the legs come on top.

    Spot: Stand to the right of the performer and place your right arm around his/her waist and lift upward as the legs swing under the right bar.

36. **Upper Arm Balance from Straddle Seat**—Mount to a straddle seat on the bars and place the hands just in front of the thighs. Lower the shoulders (upper arms) to the bars and raise the legs and hips to an inverted position balanced on the upper arms. To return, tuck the head forward, flex the hips and straddle the legs, and roll forward to a straddle seat.

    Hints: a. Keep the elbows out (away from the sides) when placing the upper arms on the bars. The hands must rotate on the bars.

             b. The upper arms should be about 10-12 inches from the hands and parallel to the floor.

             c. Keep the head up.

             d. Press downward with the hands to raise the hips.

             e. Keep the knees and hips flexed until they are above the head; then slowly extend them and arch the back. (Advanced performers keep the knees straight.)

             f. If the balance is lost forward, tuck the head, *flex the hips*, and spread the legs. Release the hands and roll across the arms to a seat.

             g. If the balance is lost backward, flex the hips and spread the legs, and resist the downward drop by pressing downward with the hands. This reduces the momentum.

             h. When rolling out of the balance, follow hints *f* to *h* in Stunt No. 30, page 148.

    Spot: a. Stand at either side of the performer and place one hand on the back as he/she straightens upward. Reach *under* the bar.

             b. Be prepared to check the fall in either direction. One hand ready at the front and the other hand ready at the back.

             c. Help to raise the legs if he *needs* help by pushing upward on the abdomen.

37. **Straddle Mount at End**—Stand at the end of the bars facing inward and place the hands on the bars. Jump upward, straddle the legs sideward and bring them over the bars and together (under the hands) in the center. Regrasp with the hands and finish in a straight arm support. This can also be done to an "L" support (legs held forward, parallel to the floor).

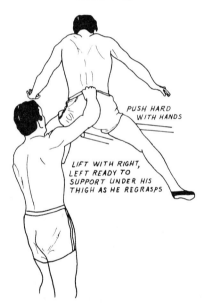

PUSH HARD WITH HANDS

LIFT WITH RIGHT, LEFT READY TO SUPPORT UNDER HIS THIGH AS HE REGRASPS

    Hints: a. Keep the arms straight and the feet directly under the shoulders.

             b. Jump straight upward and push downward vigorously with the hands at the same time. The arm push does more to get the last few inches of height than the legs do.

             c. At the same time flex the hips to bring the legs forward and straddle the legs.

             d. Lean slightly backward with the chest and shoulders.

             e. Practice the stunt to a straddle seat a few times. Pass the legs under the hands but do not bring the legs together.

             f. When ready to try the stunt, concentrate on clicking the feet together over the center of the bars.

             g. The hands must release while the body momentum is upward.

    Spot: a. Stand directly behind the performer and grasp his/her belt with the right hand and place the left hand under his/her left thigh.

             b. As he/she mounts, lift upward with both hands.

             c. Support if he/she fails to regrasp with the hands.

             d. The left hand under the thigh as the regrasp is made is important to prevent the legs from swinging back, thus kicking you.

             e. Gradually lessen the amount of assistance until finally he/she does it alone with the spotter ready for an emergency.

38. **Forward Roll from Support to Straddle Seat**—Jump to a cross support in the middle of the bars and obtain a swing. As the legs swing backward, bend the arms and place the shoulders (upper arms) on the bars in front of the hands. At the same time, flex the hips and bring them forward over the head. Spread the legs and roll across the upper arms to a "Straddle Seat."

   Hints: a. Swing fairly high (legs higher than the shoulders) before bending the arms and flexing the hips. Bending the arms too early is a common fault.
   b. The elbows must go outward (away from the body) when the arms bend. The hands rotate outward on the bars.
   c. Tuck the head forward at the same time.
   d. As the hips come forward over the head, release the hands and extend them sideward as the body rolls on the arms.
   e. Regrasp immediately with the hands in front of the shoulders.
   f. Keep the hips flexed and the legs spread and roll up to a straddle seat.

   Spot: a. Stand at the performer's right side and support the upper back from beneath the bar with your right hand as he/she places the upper arms on the bars.
   b. If necessary, push upward on the abdomen with your left hand as the legs swing backward.

39. **Backward Roll from Upper Arm Support to Straddle Seat**—Jump to an upper arm support in the middle of the bars and start to swing. As the legs swing upward in front, flex the hips and bring the legs and hips over the head. Spread the legs, release the hands, rotate on the upper arms and roll to a straddle seat.

   Hints: a. Obtain a high swing.
   b. Press downward with the hands and at the same time, whip the legs forward and upward by flexing the hips. It is a common fault to stop the downward arm pressure too early.

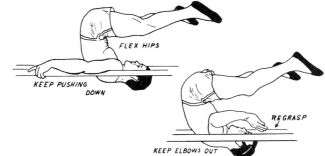

   FLEX HIPS
   KEEP PUSHING DOWN
   REGRASP
   KEEP ELBOWS OUT

   c. Keep the head forward as the legs come over the head.
   d. The elbows remain sideward as the hands shift backward.
   e. Regrasp the bar behind the shoulders as soon as possible.
   f. Spread the legs as the flexed hips come overhead.
   g. Push with hands to come to a seat.

   Spot: a. Stand at the performer's right side and place your right hand against the lower back as he/she swings forward, and push upward to help raise the hips.
   b. Place your left hand on the right elbow to keep it out, away from the body.
   c. Be ready to duck under the right arm as it extends sideward.

40. **Upper Arm Kip to Straight Arm Support**—Jump to an upper arm support in the middle of the bars and start to swing. On the forward swing, flex the hips and raise the legs over the head. (The knees should be just about over the head.) Pause a moment and then kick the legs forward and upward at about a 45° angle. At the same time, bear downward on the bars with the hands and draw the body up to a straight arm support.

   Hints: a. Practice the stunt to a straddle seat first.
   b. Pause with the hips higher than the bars and the legs straight before extending the hips.
   c. The kick must be short, fast, and snappy.
   d. With the kick, straddle the legs and come to a straddle seat.
   e. A powerful downward pressure must be exerted by the almost straight arms to aid the kick in bringing the shoulders up above the point of support.
   f. Keep the head up as the body rises.
   g. When you can land erect in the straddle seat instead of rolling into it, you are ready to try the stunt to a straight arm support.

h. The same hints apply except that the legs are kept together instead of being straddled.

Spot: a. Two spotters are needed. The spotter on the right places his/her right hand under the performer's hips and supports them as the kick is made. The left hand is on the performer's upper arm.

b. The spotter on the left places his/her right hand on the performer's left upper arm and has the left hand in readiness to put under the bar and against the performer's chest if the kick pulls him/her forward beyond the point of support.

41. **Drop to Upper Arm Kip from Straight Arm Support**—Swing forward in a straight arm support and as the legs come up in front, flex the hips, lean backward, bend the arms (elbows go outward), and land on the underside of the upper arms with the legs overhead. Pause a moment and then kick upward and outward as in Stunt No. 40.

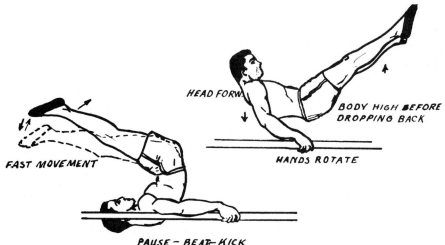

Hints: a. Wait until the legs are fairly high on the forward swing before leaning back and bending the arms. Dropping too early is a common fault.

b. However, don't stop the forward and upward momentum before dropping. Lean back just before reaching the peak of the swing.

c. Keep the head slightly forward when dropping.

d. Be sure the elbows move sideward. Rotate the hands on the bar.

    e. The hips remain well above the bars in the pike position.

    f. Pause momentarily with the hips high; then increase the flexion (dip the legs) and immediately rebound with the kick.

    g. For the kip, follow the hints in No. 40.

Spot: a. Stand to the right and as he/she drops back, place your left hand on the upper back and the right hand on his/her hips. (Both hands reach under the bar.)

    b. Give some support with the left hand and lift a little with the right as he/she drops.

    c. Spot as in No. 40 for the rest.

42. **Back Uprise**—Jump to an upper arm support in the middle of the bars and obtain a swing. As the legs swing backward and upward, bear downward with the arms and rise to a straight arm support.

    Hints: a. Don't swing backward and forward too many times. Try the stunt on the first or second swing.

    b. Obtain a large swing. Lift the flexed hips forward higher than the bars (by pressing downward with the hands) and then reach forward with the feet (arch out). Raise the hips, but not with a snap as in the kip. The upper arms remain *on* the bar.

    c. At the same time, pull with the hands to slide the shoulders forward, bringing them close to the hands and drive downward with the legs.

    d. Begin to bear downward with the hands right after the legs have passed the midpoint of their backward swing and have begun to swing upward. Use the momentum of the legs to help.

    e. Beginners are aided by a slight flexion and extension of the hips as the arms bear downward.

    f. Advanced performers will keep the back arched.

    g. Keep the head up.

Spot: a. Stand at the performer's right and place your right hand against the abdomen and push upward as he/she begins to bear down with the arms.

    b. Be sure to remove your hand as he/she swings forward in the straight arm support position so as to prevent striking your arm against the bar.

43. **Kip to Straight Arm Support**—From a cross stand frontways at the end of the bars, place the hands on the bars and, with a slight jump, lean backward with the shoulders, flex the hips, and raise the feet to a position between the hands. Hold this position while the hips swing forward. As the hips begin to swing backward, kick (extend the legs) forward and upward at a 45° angle. At the same time, press downward with the hands. This will bring the body up to a straight arm support.

    Hints: a. Place the thumbs along the sides of the bars rather than under them.

    b. Practice once or twice by jumping up and placing the feet against the uprights, bending the knees and then pushing with the legs to drive the body up to a support. The feet should be placed about hip high on the posts. After a couple of tries in this manner, proceed as follows.

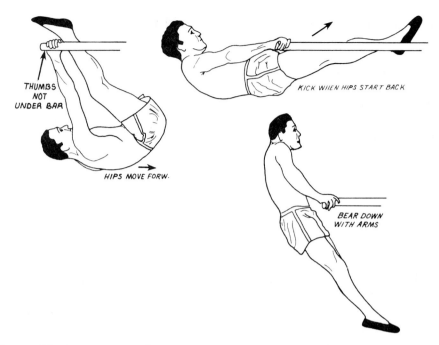

c. Start with the arms straight and the feet directly under the hands.

d. Jump from both feet and flex the hips to bring the ankles directly to the level of the hands, allowing the hips to swing forward freely.

e. A small, partial extension followed by a quick flexion of the hips aids in giving the proper timing.

f. Follow the above flexion with the kick and arm pull.

g. The common fault is to kick too soon. The hips must be moving backward before the kick is begun. As the kick (hip extension) is made, think of bringing the hips up to the hands.

h. About 1½ seconds should elapse between the start and the kick. Try to get that timing in the head before trying the stunt.

i. Another common fault is to kick too flatly. The legs must go upward at about 45° and not straight forward.

j. Keep the legs straight. The movement comes from the *hips* not the knees.

k. Lean forward—pull into the bars at the finish of the stunt.

Spot: a. Stand at the performer's right and place your left hand on the upper back.

b. As he/she drops back and raises the legs, place your right hand on the back of the right leg.

c. As he/she extends, lift with the left hand and resist the forward thrust of the legs with the right hand.

d. Be ready to place your right hand under the chest to support if he/she drops down between the bars after getting up.

44. **Upper Arm Balance from Straight Arm Support**—Jump to a support in the middle of the bars and begin swinging. As the legs swing upward in back, bend the arms (elbows out) and place the shoulders (upper arms) on the bars in front of the hands. The body continues to swing upward in the arched position to a vertical position and the balance on the upper arms is maintained. To return to an upper arm support, tuck the head forward, flex the hips slightly, release the hands and roll forward on the upper arms. Regrasp the bars in front of the shoulders as soon as possible.

Hints: a. Don't flex the arms till the backward swing is well above shoulder height, but *don't* wait till the *end* of the swing occurs.

b. Keep the head up and back arched.

c. As the arms bend, the elbows move outward. The hands rotate on the bars so that the palms are to the side of the bars and the thumbs are on top.

d. Place the shoulders about 12 inches in front of the hands.

e. Raise the head and pull with the hands if the balance tends to be lost forward.

f. Lower the head, flex the hips a little and push downward with the hands if the balance tends to be lost backward.

g. Start the roll forward by tucking the head.

h. Release the hands and extend the arms sideward as the forward movement starts and slightly flex the hips.

i. Regrasp the bars (hands in front of shoulders) as soon as possible. Rotate (roll) the arms forward as the body drops.

j. When this has been learned, try combining it with the "Back Uprise" (No. 42). As soon as the hands regrasp, start driving the legs downward for the "Back Uprise."

Spot: a. Stand at the performer's right side and reach beneath the bar with your right hand and place it against the back.

b. The left hand should be under the bar ready to check a fall in the other direction or to push up on the abdomen if there is insufficient swing.

45. **Double Rear Dismount**—Swing in a straight arm cross support in the middle and, as the legs swing backward, lean on the right arm, release the left hand, pass the legs over the left bar (hips flexed) continue the circular movement of the legs and pass them over the left bar again (in front) and on over the right bar in front of the right hand. Land in a cross stand left. Place the left hand on the right bar in front of the right hand and release the right hand just before landing.

Hints: a. Don't turn the body. Face forward all the time. Don't swing very high in back.

b. Keep the right arm straight when leaning on it. The right shoulder should be well to the right of the hand.

c. A strong push-off from the left hand will help the lean.

d. At the same time, lift (flex) the hips sharply and swing the legs left, over the bar.

e. Keep the feet as high as the hips till both bars have been passed over. Knees should be straight.

    f. The left hand (which has been raised for balance since the push-off) grasps the bar in front of the right hand and then the right hand is released.

    g. The left hand doesn't carry any weight. It just steadies the landing.

Spot: a. Stand behind the performer's right arm and grasp it above the elbow with your left hand and at the wrist with your right.

    b. Support and pull gently toward you as he/she dismounts.

    c. Be prepared to catch the upper body on your left shoulder if the feet catch on the bar.

46. Front Uprise—From a small run, jump to an upper arm support and, as the legs swing forward, bear downward with the arms and rise to a straight arm cross support.

Hints: a. Take off from both feet and dive forward. Lift the legs high in back (arch the back) but don't get the chest too high.

    b. The hands grasp the bar firmly about 18 inches in front of the shoulders.

    c. Don't sag in the shoulders. Keep the elbows even with the bars.

    d. Drive (force) the legs downward and forward instead of just letting gravity bring them down.

    e. As the legs swing upward, flex the hips slightly (the feet lead).

    f. Force the legs forward and upward hard.

    g. About three-quarters of the way up, snap the hips upward and bear downward and pull with the arms.

Spot: Stand at the performer's left and as he/she swings past the midpoint, place your right hand in the small of the back and push forward and upward.

47. Cast Back from Support to Front Uprise—From a straight arm cross support in the middle of the bars, swing, and at the end of the backward swing, bend the arms and drop to an upper arm support. As the legs swing forward, go into a "Front Uprise" as in No. 46.

Hints: a. Wait till the "dead point" of the back swing before dropping. The shoulders will be forward of the hands as in a normal backward swing.

    b. Push back from the hands as the drop occurs so the body moves backward and the upper arms land about 18 inches from the hands.

    c. Keep the head up and the elbows out.

    d. Don't sag in the shoulders when landing. Tighten the chest (pectoral) muscles.

    e. Start driving for the uprise as soon as the upper arms land.

Spot: Spot as for No. 46.

48. **Backward Upper Arm Roll**—Jump to an upper arm support in the middle of the bars and start swinging. On the forward swing flex the hips slightly, press downward with the arms and throw the head backward. As the hips rise higher than the bars, extend the body upward, throw the arms sideward and continue to rotate, supported by the upper arms. Regrasp the bar as soon as possible to prevent sliding on the bars.

Hints: a. A very large swing is needed.
      b. Keep the head slightly forward until the body is almost vertical.
      c. Start bearing down with the arms as soon as the body passes the midpoint of its forward swing and keep pressing as long as you can.
      d. Flex the hips slightly after the body passes the midpoint. Throw the legs upward.
      e. Arch the back as the body nears the top of the roll.
      f. At the same time extend the arms sideward, parallel to the floor.
      g. Keep the back arched and reach forward to regrasp the bar as the body descends.
      h. Practice the backward roll from an upper arm balance first to get used to the idea of rotating on the upper arms.
      i. Also be sure you can do the "Backward Roll from Upper Arm Support to Straddle Seat" first.

Note: This may also be done from a support and cast back as in No. 47.

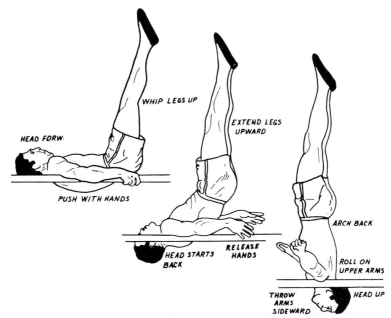

Spot: a. Stand at the performer's right side and place your right hand on the back as he/she starts swinging upward in front.
      b. Your left hand is placed on the right elbow to keep it at the same level as the bars.
      c. Duck under the extended right arm.

49. **Handbalance (Handstand)**—Jump to a straight arm cross support in the center of the bars and swing the legs backward and over the head to an inverted balance. Hold for five seconds. The arms remain straight. Lower the legs and return to a support.

Hints: a. Learn the handbalance on the floor first, then practice at the *end* of the bars facing *outward*. Keep the bars low.
      b. Place one foot on the bar behind your hand.
      c. Swing the other leg back and up and push from the foot on the bar.
      d. Bring both legs together overhead.
      e. Be sure the head remains up throughout. Do not tuck the head.

f. Use a tight grip and a lot of wrist action to fight for balance.

g. For an underbalance, bend the arms slightly, force the elbows inward and push to resist the downward pressure of the body. If this is not enough to prevent loss of balance, continue the resistance to slow down the rate of descent.

h. For an overbalance, release one hand, turn on the other and allow the legs to drop in front of the ends of the bar. Land in a side stand right (if the left hand is released).

i. When the balance can be maintained by kicking up, try swinging up (still at the end). The arms are fairly straight, the head is up. When confidence has been gained at the end, **move to the middle.**

Spot: a. Stand in front of the right arm with your left hand on the right elbow and your right hand under the right shoulder, palm up, fingers *toward* you.

b. If he/she underbalances and comes down, shift both hands to the waist to stop the forward swing before the body swings too far in front of the arms.

c. If he/she overbalances, maintain your right hand on the shoulder and support as he/she twists and brings the feet down. He/she may want to twist off in the other direction in which case you would reverse your hand positions and support the left shoulder.

50. **Forward Double Leg Cut Under One Hand**—From a straight arm support in the middle of the bars, swing the legs backward then circle them over the left bar, under the left hand as it is released and back over the left bar in front as the left hand regrasps. Maintain the right grip at all times. This can finish in either a held "L" position (trunk erect, legs parallel to the floor) or in a backward swing.

Hints: a. When learning this, keep the bars low and start at the *end* of the bars facing inward.

b. Don't swing very high.

c. Begin raising (flexing) the hips as the legs pass through the vertical position.

d. As the hips continue upward lean on the straight right arm and push off with the left.

e. The shoulders should be slightly ahead of the hands.

f. As the legs pass under the left hand, lower the hips a little and raise the feet.

g. Regrasp with the left hand as soon as possible.

h. When it has been learned on the end, move to the middle.

Spot: a. Stand slightly behind the right arm and place your right hand on the biceps.

b. Pull slightly on the arm and place your left hand under his/her right thigh and push upward.

51. **Forward Straddle Cut Under Both Hands (from Support)**—Swing backward in a straight arm support and at the end of the swing, straddle the legs over the bars and bring them forward under the hands. Bring the legs together again in front and regrasp with the hands. Finish either in a backward swing in support or in an "L" support.

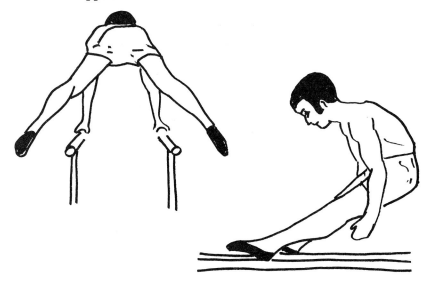

Hints: a. To learn, start at the end of the bars, facing inward with the bars at a low height.

b. Don't swing very high.

c. Raise the hips (flex them) as the body swings backward.

d. At the *end* of the back swing (slight pause) snap the heels upward (extend the hips to an arched position, body parallel to bars).

e. React against this hip snap with a hard, downward thrust against the bars and "bounce" the hands off the bars. Keep the arms straight—the thrust comes from the shoulders.

f. Don't lean too far forward. The shoulders are just slightly ahead of the hands.

g. With the downward push, straddle the legs and snap them forward.

h. Bring the legs together in front and regrasp with the hands. Concentrate on clicking the feet together.

i. Keep the head up throughout.

52. **Forward Straddle Cut Under Both Hands (From Back Uprise)**—Jump to an upper arm support in the middle of the bars, obtain a large swing and on the back swing do a back uprise to support while straddling the legs and bringing them forward under the hands as in stunt no. 51.

Hints: a. A very vigorous, high backward swing is needed.

b. Just before the end of the upward swing, pike (flex) the hips, straddle the legs, and snap the feet forward. Do *not* pause as in *d* of stunt No. 51.

c. The arms push against the bars for the "Uprise" and *continue* to push, coming right off the bars. This is *one* movement.

d. The shoulders are *behind* the hands at the moment of thrust.

e. With the arm push, raise the upper body.

f. Concentrate on clicking the feet together in front.

g. Reach for the bars with straight arms. Keep the head up.

Spot: No spotting needed.

Routines:

Work on the "Beginner's Routine" till it can be done in a flowing, continuous manner with no pauses (except where indicated) and no extra swings. Each movement should be part of the one preceding it and flow into the next one. Try small sequences of two or three stunts then keep adding till all can be done. When this is done with good form, start working on the next routine.

53. **Beginner's Routine**—Jump to upper arm hang, back uprise, drop back to kip position, kip, swing to upper arm balance and hold for 2 seconds, roll forward and back uprise with straddling of legs to straddle seat on bars behind hands. Place hands behind hips, swing left leg forward and between the bars, place the right hand on the left bar (body supported by right leg and both hands), left leg swings left sideward and upward while the left hand pushes off and the weight is carried by the right arm as the legs scissor to a straddle seat facing in opposite direction. Place hands in front of legs, swing legs backward and bring them together, then forward between the bars to an "L" position (hips flexed, legs parallel to floor) and hold. Press to upper arm balance, keeping the legs straight. Hold. Back roll to front uprise. Swing backward and front dismount right with half twist right to stand with right side toward bar. Note: Whenever a specific leg, arm, or direction (left or right) is mentioned, the performer may use the opposite one if he desires. If the first move of a series is reversed, all directions for the particular series must be reversed.

Hints on Individual Moves:

1. Back Uprise: Dive into the upper arm hang trailing the legs behind. When the upper arms and hands strike the bars, swing legs forward and upward and pike the hips slightly. Then arch out by raising the hips and reaching forward with the legs (extend the body). *Drive* downward, backward, and upward with the legs and body. Don't "sag" in the shoulders. As the body passes the vertical position, begin the downward pressure with the arms to bring yourself up to the straight arm support. A slight pike and immediate extension of the hips as the body is rising will aid the beginner, but with practice, it can be done with an arch all the way.

2. Upper Arm Kip: Swing forward in a straight arm support. As the legs swing higher than the bars, flex the hips, lean backward with the shoulders, drop to the upper arms (elbows move outward away from the body), and land in an upper arm kip position. Don't drop too early—wait till the legs are fairly high. The hips are higher than the bars, the legs are straight and above the head, the head is slightly forward, the hips are flexed, and the hands grip the bars tightly, well forward of the shoulders. Pause momentarily, then slightly increase the pike (dip the legs downward) and immediately rebound upward with a sharp, snappy extension at an upward and forward angle of 45°. At the same time, bear downward with the arms to bring yourself up to a straight arm support.

3. Upper Arm Balance: Swing backward in a straight arm support and, as the legs swing above the bar in back, bend the arms (elbows move out, away from the body) and land on the upper arms with the arched body extending upward. The head *remains up* throughout the stunt. Don't bend the arms *too soon*. Rotate the hands outward on the bars as the arms bend.

4. Roll Forward and Back Uprise to Straddle Seat: From the upper arm balance, tuck the head forward, release the hands and extend the arms sideward as the body rolls forward. Regrasp with the hands (about 15 inches in front of the shoulders) as *soon* as possible. When the hands regrasp, drive downward and backward with the legs as in the back uprise (No. 1). Beginners will flex the hips to some extent when starting the roll forward, but practice will enable you to keep the body extended. Just before the high point of the back uprise is reached, pike the hips, spread the legs, and land in a straddle seat with the legs behind the hands.

5. Follow the directions in the routine description up to the "L" position.

6. Press to Upper Arm Balance: From the "L" position, raise the hips backward and upward by leaning forward with the shoulders, bending the arms (elbows stay close to the body) and hunching (raising) the upper back. As the hips come overhead, rotate the hands outward on the bars and bring the elbows sideward. The head must remain up throughout the stunt. The knees may

be bent to make it easier to begin with but practice till it can be done with perfectly straight legs. As the shoulders come to the bar, extend the legs upward. The tighter the pike (bent hips) the easier the stunt. *Don't* extend the hips till they are above the head and the shoulders are on the bar.

7. Back Roll to Front Uprise: From the upper arm balance, extend the arms sideward (keep the head up), begin the backward roll using the upper arms as an axis and regrasp the bar about 15 inches in front of the shoulders as *soon* as possible. Keep the body extended. When the hands regrasp, drive the body forward and upward, piking slightly when passing through the vertical position. Continue the upward surge and bear down hard with the arms. As the arms downward pressure raises the body, snap the hips upward to eliminate the slight pike at the hips. The shoulders remain somewhat behind the hands as the body comes to a straight arm support.

8. Front Dismount Right, Half Twist Right: As the body swings backward and upward, lean on the right arm, transfer the left hand to the right bar in front of the right hand and push off with it as soon as it lands. At the sime time, swing the right arm sideward to the right and behind you to regrasp the bar with the right hand after completing the half twist. Turn the head to the right as the right arm swings sideward and back.

54. **Intermediate Routine**—From a cross stand frontways at the end of the bars, jump to a straddle mount to an immediate drop kip. Swing through a momentary upper arm balance and roll forward to a back uprise. Dip Swing Jump into an immediate swing to a handstand. Swing downward and forward to a stütz (release bars on forward swing, execute a half-turn in air and regrasp bars facing other way), cast to an upper arm hang and back uprise to an "L" support for 2 seconds. Press a bent arm (or straight arm) straight leg handstand. Execute a one-quarter turn to a handstand on one bar and do a squat (or straddle, or stoop) dismount.

22

Vaulting

The same horse is used for vaulting as for pommel horse work except that the pommels are removed. Place wooden plugs into the holes made for the pommel shafts or cover the holes with tape to prevent the vaulter's fingers from going into the holes as the hands are placed. If plugs are used, they must be flush with the top of the horse.

Competitive vaulting is done over the length of the horse for men and boys and over the width of the horse for women. The horse height for men is 53 inches and since 1979, it is the same for high school boys. Women's vaulting height is 47 inches. For physical education class vaulting, a waist high horse is fine for both boys and girls. Adjust the height according to the abilities of the group.

It is recommended that vaulting for *all* beginners be started over the horse placed sideways rather than over the long horse. Also, beginners will be aided by the use of the pommels rather than vaulting with the pommels removed. A take-off board is used for competitive vaulting but not required for class work because of the reduced height.

A double take-off (spring from both feet at the same time) is important as is landing on both feet simultaneously. Stress bending the knees to absorb the shock of landing. Suggest to primary children that they touch the floor with their hands as they land. There is no virtue in touching the floor, but it will insure that the youngsters bend their knees when landing.

When vaulting over the long horse (horse placed lengthwise) the concept of height, flight, and distance must be kept in mind. Have confidence in your ability. Run hard, don't hesitate just before taking off. The simpler vaults are *not* as difficult as they appear to be. *Dive* for the far end of the horse and *raise* the legs behind you. Work for a body position that is at least parallel to the horse. For all vaults, the legs should remain together until the hands hit and push off—even for straddles and scissors.

The vaults listed can also be done with the hand placement and push-off at the croup (near end) but they are harder. They can be learned after they are done from the neck.

If a horse is not available, many of the vaults can be done over a vaulting box, a balance beam, a low horizontal bar, over one rail of a parallel bar with the second rail removed, or even over a narrow stack of mats piled up waist high.

Pommel Horse Vaulting:

Young boys and girls should start vaulting with the pommels in place as described in the following vaults. As proficiency is gained the pommels may be removed. Later, the height of the horse may be increased. As a lead up, some mounts with jump dismounts are described as lead ups to the vaults. Practice these in sequence.

The spotters will stand on the "far" side of the horse (side where the performer lands) unless told not to in the spotting hints. They must stay close or they will not be effective.

1. **Squat Mount, Jump Dismount**—Jump to a squat mount in the saddle (feet on the horse, knees and hips flexed, hands on the pommels) and immediately jump upward and forward to a side stand rearways. (Back toward the horse.)

   Hints: a. Keep the head up on the mount. The arms are straight and support the weight.
   b. On the dismount, jump for height, not distance forward.
   c. Coordinate the straightening of the legs with an upward swing of the arms.
   d. Keep the head up. Look straight forward.

   Spot: a. Stand close to the horse and slightly to the right of the performer as he/she approaches and be ready to grasp the right upper arm to prevent falling forward if he/she catches the toes on the horse at the mount. If a toe is hooked, catch the chest on your right shoulder.
   b. Step back as he/she jumps and be prepared to steady the landing. Brace the chest with the right hand if he leans forward and place the left hand at the back if he/she leans backward.

   Note: For variety, twists may be added to the jump dismounts. When spotting for a ½ twist, the spotter stands close for the mount then moves in front of the saddle and braces the gymnast's hips as he/she lands.

2. **Knee Spring Dismount**—Jump to a kneeling position in the saddle with the shins on the horse and the hips and knees flexed. Swing the arms backward then vigorously forward and spring off forward to a side stand rearways.

   Hints: a. Lean slightly forward as the arms swing backward.
   b. A quick, partial extension of the hip and knee joints must be coordinated with the vigorous forward and upward arm swing.
   c. Keep the head and chest up. Look forward.
   d. Push off from both shins at the same time.
   e. As the spring is made, draw the feet under the body to land.

   Spot: Stand to the right of the performer and place your right hand against the chest if there is danger of catching a toe on the horse.

3. **Knee Spring Dismount with Half Twist**—Same as the "Knee Spring Dismount" except for the addition of a half twist as the spring is made. The twist must occur as the body is in the air. Land in a side stand frontways (facing the horse).

   Hints: a. Lean slightly forward.
   b. The arm swing is forward, upward, and to the left (or right) with the elbows bent and the arms close to the body.
   c. Look over the left (or right) shoulder as the spring is made.

   Spot: Stand directly in front of the saddle and brace the performer's hips as he/she lands.

4. **Squat Vault**—From a short run, place the hands on the pommels and spring upward. Draw the knees to the chest, push downward with the arms, and pass over the horse to land on the far side in a side stand rearways.

   Hints: a. Take off from fairly close to the horse.
   b. Coordinate a strong, downward arm push with the spring from the legs. The push is as important as the spring from the legs.
   c. Release the hands while the body momentum is still upward.
   d. Draw the knees tightly against the chest.
   e. Lean slightly forward. Keep the head up and the chest raised. Look forward.
   f. If the arm push is *downward,* balance can be held when landing.
   g. *Don't* snap the hips forward to clear the horse. Depend on the momentum and arm push to get across.
   h. Straighten the body for landing. Think of raising the chest instead of lowering the legs to straighten out.

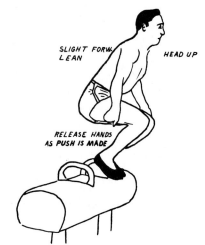

SLIGHT FORW. LEAN HEAD UP

RELEASE HANDS AS PUSH IS MADE

Spot: Stand close to the horse on the performer's right. Be ready to grasp the right arm above the elbow with both hands to prevent falling forward if he/she catches the toes on the horse.

5. **Flank Vault**—From a short run, place the hands on the pommels, spring upward and swing the legs and body left sideward over the horse. Release the left hand as the body passes over the horse. Release the right hand just before landing in a side stand rearways.

   Hints: a. Keep the right arm straight and stiff. It supports the weight.
   - b. The right shoulder should be directly over the right hand (arm perpendicular to floor) when the body is passing over the horse.
   - c. The side of the body must be toward the horse.
   - d. Get a good push-off from the left arm as the legs swing upward.
   - e. Advanced performers can straighten the hips (arch out) as they pass over the horse.

   Spot: a. Stand at the performer's right arm and grasp it above the elbow if there is a tendency for it to bend.
   - b. Resist the tendency for the shoulder to move to the left. (Keep the shoulder over the hand.)

6. **Front Vault**—Same as the "Flank Vault" except that at the takeoff, the body makes a quarter twist to the right as the legs swing left sideward so that the front of the body is toward the horse as it passes over it. Land in a cross stand right. (Right side toward the horse.)

   Hints: a. Execute the quarter turn at the takeoff.
   - b. Keep the shoulders directly over the saddle.
   - c. Get a good spring from the legs and raise the feet high to arch the back. Keep the head up. The body should not be bent at the hips.
   - d. The left arm supports the weight and the right arm pulls slightly to counteract the weight of the legs. Release the left arm just before landing.

   Spot: Stand at the shoulders and support them if necessary.

7. **Rear Vault**—Place the hands on the pommels. At the takeoff, swing the legs left sideward and add a quarter twist to the left so that the rear of the body is toward the horse as it passes over it. Land in a cross stand left. (Left side toward the horse.)

   Hints: a. Bring the hips close to the supporting right arm. The right arm must be straight and perpendicular to the floor.
   - b. Very little forward momentum is needed.
   - c. Push off from the left hands as the jump is made.
   - d. Flex the hips as the turn is made. The legs are straight and parallel to the floor.
   - e. Don't jump too high. The hips should just clear the pommels. The feet are at least as high as the hips.
   - f. Keep the hips close to the right wrist. Lean back on the *right arm.*
   - g. As the body passes over the horse, reach back with the left hand, place it on the horse, and release the right.

REACH BACK WITH LEFT

LEAN ON RIGHT THEN RELEASE

LEGS PARALLEL TO FLOOR

   Spot: Stand by the performer's right arm and brace it if he/she has too much forward momentum.

8. **Straddle Mount, Jump Dismount**—Place the hands on the pommels, spring upward and spread the legs sideward, placing one foot on the neck and the other on the croup. Keep the legs straight. Straighten up and jump off forward, landing in a side stand rearways with the legs together.

   Hints: a. Flex the hips and raise them high.
   - b. Keep the arms straight and let them bear the weight.
   - c. Straddle the legs wide and keep them straight.
   - d. Keep the head up.

   Spot: a. Stand very close, directly in front of the saddle. If the performer begins to fall forward, brace both shoulders with your hands immediately. Don't wait till he/she gathers momentum.
   - b. As he/she jumps, step left sideward and be prepared to brace the landing with your right arm.

9. **Straddle Vault**—From a short run, place the hands on the pommels and vault over the horse with straddled (spread) legs. Land in a side stand rearways with the feet together.

   Hints: a. Take off close to the horse, keeping the hips directly under the shoulders instead of protruding backward.
       b. Raise the hips high and flex them as much as possible. Keep the legs straight.
       c. At the same time straddle the legs and *push hard* with the arms.
       d. The push is straight downward and aids in the upward momentum of the body. Release the hands as the push is made to allow the body to rise.
       e. Lift the chest and bring the hips forward as the push is made. The hips should not *snap* forward.
       f. Keep the head up.
       g. Bring the feet together and straighten up before landing.

   Spot: a. Stand very close and directly in front of the saddle.
       b. If the performer strikes the toes, brace both shoulders with your hands immediately.
       c. If he/she clears the horse without trouble, quickly step back out of the way.

10. **Squat Vault with Half Twist**—Same as the "Squat Vault" except for the half twist which is made just after the body passes over the horse. Land in a side stand frontways.

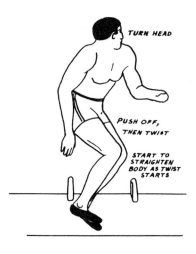

   Hints a. All hints for the "Squat Vault" pertain to this stunt.
       b. *After* the vigorous push-off from both hands, turn the head sharply in the direction of the turn. Do not pivot on one arm.
       c. If the head and shoulders twist to the left, the arms must be thrust to the *right*.
       d. As the twist is made, straighten the legs downward.
       e. Reach for the pommels and regrasp them when landing. This will be possible if the arm push is downward and there is not much forward momentum.

   Spot: a. Stand about two feet from the horse, directly opposite the saddle.
       b. Brace the performer's hips with both hands as he/she lands after the twist.
       c. Also, be prepared to catch under the arms if the toes hit the horse on the way over.

11. **Straddle Vault with Half Twist**—Same as the "Straddle Vault" except for the half twist which is made just before landing. Land facing the horse with the feet together and the hands on the pommels.

   Hints: a. The hints for the "Straddle Vault" pertain here.
       b. After the hands have released the pommels (body momentum is still upward), turn the head sharply in the direction of the twist with the arms starting in the opposite direction.
       c. At the same time, bring the legs together.

   Spot: Spot as for the "Squat Vault With Half Twist" but stand a little closer to the horse.

12. **Thief Vault**—From a short run, take off from *one* foot, swing the other foot forward, and quickly bring the takeoff foot up to join it. Both legs precede the body and pass over the horse before the hands contact the pommels. As the hands contact the pommels, push off to a stand.

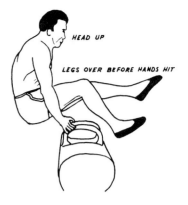

Hints: a. Take off from a little further back than usual.
      b. Practice by taking off from the left foot, putting the right foot against the side of horse and then bringing the left foot up too, before bringing the right one down. This can also be practiced against a wall.
      c. Raise the legs forward (one leg at a time) to a position parallel to the floor.
      d. The hands contact the pommels just as the hips pass over horse (legs have already passed).
      e. Push downward and backward with the hands as soon as they contact the pommels.
      f. Keep the head up—look forward.

Spot: a. Stand at the performer's right, ready to grasp and support the right arm if he/she should catch a toe on the horse.
      b. A second spotter stands on the *near* side (behind left arm) ready to prevent the performer's falling backward if he/she gets the feet up but has insufficient momentum to carry forward.

Note: This can be used as a mount for girls on the beam.

13. **Delayed Squat Vault**—From a short run, take off and swing the legs and hips backward and upward so that the body is raised parallel to the floor in a momentary free support. Then quickly flex the knees and hips and squat through between the arms to a side stand rearways.

    Hints: a. A forceful spring from the legs is required.
      b. Lean forward (shoulders in front of the hands) and arch the back as the legs are raised. The heels should be higher than the hips.
      c. Bend the arms *slightly.*
      d. Raise the hips as the knees are drawn to the chest. Hunch the back.
      e. The flexion should be very rapid and snappy.
      f. As the hips are flexed, push downward vigorously with the arms and lift the chest.
      g. Keep the head up.
      h. Depend on the arm push to carry you clear of the horse. Do not snap the hips forward.

    Spot: a. Stand to the right of the performer and grasp the right upper arm with both hands.
      b. Lift upward and pull forward as he/she brings the knees forward and pushes from the hands.

    Note: This is similar to the "Layout" vaults done by women in competitive vaulting over the high (47") horse.

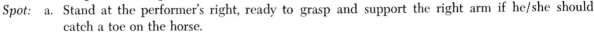

14. **Handspring Vault**—From a short run, place the hands on the pommels and take off. Swing the legs upward and pass them over the head through a handbalance position and down to a side stand rearways on the far side of the horse.

Hints: a. Use a vigorous takeoff from close to the horse.
        b. Flex the hips as the legs go upward and tuck the head forward.
        c. *Lean forward* slightly with the shoulders. The shoulders must be ahead of the hands before the hips pass over the head.
        d. Keep the arms fairly straight.
        e. As the feet pass overhead, snap the back into an arch and push from the hands.
        f. Snap the head back as the back is arched.

Spot: a. Stand opposite the right pommel and place your right hand under the performer's right shoulder and your left hand on the right arm with a hook grasp just above the elbow.
        b. Don't permit the shoulders to drop too low.
        c. Lift upward on the shoulder as he/she arches over.
        d. The left hand's grasp is to prevent falling forward as he/she lands if the push or arch is too vigorous. Keep this grasp till he/she lands.
        e. If the head and shoulders are on the near side of the horse (away from you) block the hips with your hands to prevent his/her finishing the vault because he/she might land with the back across the horse.
        f. For beginners, a spotter at each arm can be used.

15. **Stoop Vault**—From a short run, place the hands on the pommels and spring upward, flexing and raising the hips high and drawing the legs over the horse between the arms. Keep the *knees straight* and land in a side stand rearways.

Hints: a. Take off from close to the horse.
        b. Push vigorously downward with the arms.
        c. As the hips are flexed and raised, keep the head up.
        d. When pushing off from the hands, bring the hips forward and lift the chest upward for the landing. The *opening* from the pike position is an important phase of the vault.

Spot: Stand beside the croup and support the performer's right arm.

Note: This may also be done from a laid-out position as in the "Delayed Squat Vault."

16. **Sheep Vault**—From a short run, place the hands on the pommels and spring upward and over the horse, keeping the *hips extended* and the knees flexed. The body passes between the arms and lands in a side stand rearways.

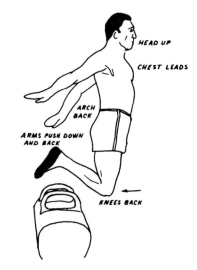

Hints: a. Keep the head and chest up. The chest leads the way.
        b. The arm movement is downward and backward with fairly straight arms. The propulsion occurs at the *moment of takeoff* and must be very vigorous.
        c. Take off a little further from the horse than usual. Lean *slightly* forward.
        d. As the vault is made, push the knees backward and raise the feet backward and upward (arch the back).

Spot: a. Stand directly in front of the saddle, fairly close.
        b. If the performer's toes or knees catch on the saddle, support under both arms with the hands.
        c. If he/she clears the horse, step back out of the way.

Note: This is a lead up for the Hecht (Swan) Vault.

17. **Hecht (Swan) Vault**—This is like the Sheep Vault except that the knees are extended as well as the hips. It is a very difficult vault, especially without a spring board. It should be attempted only after proficiency on the other vaults has been gained.

Long Horse Vaulting (men)

The first stunts are not vaults but are used as lead up for the vaults. Most of the vaults are the same as in the previous section but are more difficult now because of the greater distance that must be traveled. A fast, hard run is required.

1. **Straddle Dismount from Croup**—Jump to a squat stand on the croup, straighten to a stand and fall forward to a front leaning support with the hands on the neck. Push off from the hands, straddle the legs sideward, and pass over the neck to a cross stand rearways.

    Hints: a. Lean well forward (shoulders ahead of hands) in the front leaning support.

    b. Keep the head up and the arms straight. The toes should be tucked under.

    c. Push downward and backward with the hands and push with the toes at the same time.

    d. Flex the hips as the push-off is made.

    e. Look straight ahead.

    Spot: a. Stand in front of the performer and grasp his right arm with the right hand close to his shoulder and the left hand on his wrist.

    b. As he dismounts, lift upward on his arm and step backward out of his way.

2. **Straddle Vault**—From a fairly good run, dive forward, place the hands on the neck, straddle the legs and pass over the horse to a rear stand. Only the hands contact the horse.

    Hints: a. Keep the eyes on the takeoff spot. Just before the feet hit the takeoff spot, shift the eyes to the neck of the horse.

    b. Reach for the far end of the horse. The legs trail behind.

    c. The palms of the hands should land beside each other with the fingertips just over the edge of the horse.

    d. *The shoulders should be slightly ahead of the hands for beginners.*

    e. Advanced performers have hands ahead of shoulders and "block" for height.

    Note: The four hints above pertain to all vaults unless otherwise stated in the hints.

    f. Push downward and backward with the hands.

    g. The legs should be together and above the horse in a horizontal position until the hands touch, but this comes with practice only. The beginner will have his legs in a vertical position. Straddle the legs when pushing off from the hands.

    h. Keep the head and chest up.

    Spot: a. Stand in front of the horse facing the neck and grasp the performer's right arm with the right hand close to his shoulder and the left hand on his wrist just as his hands contact the neck.

    b. Lift upward and step backward immediately.

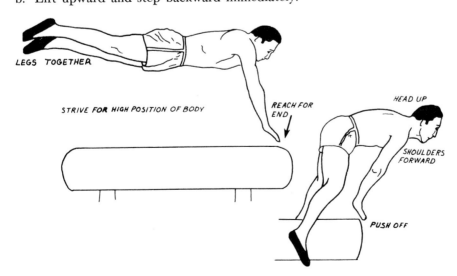

LEGS TOGETHER

STRIVE FOR HIGH POSITION OF BODY

REACH FOR END

HEAD UP

SHOULDERS FORWARD

PUSH OFF

3. **Squat Dismount from Croup**—Mount to a front leaning support as for the "Straddle Dismount from Croup." Push off from the hands, draw the knees to the chest and pass the legs over the horse to a cross stand rearways.

    Hints: a. Lean well forward in the front leaning support position and keep the head up and the arms straight. Keep the toes tucked under.

          b. Sag at the hips and then whip them upward.

          c. At the same moment, push downward with the arms and backward with the toes.

          d. Draw the knees to the chest as the hips whip upward.

          e. Keep the head up; look forward.

    Spot: Spot as for the "Straddle Dismount."

4. **Squat Vault**—This is the same as the "Straddle Vault" except that the legs are kept together and pass over the horse between the arms.

    Hints: a. The legs must be kept *above* the horse. The body should be in a horizontal position.

          b. As the hands hit the neck, raise and flex the hips and draw the knees to the chest.

          c. At the same time, push downward and backward with the hands to raise the chest.

          d. Keep the head up.

    Spot: Spot as for the "Straddle Vault."

5. **Scissors Dismount from Croup**—Mount to a squat stand on the croup and drop to a front leaning support with the hands on the neck. Place the left leg on the right side of the horse (under the right leg) and push off from the hands, executing a half turn in the air and land in a cross stand frontways with the hands on the neck. The left leg remains on the right side and the right leg slides over to the left side.

    Hints: a. Lean well forward in the front leaning support.

          b. Place the left hand in the center of the neck, fingers just over the end.

          c. Remove the right hand and raise it sideward, pivot on the left arm, and execute the half turn to the right (facing to the rear).

          d. Simultaneously push with the left hand and dismount.

          e. Then learn to do it starting with both feet on the croup instead of sliding the left leg to the right at the start.

          f. Next, start from a stand on the croup, drop forward (body straight) and execute the scissors the moment the hands hit the neck.

    Spot: Stand about two feet in front of the neck and be prepared to catch the performer under both armpits if his legs drag on the horse.

6. **Scissors Vault**—From a medium run, dive forward, place the hands on the neck, push off from the hands with a half twist to the left to a cross stand frontways, and replace the hands on the neck. The right leg cuts under the left leg to the left side of the horse and the left leg passes over the right to the right side of the horse while the body is above the horse.

    Hints: a. Practice the stunt from a front leaning support on the horse till it is well learned.

          b. The legs must be higher than the horse when the hands hit. Don't flex the hips.

          c. As the hands push off, twist the head and hips to the left.

          d. The body simply revolves while in a horizontal position.

          e. As the twist is executed, straddle the legs.

          f. Keep the head up till the twist is made, then hold it forward.

          g. Keep the legs straight.

    Spot: Spot as above.

LEGS BACK
TILL HANDS
PUSH-OFF

7. **Stoop Vault**—This stunt is the same as the "Squat Vault" except that the knees must remain straight.
   Hints: a. A harder and higher takeoff is required.
   b. The legs should be higher than the head, the back arched, and the body laid out above the horse until the hands hit the neck.
   c. As the hands contact the horse, draw the hips upward and bring the feet forward to a jackknife position.
   d. A strong push from the hands is required.
   e. As the feet pass over the neck, open up by raising the head and chest. The straightening out is an important part of the vault.
   Spot: Spot as for the "Squat Vault."

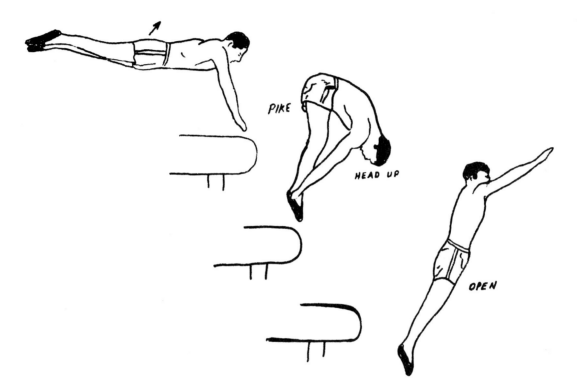

8. **Sheep Vault**—This stunt is the same as the "Squat Vault" except that the hips remain extended. The knees are flexed (the feet are held backward). (This vault is not done in competition but it is a good lead up to the Hecht Vault.)

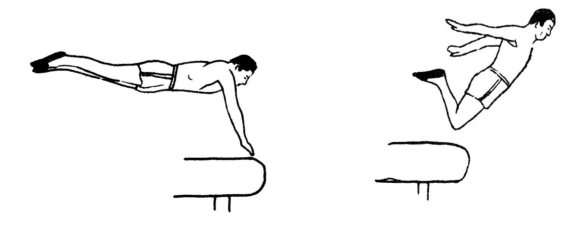

Hints: a. Keep the body straight and extended above the horse until the hands hit. The shoulders are behind the hands at the moment of impact.

b. Then raise the head and chest immediately by an extremely strong push from the hands.

c. At the same time raise the feet backward. The back must be arched.

d. Think of trying to touch the back of the head with the soles of the feet to get the proper position.

Spot: Be prepared to place your right hand under his chest and lift.

9. **Hecht (Swan) Vault**—This is like the "Sheep Vault" except that the knees as well as the hips remain extended. The body is in a laid out position all the way.

Hints: a. Maximum speed in the run is required.

b. The body should be about parallel to the horse when the hands hit.

c. There should be a slight pike in the hips till the hands hit.

d. The hands should be ahead of the shoulders at the moment of impact.

e. Push *hard* as soon as the hands hit (extend the shoulders), lift the head and chest and arch the back.

Spot: Stand in front of and to the right of the neck, place your right hand on his chest and lift.

10. **Handspring Dismount from Croup**—Mount to a squat stand on the croup and straighten to a stand. Whip the hands downward toward the neck, push off from the feet, bring the feet over the head to the mat and land in a cross stand rearways beyond the horse.

Hints: a. Keep the left foot in front of the right and swing the right foot upward as the hands go downward.

b. Push off from the left foot as the hands touch the horse.

c. The arms should be fairly straight with the shoulders slightly in advance of the hands.

d. Arch the back as the legs go over the head.

e. Push from the arms.

Spot: a. Stand to the left of the neck facing the performer.

b. Place the right hand on his right shoulder and the left hand on his right upper arm in a reverse grasp (twist the left hand to the left) as he places his hands on the neck of the horse.

c. Support his shoulder with the right hand as his feet go over the head and hold on to his right arm to prevent his falling forward as he lands.

11. **Handspring Vault**—From a fairly hard run, dive forward and place the hands on the far end of the horse. The legs continue upward and forward and pass over the head and then downward to a stand. The arms remain fairly straight.

    Hints: a. At the takeoff, concentrate on raising the heels high above the head.
    b. As the hands reach for the neck the body should be at a 45° angle pointing downward
    c. When learning, flex the hips and bend the arms slightly as the hands hit. (Advanced performers will hold the arch and keep the arms straight.)
    d. Tuck the head forward till the body overbalances. (Advanced performers keep the head up throughout the vault.)
    e. Then arch the back, snap the head back and push from the arms.

    Spot: a. Spot as for the "Handspring Dismount from Croup" (Stunt No. 10).
    b. Another spotter can stand at the near end and push upward on the gymnasts legs as he dives for the neck.

12. **Yamashita (Piked Handspring) Vault**—This is like the "Handspring Vault" except that the hips are piked (flexed) sharply during the vault and then extended for the landing.

    Hints: a. The general hints for the "Handspring Vault" pertain.
    b. The extension for the landing should be definite and vigorous.

    Spot: Spot as for the "Handspring Vault."

13. **Handstand Pivot Cartwheel Dismount**—Mount to a stand on the croup. Kick up to a momentary handstand with the hands on the saddle, raise one hand, pivot on the other a quarter turn and place the raised hand on the neck. Continue on over the end of the horse as in a cartwheel but keep the legs together. Land with your side to the horse.

    Hints: a. Practice the pivot on the floor a few times before moving up to the horse.
    b. Get a lot of momentum when kicking to a handstand. Kick with a straight rear leg and push from the front one.
    c. Keep the head up.
    d. Don't pause in the handstand. Lift one arm and pivot while the momentum continues.
    e. Push down (extend the shoulder) on the arm placed at the neck.
    f. Stretch the whole body upward and outward.
    g. The legs remain together.

    Spot: a. Determine which side he prefers to pivot to and stand behind his back (when he completes pivot).
    b. If he pivots on his right arm and places his left hand on the neck, put your right hand on his left hip and support it as he turns over.
    c. Your left hand is on his left upper arm and lifts to help him over.

14. **Handstand Pivot Cartwheel Vault**—This is performed as Stunt No. 13 except it starts from a spring from the floor instead of a kick up from the croup.

    Hints: a. Dive as for a "Handspring Vault" except the hands are placed on the saddle instead of on the neck.
    b. Use the momentum of the takeoff to go right into the pivot. Keep the arms straight.
    c. The head remains up throughout and the legs stay together.

    Spot: Spot as for Stunt No. 13.

15. **Giant Cartwheel (Hollander)**—Run hard, take off lifting the heels and turning the body a quarter turn right so that the side of the body is facing forward as the left hand lands about the middle of the horse. The right hand is then placed at the neck (far end) of the horse as the feet go over head. Push off from the right hand and land in side stand right (This may of course, be done to the other side.).

    Hints: a. Practice #14 first.
    b. Then simply turn the body earlier (before the first hand lands).

    Spot: Spot as for Stunt No. 13.

There are no combinations or routines done in vaulting. As expertise is gained, strive for additional height and distance. Half and full turns can be added to these vaults to increase the difficulty.

23

Rings

Girls and women do not work this event competitively because of general lack of strength in the upper body and arms. However, some girls will be able to do some of the skills—especially on the *swinging* rings.

Swinging ring work is no longer used in competition even for men but for class purposes, it has its place. Still ring work requires a great deal of strength—more than many beginners have acquired by the time they start ring work. Stunts on the swinging rings can be used to develop the strength needed for still rings. It is wise to institute a supplemental program of push-ups, chins, and dips as an additional aid. Swinging rings are generally more enjoyable—more thrilling and exhilarating. A good sense of timing can be developed in this way. Some stunts (back uprise, front uprise, dislocate, etc.) can be performed more easily while swinging than from a still hang. Therefore, some swinging ring work is presented in this text.

The rings are a unique event because the performer must learn not only to control his body, but the rings as well. Unlike other apparatus, the rings do not offer a solid, stationary support. They are suspended from cables and therefore are movable. This will be quite evident when a novice attemtps to hold his first simple straight arm support. Each ring seems to have a will of its own and be determined to move forward, sideward, or backward. For this reason, spotters must be prepared to steady the performers.

When swinging ring stunts are used, be sure that the mat extends out beyond *both* ends of the swing. A spotter should stand to the side of each end of the swing and be prepared to "tackle" the performer's waist or upper body. Don't grab for the legs. Carbonate of magnesium should be applied to the hands to keep them dry. Sweaty hands can result in a loss of grasp. Stunts should be learned first while at a still hang where assistance can be given and spotting is easier. Then they should be attempted with a *small* swing and the height gradually increased. To dismount, drop off at the *end* of the *backward* swing when the momentum has stopped. It is a good idea to use a crash pad (specially made mat 8 inches thick) if one is available.

In competitive ring work the competitor's feet do not touch the mat when he is in a hang. However, for classwork most of the stunts should be done with the rings about head high. Modern ring equipment cannot be quickly adjusted for height, so a fast method of changing the height to accommodate different sized individuals is needed. One such method is to have several small mats handy so that they can be placed under the rings for short individuals and pulled out for tall ones.

1. **Obtain Swing**—Jump to a hang and work up to a fairly high swing by using a "two-step takeoff" in the middle of the swing (directly under ring supports). Push off on both the forward and backward swings. Drop off at the *end* of the backward swing.

   Hints: a. Push off with the left, then right foot.

         b. Keep the left foot back after its push-off until the right foot comes back after its push-off. Then whip both legs forward hard while swinging forward.

         c. Keep the legs forward (hips slightly flexed) until the end of the forward swing.

         d. As the backward swing begins, whip the legs backward (arch the back) forcibly and step off with the left and right foot at the middle.

    e. Push off in a quick rhythm and bring the legs together in front (hips flexed) as the right foot pushes off.

    f. Immediately swing them backward hard (arch the back) and hold them back until the end of the backward swing.

    g. Then whip them forward together as the forward swing starts and raise the right leg a little higher than the left to push off with the left, then right foot.

    h. Continue as above until a high swing is obtained.
       The arms remain extended.

    j. Drop off at the "dead point" of the *backward* swing when you are moving neither forward nor backward.

    k. Just before the end of the swing, pull up slightly with the arms to bring the body to a vertical position.

Spot: No special spotting is required, but spotters should stand at either end of the swing opposite (not behind) the performer in case the performer loses his grasp. Be alert.

2. **Bent Arm Hang Swing**—Jump to a hang and work up a fairly high swing. At the end of the forward swing, bend the arms till the head comes up between the hands. Hold the bent arm position for two complete swings and straighten the arms at the *end* of the backward swing and drop to a stand.
  Hints: a. Keep the rings close to the chest with the hands right in front of the shoulders.
      b. Let the body hang. Do not attempt to swing the body.
  Spot: Same as for the previous stunt.

3. **Inverted Squat Hang**—Jump to a hang, raise the legs and hips upward and turn over backward till the feet are above the head. Keep the knees against the chest and the arms straight. Return to a stand by reversing the movement.
  Hints: a. Bend the arms and draw the knees to the chest.
      b. At the same time, lean backward with the head and shoulders and thrust the arms forward.
      c. Hold the head forward when in the inverted position. The back should be rounded.
      d. Flex the arms and let the hips drop forward slowly when returning to a stand.
  Spot: a. Stand at the performer's left and grasp his left wrist with your right hand. Place your left hand under his hips and lift upward *if* he needs help.
      b. When he reaches the inverted hang, transfer the left hand to his wrist and use the right to prevent his turning on over if he starts to do so.

4. **Swinging Inverted Squat Hang**—Jump to a hang and obtain a small swing. At the end of the forward swing turn over backward to an "Inverted Squat Hang." Hold the position for two swings and return to a hang at the end of the backward swing. Swing forward and backward and drop off at the end of the backward swing.
  Hints: a. Do not swing high while learning the stunt.
      b. Be sure to keep the knees close to the chest.
      c. Use the forward whip of the legs that follows the push-off to aid in turning over.
      d. Turn over slowly. Keep control of the turn in the arms. Don't let the weight control the turn.
      e. Squeeze the arms against the sides, tense all the muscles, and hang on if the balance is lost backward.
  Spot: a. The front spotter stands a little behind the front end of the swing to support the performer's bent knees to prevent his losing his balance backward.
      b. The rear spotter must be alert for the same possibility.

5. **Nest Hang**—Jump to a hang and raise the feet overhead to hook the toes in the rings. Push the hips through between the arms and arch the back. The body is supported by the hands and toes. Return by flexing the hips and turning forward.
  Hints: a. Turn over to the "Inverted Squat Hang" first.
      b. Then hook the toes through the rings.
      c. Keep the head forward while pushing the hips through between the arms.
      d. Arch the back and raise the head.
  Spot: Grasp the performer's wrist with one hand and place the other hand on his abdomen to support him if his feet should slip out of the rings.

6. **Inverted Straight Hang**—From a hang, turn over to an "Inverted Squat Hang" and then extend the legs upward and arch the back. The arms are straight and the head is back.

   Hints: a. Follow the hints for the "Inverted Squat Hang" first.
         b. Keep the head forward while extending the legs upward. Extend legs slowly after first obtaining a good balance. If you have trouble, put the feet against the ropes when extending legs upward and then bring them together.
         c. Lay the head back after the back is arched.
         d. Keep the rings close to the sides.
         e. If no spotter is present, double up (tuck head, knees, and hips) if balance is lost.

   Spot: Stand beside the performer and place one arm in front and one arm in back of him to steady him.

7. **Skin the Cat**—From a hang, bring the legs and hips over the head, pass *through* the "Inverted Squat Hang" position and extend the legs downward. Reach downward as far as possible with the feet before returning to a stand by reversing the movement.

   Hints: a. Turn over as in the "Inverted Squat Hang."
         b. Continue around, passing the hips between the arms *with the knees close to the chest.*
         c. Extend the legs downward *after* the maximum rotation has been made. Keep the head up.
         d. Tuck the head forward, bring the knees to the chest and raise the hips to return to a stand.
         e. Advanced performers can do this by flexing the hips but keeping the knees straight.

   Spot: a. Stand at the performer's left and place the right hand on his knees as he starts downward with them after passing them between the arms.
         b. Make sure that the knees are against the chest and check a too rapid descent.
         c. Lift upward on the knees if he needs help in raising the hips to return.

8. **Half Crucifix**—From a hang, pull up (bend the arms) till the shoulders are level with the hands. Then extend the left arm sideward, hold it momentarily and return it to the shoulder. Then extend the right arm sideward and return. Straighten the arms to a hang and drop off.

   Hints: a. Keep the rings close to the chest.
         b. Shift the weight to the right arm when extending the left hand.
         c. Turn the palm of the left hand downward and press downward with the hand.

   Spot: If necessary the spotter can give some assistance by grasping the performer's thighs and lifting upward slightly. Don't help too much. Make the performer bear as much weight as he can.

9. **Forward Single Leg Cut and Catch**—Turn over backward to an "Inverted Squat Hang" and straighten the knees. The hips remain flexed and the legs are above the head and parallel to the floor ("Kip Position"). Straddle the left leg, swing both legs forward, release the left hand and pass the left leg between the ring and the hand and regrasp with the left hand as the legs drop down to a hang. Repeat the stunt using the right hand and leg.

   PAUSE IN KIP POSITION

   PULL WITH RIGHT, RELEASE LEFT

   HEAD FORWARD

   SUPPORT BACK

   Hints: a. Pause in "kip" position before bringing the left leg forward.
         b. Keep the arms slightly flexed.
         c. Take all the weight on the right arm *before* releasing the left.
         d. Don't push the ring away. Simply let go of it with the left hand. The ring should not move much.
         e. Keep the head forward and the back round.
         f. Regrasp as soon as the leg passes the ring.

   Spot: Stand at the performer's left and place the right hand under his neck and the left hand under his back on the first few attempts. Gradually decrease the support.

10. **Muscle Up**—Jump to a hang using the false grasp. (Grasp the rings on the heels of the hands.) Pull up (bend the arms) as far as possible, shift the hands so the wrists are above the hands and push downward to a straight arm support.

    Hints: a. Keep the rings and elbows close to the body all the way. The knuckles are right in front of the shoulders.

           b. Turn the rings outward (little fingers of hands turn away from each other) when shifting the hands.

           c. Hunch the shoulders and flex the hips (raise them) slightly but rapidly as the shift is made

           d. Bring the rings behind the hips to maintain the support.

    Spot: a. Assist by raising upward on the performer's legs if assistance is needed.

           b. Steady him when he is in the support position.

11. **"L" Support**—Mount to a straight arm support using the "Muscle Up" (with help, if needed) and raise the legs till they are parallel with the floor. The arms and legs remain straight.

    Hints: a. Press the arms against the sides for steadiness. (With practice this pressure can be eliminated.)

           b. Lean *slightly* backward with the shoulders.

           c. Keep the head up. Don't sag in the shoulders.

           d. If you *can't* hold the "L" with straight legs, bend the knees slightly.

           e. If you still have trouble, work on abdominal strength (sit-ups) and hip flexibility (touch floor with hands, keeping knees straight).

    Spot: No *special* spotting needed.

12. **Forward Roll from Support to Hang**—Mount to a straight arm support by using the "Muscle Up" (with assistance if necessary). From the support, tuck the head, raise the hips and turn over forward to a hanging position.

    Hints: a. Hold the rings close together in front of the hips. (Arms slightly bent.)

           b. Tuck the head, lean forward with the shoulders and raise the flexed hips. Bending the knees makes it easier, but *try* to keep them straight.

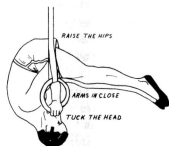

           c. The arms support the weight.

           d. Keep the hips moving forward, and extend the hips as they start downward.

           e. The arms remain flexed until the legs are almost down.

    Spot: a. Stand at the performer's right and place the left hand on his abdomen and push upward if he has trouble raising the hips.

           b. The right hand should be just under the shoulder to slow down the descent.

13. **Inlocate from a Jump**—Adjust the rings or stand on a rolled mat so the rings are about head high. With a slight jump, flex and raise the hips upward, draw them forward between the arms and continue turning over forward to a hang. The arms are flung sideward and the head is tucked forward as the jump is made.

    Hints: a. The "feel" of the movement can be obtained by stretching the arms overhead, rolling the arms forward and bringing them sideward and backward. Keep the hands as high as possible. Do this twice, then grasp the rings and proceed.

           b. Think of raising the hips above the head.

           c. The hands, arms, and shoulders rotate forward as the arms move sideward.

           d. Bear downward on the rings at the same time.

           e. Flex the hips well as they are raised.

           f. Let the hips lead. The legs follow behind.

           g. Bend the arms as the hips start downward after passing between the arms.

Spot: a. Stand to the performer's right and place the left hand on his abdomen and the right hand on the back of his neck from in front of his right arm.

b. Push upward with the left hand as he jumps and support his head slightly as it drops forward.

14. **Inlocate from Kip Position**—From a hang, flex the hips and bring the legs up between the arms (knees straight) with the legs about parallel to the floor. Drop the legs downward, swing them backward and upward while flexing the hips, extending the arms sideward, and rolling forward as in the previous stunt. It can be done with a *straight* body but this is much harder. Learn it with a pike first, then try to keep the body straight and drive upward with the *heels* instead of the hips.

Hints: a. From the "Kip Position," extend the legs upward and forward smoothly. Do *not* snap into the extension.

b. Tuck the head slightly as this is done.

c. Continue the leg movement with a vigorous downward and backward drive. Lift the heels and arch the back.

d. When the body is almost parallel to the mat, increase the head tuck as much as possible, *sharply* pike the hips to take the strain off the shoulders, and spread the arms, rolling the hands forward.

e. The movements in *d* are *part* of the upward rise of the body. Do *not* let the upward momentum die before piking.

f. As the shoulder rotation occurs, bring the arms toward each other again, keep the head forward, and return to the "Kip Position."

Spot: Stand at the performer's left, place the right hand on his abdomen and lift as his legs pass the vertical position. At the same time, place the left hand on the back of his neck and push downward, to your right, and upward in an arc.

15. **Backward Double Leg Cut Dismount**—Adjust the rings so the performer has to jump to reach them. Whip the legs back and forth (flex and arch) several times to gain momentum. As the legs swing forward, raise the body upward, pivoting at the shoulders. At the same time, spread the legs, lay the head and chest back and turn over to a stand. Release the rings as the legs pass over the head.

Hints: a. Bend the arms slightly (pull upward as the legs come up for the cutoff).

b. Flex the hips as they move upward. (Advanced performers can keep the hips extended.)

c. Throw the head vigorously backward just as the rings are released.

d. Keep the head up and look forward when descending. Reach forward with the arms.

e. Do *not* wait till backward momentum is lost before releasing hands.

Spot: a. Stand at the performer's left side and place your right hand on his shoulder from behind his arm.

b. Push upward and backward on the hips with the left hand.

c. If he cuts off too soon, support his shoulder till he completes his turn.

d. Us another spotter on the right side. He puts his left hand on the performer's shoulder.

PULL ON ARMS,
RELEASE HANDS,
AND WHIP HEAD BACK

PUSH
HIPS

SUPPORT
SHOULDER

16. **Forward Double Cut Dismount**—Assume the kip position. Then spread the legs and cut them forward. As the legs come to the arms release the rings, continue forward with the legs, and drop to a stand.

Hints: a. Practice the stunt a few times without letting go of the rings.
      b. Flex the arms at the elbows as the legs are brought forward.
      c. Throw the head vigorously forward as the legs come to the arms.
      d. When you can roll well forward on to the arms, practice the stunt with the releasing of the rings. *Be sure* you are spotted.
      e. Release the hands just as the legs contact the arms.
      f. Keep the head forward all the way.

Spot: Stand behind the performer with your right hand on the back of his neck and the left hand on his buttocks to brace him as he descends.

17. **Swinging Front Uprise**—Obtain a fairly high swing in a hanging position. At the end of forward swing, swing the legs and body forward and upward and at the same time bear downward with the arms and rise to a straight arm support. Bring the rings behind the hips and swing backward in the support position. At the end of the backward swing, swing the legs backward and drop to a hang. Swing forward, drag the feet in the middle of the backward swing and drop off at the end of the backward swing.

    Hints: a. Obtain an early beat. (Push off with both feet together just before reaching the center of the forward swing, and arch the back. Legs trail behind.)
        b. Whip the legs forward after the beat (flex the hips slightly), raise the legs and start pulling with the arms at the same time.
        c. Keep the arms as straight as possible. Bear downward with the hands and bring them to the hips. Turn the hands so the thumbs are toward each other.
        d. Lean forward and keep the head slightly forward.
        e. Use the impetus of the forward swing upon the movement of the body.

    Spot: No *special* spotting needed. Be especially alert if the performer gets almost to the support but fails. Be ready to tackle him.

18. **Front Uprise from a Hang**—Adjust the ring height so the performer must jump to reach them. Develop a "pendulum" swing (legs whip forward and backward while the shoulders remain relatively in the same place). On one of the forward swings, bear downward with the arms and raise the body to a straight arm support.

    Hints: a. For the pendulum swing, push forward with the arms to bring the body forward and upward. The hips can flex somewhat, but the movement is initiated at the shoulders.
        b. Gravity brings the body downward, then swing it backward and upward by pushing backward with the arms. Lift the heels as high as possible, but *don't* bend the knees. Arch the back.
        c. The rings actually move forward slightly when the legs swing backward.
        d. Work up as big a swing as possible by this forward and backward whip.
        e. Then force the legs forward and upward with a slight pike at the waist and bear down hard with the arms. The head tucks a little.
        f. The arms move slightly sideward and the hands are well in front of the shoulders.
        g. A little upward thrust of the hips just before the upward momentum is lost will help.
        h. Bring the arms to the side.

    Spot: a. Stand to his right, place your right hand on his buttocks, your left hand on his upper back as he goes for it and push upward with both hands.

19. **Back Uprise from a Hang**—Ring height as in No. 18.) Pull to a "Kip Position" and start the hips forward and downward while partially extending them. Drive them backward and upward and pull on the arms to bring the body up to a straight arm support.

    Hints: a. Though the hips are extending as the body descends, there is still some pike left as it hits the bottom and starts backward and upward.
    b. At the bottom of the swing, snap the heels backward (arch out) and drive them upward without bending the knees.
    c. As the body rises, bear down on the arms and pull them to your sides.
    d. The greater the momentum, the greater the ease of movement.
    e. Advanced performers can keep the arms straight, but a bent arm pull is easier.

    Spot: Stand at his left, place your right hand on his left thigh and your left hand on his chest as his body pases the vertical and push upward.

20. **Forward Roll from Support to Support**—From a hang, mount to a straight arm support by using the "Muscle Up." Then raise the hips, tuck the head and shoulders forward and roll, bringing the hips over the head. Keep the arms bent and continue around, bringing the head and shoulders on up to a straight arm support.

    Hints: a. Bring the rings in front of the hips (bend the arms).
    b. Hunch the shoulders and move the elbows outward.
    c. At the same time, flex and raise the hips. The arms support the weight.
    d. As the hips go forward over the head, keep the chin against the chest and keep the hips flexed.
    e. Bending the knees makes it easier, but better performers can keep them straight.
    f. The arms remain flexed and the rings remain in the pit of the abdomen. (The body is curled around the rings.)
    g. Pull with the arms and lean forward as the head and chest come up.
    h. At the last moment, swing the legs backward and upward (arch the back) to complete the stunt.

    Spot: Stand at the performer's left side. Place your right hand under his upper back as his head comes below the rings and place the left hand under his buttocks. Assist him by lifting if he needs help.

21. **Press to Shoulder Balance**—From an "L" support, raise the hips, bend the arms and extend the legs upward between the ropes, but not touching them.

    Hints: a. To raise the hips push downward and forward on the rings and draw the hips backward. Hunch the shoulders.
    b. Bend the knees to start with, but as you practice try to do it with the knees straight.
    c. Bend the arms and lower the shoulders as the hips go up. The shoulders move forward.
    d. Keep the head up.
    e. As the hips come over the head, pause momentarily to "feel" the balance.
    f. Slowly extend the legs upward, feeling the balance all the way.
    g. Stretch upward with the body, but sink deeply in the arms with the shoulders close to the hands and just a little in front of them.
    h. The elbows point outward slightly.
    i. Adjust for balance by pushing the rings forward or backward as needed.
    j. Beginners can press the legs against the cables at first and use the elbows against the straps for support.
    k. If the balance is lost and no spotter is present, tuck into a ball and hang on.

    Spot: a. Keep the rings low or stand on a table or pommel horse beside the rings.
    b. *If* he needs help, push up on his legs to help get his hips overhead.
    c. Help maintain his balance with a hand in front and one behind.

22. **Dislocate**—From a kip position, extend the legs upward and *backward* at a 45° angle and arch the back. At the same time extend the arms sideward and rotate them backward (little fingers turn toward each other) and descend to a straight hang. This may be done in a hang or at the end of either the forward or backward swing. Expert gymnasts can do it in the middle of a swing as well.

Hints: a. Try it several times from a hang and in slow motion first. Use two spotters to support the performer and "lift" him through the stunt. Push upward on the shoulders (to take the body weight off the shoulder joints) and support the thighs (to prevent a too rapid drop).
  b. Later, the extension should be forceful and snappy.
  c. Throw the head backward and arch the back as the extension is made.
  d. Keep the arms bent while learning.
  e. Wait until the "dead point" of the swing when doing it on the backward swing.
  f. Extend the legs just before the end of the swing when doing it on the forward swing.
Spot: a. From the hang, push upward on the performer's shoulder and place the other hand on his thigh to support him there.
  b. Be ready to tackle the performer if he needs help when attempting the stunt while swinging.

23. **Kip**—Jump to a hang and raise the legs to a Kip position. Extend the hips sharply (shoot the legs upward and forward at a 45° angle) and at the same time, bear downward on the arms. This should bring you to a straight arm support.
  Hints: a. Learn the kip on the horizontal bar and parallel bars first.
    b. Then try it on the rings.
    c. Keep the head forward while in the Kip position.
    d. The leg kick is forceful and snappy.
    e. When bearing down hard with the arms, turn the hands so the knuckles are upward.
    f. Shift the hands as the body rises so that the wrists are on top.
  Spot: a. Stand to the left of the performer and place your right hand on the upper back and your left on his hips.
    b. As he snaps and pulls, push upward hard on his back and pull the hips back under the shoulders.

Every good ring routine should have a static hold move of some kind in order to meet the composition requirements for competition. All of these holds are difficult. The "Back Lever" is the easiest.

24. **Back Lever**—Start from an inverted hang. Lower the straight body slowly till it is parallel to the mat then stop it in that position and hold for at least 2 seconds. With a lot of practice, the straight body can be raised again to the inverted position.

Hints: a. The body *should* be straight, but a slight pike will make it easier.

b. If it can't be held in a parallel position, stop the descent a little earlier and hold. As you practice, get lower each time till it is done correctly.

c. As the body lowers, resist the pull of gravity by pressing downward. The inside of the elbow (hollow) should be facing downward.

d. The head is in a neutral position, directly in line with the body.

e. Bring the rings a little closer together behind the back—squeeze the arms against the body.

Spot: a. Stand at the side and give support to the legs as *needed*—make the performer do most of the work.

b. If (after trying) he *can't* hold a horizontal position, stop him while still at an angle, tell him to hold it there.

Routines:

Practice the stunts at low ring height first. Learn each individual stunt, then combine. These ring routines will probably be harder to do than the routines on the other equipment because of the nature of the event.

Beginning Routine:

Jump to a hang and turn over to an inverted squat hang (No. 3). Hold for 2 seconds. Place the feet in the rings and push the hips between the arms to a nest hang (No. 5). Hold. Return to an inverted straight hang (No. 6). Flex the hips to a kip position and execute a forward single leg cut and catch (No. 9) and come to a hang. Change the grip to a "false grip" (one hand at a time) and do a muscle up (No. 10). Raise the legs to an "L" support (No. 11), hold for 2 seconds. Roll forward to a hang (No. 12) and let the legs swing backward as far as they will then force them forward and upward into a backward double leg cut dismount (No. 15).

Intermediate Routine:

Jump to a hang and begin a pendulum swing. On the forward swing pull up to an inverted hang (with a straight body, if possible). Immediately drop the legs to a pike and execute an inlocate from a kip position (No. 14) than kip to a straight arm support (No. 23), and roll forward from support to support (No. 20) and raise the legs to an "L" support (No. 11). Hold for 2 seconds. Press a shoulder balance (No. 21) and hold for 2 seconds. Tuck the head, flex the hips, and lower the body between the rings to a kip position. Extend the legs upward to an inverted hand and lower the straight body to a back lever (No. 24) and hold for 2 seconds. Drop the legs by flexing the hips, then pull back to a kip position. Dislocate (No. 22) to an immediate backward double leg cut dismount (No. 25.).

24

Low Horizontal Bar

This is another event in which girls and women do not compete. In fact, boys and men do not compete in the *low* horizontal bar either. However, many skills done on the regulation (high) horizontal bar can and should be *learned* on the low bar because the spotter can assist and protect the gymnast more advantageously and the learner feels more confident and secure at the lower height.

Though women use neither high nor low horizontal bar, they do have a similar event—the uneven parallel bars upon which they execute many of the same stunts. If no unevens are available, girls can practice and learn the skills on the low horizontal bar. If no horizontal bar is handy, boys can use the unevens. In fact, if only a boys' regulation (even) bars is useable, both sexes can use it by removing one of the rails and working the other.

There is, of course, a big difference in the diameter of the "P" bars and the horizontal bar and one must get used to the grip. Boys are cautioned to grasp the bar between the thumb and fingers while girls normally use a "hook" grasp (thumb on same side of bar as fingers). For both, the hands should be in an *upper* grasp (palms down) when circling in a backward direction and in an undergrasp (palms up) when circling forward. It is very important to follow this rule. Generally, the hands should grasp the bar shoulder width apart and the bar should be about chest high.

For stunts that start from a seat on the bar or from a rear support, time can be saved by having the performers stand in front of the bar with their hands reaching back to the bar and one foot raised forward. The spotter grasps this foot with both hands and lifts the performer into position. However, if there aren't many in the squad and time isn't an important consideration, it is good to have them jump to a front support, swing one leg over the bar, sit on that thigh and then bring the other leg forward over the bar. The involvement and development of the balance factor is frequently worth the extra expenditure of time.

Use carbonate of magnesia on the hands to prevent sweaty hands. Sandpaper the bar regularly to remove caked magnesia. Palm guards (hand grips) are worn by most gymnasts to reduce the friction between the bar and the hands which will increase the length of time they can work out without getting sore hands. For class work, this is usually not necessary.

The bar can be used for vaulting but the vaults will not be described in this chapter since they are covered in the chapter dealing with vaulting. If you wish to include vaulting in your horizontal bar lessons, refer to Chapter 21.

Of course there are many women's maneuvers that can't be performed on the horizontal bar. For this reason a separate chapter for uneven bar work is included.

Always spot from the *far* side of the bar unless specifically told to stand on the *near* side in the spotting hints.

1. **Underswing from Stand**—From a side stand frontways with the hands in an uppergrasp on the bar, take a slight jump, and bring the thighs to the bar. At the same time, lean backward with the head and shoulders and allow the hips to swing forward and upward. As the hips move forward, extend the legs

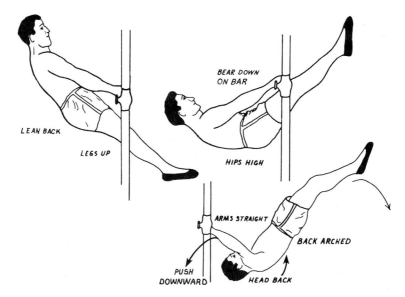

upward and forward on the far side of the bar by arching the back. The shoulders and head follow the path of the legs and hips and the hands release the bar before the feet complete the arc to the floor. Land in a side stand rearways. Repeat the stunt with the addition of a half twist while the body is in the air. Land in a side stand frontways.

Hints: a. Stand with the feet fairly close to the bar. The body should be leaning backward when the arms are straight. Keep the hips extended.

        b. Push off from the feet and drop straight backward with the shoulders as the thighs are brought to the bar.

        c. *Keep the arms straight.* Bending the arms may cause you to hit your head on the bar.

        d. Bear downward with the arms to bring the hips close to the bar. The body should be almost horizontal. Do *not* drop the hips.

        e. Drop the head backward as you arch the back.

        f. A backward thrust with the arms as the back arches will give greater height and distance.

        g. Release the hands as the thrust is made and the arms are as far back as they can go.

Spot: a. Stand to the performer's right and reach under the bar to grasp the right wrist with your left hand (palm facing downward).

        b. Pull forward on the wrist as he/she brings the legs toward the bar.

        c. Place your right arm under the lower back and lift upward as the back arches.

        d. Maintain your grip on the right wrist to prevent falling forward as he/she lands.

Note: a towel or sponge rubber pad can be taped to the bar between the hands as a safety precaution to prevent injury in case the arms bend and the head hits.

2. **Underswing Dismount from Support**—This is like stunt No. 1 except that the starting position is a front support. To start, swing the legs back away from the bar, then, as they return and pass under the bar, lay backward with the shoulders and continue as in No. 1.

Hints: a. In the front support the body and arms are straight and the shoulders are leaning forward over the bar.

        b. Bend the arms slightly, flex the hips (legs move forward under the bar) but the shoulders *stay* forward.

        c. Whip the legs backward (body leaves bar) and straighten the arms. The shoulders remain forward.

        d. As the body starts back toward the bar, lay back with the shoulders. The head is slightly forward.

        e. Bring the hips close to the underside of the bar by bearing down hard with the arms and continue as in No. 1.

Spot: Spot as for No. 1.

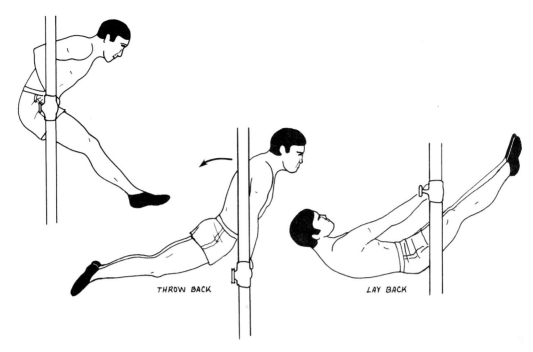

THROW BACK   LAY BACK

3. **Flank Dismount from Support**—Jump to a straight arm support. Swing the legs backward slightly then left sideward and forward over the bar to a rear stand. Release the left hand as the body is raised sideward and release the right hand just before landing.

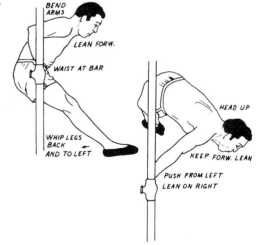

BEND ARMS
LEAN FORW.
WAIST AT BAR
WHIP LEGS BACK AND TO LEFT
HEAD UP
KEEP FORW. LEAN
PUSH FROM LEFT LEAN ON RIGHT

   Hints: a. Lean forward slightly and swing the legs backward.
   b. Bend the arms as the legs return to the bar and flex the hips as the waist strikes the bar. This gives the needed momentum. Keep the shoulders forward over the bar.
   c. Now swing the legs backward again and straighten the arms. Lean on the right arm and swing the legs to the left at the same time. Both shoulders stay forward of the bar.
   d. The legs swing backward, to the left and forward in a smooth, continuous circle.
   e. Keep the right shoulder directly above the right hand and push off hard with the left hand.
   f. Arch the back when passing over the bar.
   Spot: a. Stand to the right of the performer and support the right arm above the elbow with your right hand. Resist the tendency for the arm to move to the left.
   b. If needed, reach over the bar and place your left hand on the right hip and push.

4. **Squat Dismount from Support**—Jump to a straight arm support. Swing the legs backward, draw the knees to the chest and bring the feet between the arms, over the bar, and land in a side stand rear ways.
   Hints: a. The hands should be shoulder width apart.
   b. Obtain the momentum as for the "Flank Dismount from Support."
   c. Keep the weight well forward as the legs swing backward.
   d. Raise the hips and bring the knees to the chest.
   e. At the same time, push hard from the hands as the arms are vigorously straightened.

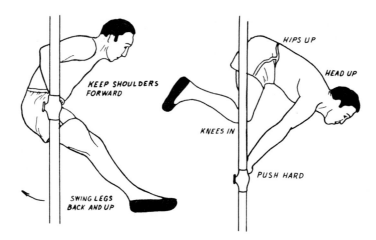

f. The hands release the bar while the body momentum is upward and forward.

g. With the push, lift the chest to bring the shoulders over the hips. Don't snap the hips forward to get them clear of the bar.

h. Keep the head up.

Spot: a. Two men, one in *front* of either arm, support the performer's arms during the vault. They grasp the arms close to the shoulders. The spotter on the right arm has the right hand high and the other spotter has the left hand high.

b. They catch the performer on their shoulders if his/her toes hook on the bar.

5. **Straddle Dismount from Support**—Jump to a straight arm support, swing the legs backward, straddle them and bring them forward over the bar to land in a side stand rearways. Bring the legs together before landing.

Hints: a. Obtain the needed momentum as for the preceding stunt.

b. Raise the hips upward and flex them to bring the legs toward the bar. Spread the legs as far as possible.

c. Lean *forward* and shove downward very hard from the hands at the same time that the hips flex.

d. *Keep the head up.*

e. Raise the chest upward and bring the feet together after they pass over the bar.

f. Keep the legs straight.

Spot: a. Two spotters, one in *front* of each arm, grasp the performer close to the shoulders. The one on the right arm has the right hand high.

b. As he/she straddles, lift upward and step back.

c. If only one spotter is available catch the performer on your shoulder if the toes strike the bar.

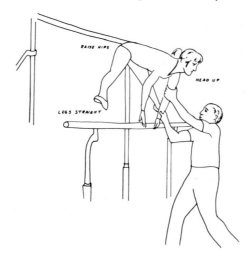

Note: For all of the "Knee Circle" stunts (stunts No. 6, 7, and 11) a towel can be folded several times and taped to the bar to prevent "burning" the knee joint. The towel must be fixed so that it will revolve easily around the bar. The performer puts his knee, or knees, on the towel and his hands on both sides.

6. **Backward Single Knee Circle**—Jump to a support and place the left leg over the bar between the hands. Sit on the left thigh. Swing the right leg backward, then vigorously forward and circle around the bar supported by the left knee and both hands to return to a seat on the thigh.

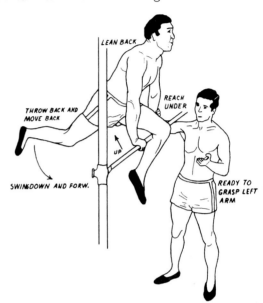

    Hints: a. Shift the entire body backward when swinging the right leg backward.
          b. Hook the left knee tightly against the bar as this is done.
          c. Lean backward and throw the head back as the right leg starts forward.
          d. Reach downward as well as forward with the right leg.
          e. Keep the arms extended while going backward and downward.
          f. Bend the arms if necessary as the body circles upward on the far side of the bar.
          g. Stop the momentum as you come up by squeezing the bar tightly with the hands and moving the bar from the knee joint to the thigh. (It will be impossible to stop on top if the knee joint remains at the bar.)

    Spot: a. Reach under the bar with your right hand (thumb down) to grasp the performer's left wrist.
          b. Place your left hand on his/her left knee and push it back as the right leg swings back. This push assures that the body will move back as it should.
          c. Pull downward and forward with your right hand as he/she starts to circle and lift upward on the left upper arm with your left hand as he/she starts up on the far side of the bar.

7. **Forward Single Knee Circle**—Jump to a support and place the left leg over the bar between the hands. Sit on the left thigh. The hands are in an *undergrasp.* Lean forward, circle under the bar supported by the hands and the left knee and return to a seat on the left thigh. Swing the right leg over the bar and dismount with a quarter turn left to a cross stand left.

    Hints: a. Raise the hips (take the weight on the arms) and hook the left knee when leaning forward.
          b. Tuck the head to the chest.
          c. Bend the arms slightly.
          d. Swing the right leg upward and forward as the circling begins.
          e. Then whip the right leg downward and backward very vigorously.
          f. Flex the arms slightly and lean forward when coming up again.
          g. Also, move the bar from the knee back to the thigh.

    Spot: a. Stand on the *near* side of the bar to the performer's left. Reach under the bar to grasp the left wrist with your left hand (knuckles toward you).
          b. Reach under the bar with the right hand too (palm turned toward you) and place it on the left knee as he/she raises and leans forward. Pull back with your right hand to help hook the knee.

c. Pull downward and toward you as he/she circles under the bar and shift your right hand to the left upper arm as he/she comes around to help in coming up to a seat on the left thigh.

Note: Both No. 6 and 7 can be done with the forward leg straight rather than hooked on the bar. Girls on the unevens usually do them this way. When both legs are straight the stunts are called "Mill Circles."

8. **Squat from Front Support to Rear Support**—Jump to a straight arm support, hands in an uppergrasp. Swing the legs backward, draw the knees to the chest and pass the feet over the bar between the arms. Straighten the legs downward and maintain the rear support. Change the left hand to an undergrasp, release the right hand, pivot around the left arm and face the bar, regrasping with the right hand in a front support. Drop to a stand.

Hints: a. Obtain the leg swing as for the "Squat Dismount from Support."
b. Lean forward, draw the knees to the chest and raise the hips high. "Hunch" the back.
c. Lean *backward* slightly with the shoulders as the feet pass over the bar.
d. Do not release the hands. Grasp tightly to check the forward momentum.

Spot: a. Grasp the performer's right arm and hold back on it to prevent the momentum from carrying him/her off the bar.
b. Catch the body on your right shoulder if the toes hit the bar.

9. **Kick Up to Backward Hip Circle**—Stand with one foot under the bar, the other leg back, and the arms and body straight. The body is leaning backward. Swing the rear leg forward and upward, push off from the forward foot and circle the legs up and around the bar to a front support position.

Hints: a. Don't sag at the hips in the starting position.
b. Swing the rear leg up and push hard from the forward foot.
c. At the same time, lay back with the shoulders and pull with the arms.
d. Pull the hips directly to the bar. Don't let them drop.
e. Bend at the waist as it hits the bar.
f. Revolve the hands on the bar. Snap the wrists to the top.
g. The head is forward as the shoulders go backward but it is lifted as the chest rises to the support.

Spot: a. Stand to the performer's right, reach under the bar to grasp the right wrist with your left hand. Your knuckles face upward.
b. As he/she kicks upward, place your right hand under the thighs and lift.
c. Pull down, to your right, and upward on the right wrist—especially upward.

10. **Backward Hip Circle from Front Support**—Jump to a support, hands in an uppergrasp, and swing the legs backward for momentum. Bring the body back to the bar and circle around it (bar at the hips) and return to a front support position. Drop to a stand.

Hints: a. Lean forward as the legs are swung backward.
b. Start leaning backward as the body returns to bar. Keep the head forward just a bit.

c. Bend the arms slightly, so that the bar strikes at the belt. (Advanced performers keep the arms straight.)

d. Throw the hips toward the bar. Don't let them drop and *don't* bend the knees.

e. Shift the wrists downward and forward and strike the undersurface of the bar with the abdomen rather than the top or back surface.

f. Throw the head backward and arch the back as the head and shoulders start rising on the far side.

Spot: From the right side reach under the bar with your left hand and place it on the hips as they come to the bar. Pull forward and keep him/her *close* to the bar.

11. **Backward Double Knee Circle**—Mount to a seat on the bar with the hands in an uppergrip outside of the legs. Lean backward, hook the knees and circle under the bar and up on the other side, to return to seat. Push off forward to a stand.

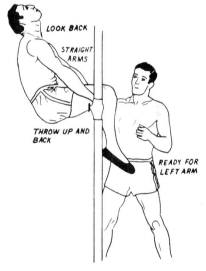

Hints: a. Shift the hips *upward* and *backward* to hook the knees. The arms support the body.

b. As the knees hook, lean backward and throw the head vigorously backward.

c. Keep the arms extended until the body passes under the bar.

d. Flex the arms and increase the hip flexion as the body rises to the seat.

e. Snap the wrists upward (knuckles on top).

f. At the same time, slide forward on the bar so that the thighs rest on the bar rather than the knee joints.

Spot: a. Grasp the performer's left wrist from under the bar with the right hand and give impetus to the circling by pulling on the wrist as he/she starts around and lifting on it at the finish.

b. Place your left hand on the left knee and push back as it hooks and make sure that it remains hooked.

c. As he/she rises to a seat help him/her to the siting position by shifting your left hand to the upper arm.

12. **Kip**—From a front stand with the hands in an uppergrasp, take a slight hop and flex the hips to bring the feet directly to the bar. Hold that position while the body is moving forward. As the hips start the return swing, kick upward and outward at a 45° angle with the feet (extend the hips). At the same time bear downward with the arms and rise to a front support position. Drop to a stand.

Hints: a. Keep the arms straight and start with the feet almost under the bar.

b. Take a slight jump from both feet and flex the hips.

c. At the same time, lean backward with the head and shoulders. Keep the arms straight.

d. Let the hips move forward freely. They should drop low.

e. The kick (extension) must be snappy and vigorous and it occurs as the hips move backward.

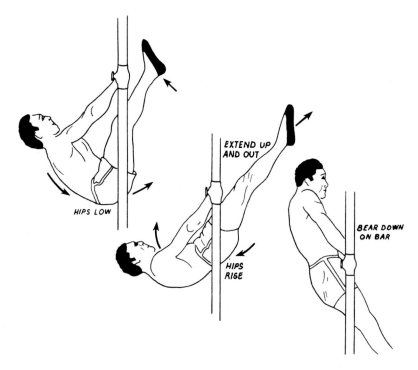

f. The arm pull is actually a downward pressure which raises the body and draws it toward the bar. The arms remain straight.

g. Snap the wrists upward as the arms pull. The wrists are above (not behind) the bar as the movement finishes.

h. Coordinate the leg kick and arm pull.

i. Lean forward and keep the head forward when coming up to the support.

j. Two main faults are kicking too soon and kicking too flatly. *Wait* till the hips move back and kick at a 45° angle.

Spots a. Stand at the performer's right and place your right hand against the calves as he/she brings the legs to the bar and your left hand on the small of the back.

b. At the kick, resist it with the right hand (so there is something to kick against) and lift with the left hand.

13. **Forward Heel Circle Dismount**—(Bar shoulder high.) Mount to a rear support with the hands in an undergrasp. Flex and raise the hips till the heels are brought to the bar. At the same time, lean forward, tuck the head to the chest and circle the bar. As the body rises on the other side of the bar, release the bar with the hands and slide the heels off of the bar. As the feet clear the bar, extend the legs downward and come to a side stand frontways.

Hints: a. Move the hips backward over the bar as well as upward when drawing the heels to the bar.

b. Keep the knees straight. Press against the bar with the heels.

c. Do not flex the arms.

d. Release the bar just before the height of the upward movement of the body is reached. The momentum of the circle will pull you off the bar.

e. Keep the hips flexed (sitting position) until the feet clear the bar.

f. Bring the legs under the body by extending the legs downward.

g. Keep the head forward.

h. On the *first* trial, don't release the hands. Each spotter *must* support an upper arm. After a "feel" for the stunt has been acquired, release the hands.

Spot: a. Use two spotters. They stand on the *near* side. Reach under the bar and grasp the performer's wrist with the hand nearest the bar. As he/she rises on the near side, grasp the upper arm with your other hand.

b. Step back with him/her as he/she releases the bar.

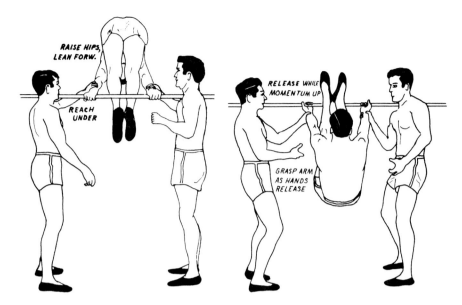

c. Guard against an early release. Lift upward on the upper arm if that happens.

d. Also watch for a too late release. Since the momentum will be lost, support the upper arms till the feet can be released.

14. **Backward Sole Circle Dismount**—(Bar shoulder high.) Jump to a front support with the hands in an uppergrasp. Swing the legs backward, flex the hips, place the soles of the feet on the bar between the hands and circle backward (hips leading) under the bar. Just past three-quarters of the way around, release the bar with the hands, straighten upward and push off from the bar with the legs to a side stand rearways.

Hints: a. Keep the head up as the hips and knees are flexed to place the arch of the feet on the bar.

b. The shoulders should be slightly ahead of the hands.

c. Straighten the legs and thrust the hips backward and upward as soon as the feet are placed on the bar.

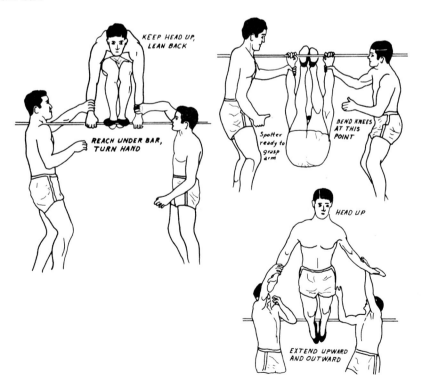

    d. Throw the head back.

    e. Bend the knees as the body starts to rise on the far side.

    f. Do not relase the hands on the first attempt. The spotters must support the shoulders. This is to get used to the position.

    g. *Raise the head* and chest and release the hands at the *height of* the upward swing.

    h. Jump off just as the upward momentum is lost.

Spot: a. Use two spotters. They stand in front of and to the side of each arm, reach under the bar to grasp a wrist with the nearest hand and are prepared to brace the performer's shoulders with the other hand to prevent his/her falling forward as the feet are placed on the bar.

    b. Step to the side as the hips come up on the far side.

    c. Step in as soon as they have passed and grasp the upper arms with your free hand and push him/her up to a squat stand on the *first* attempt.

    d. Support the shoulders and move along with him/her as he/she releases the bar and pushes from the feet for the dismount.

15. **Glide Kip**—From a front stand with the hands in an uppergrasp, flex the hips, and let the shoulders sink so that the head is between the arms and the hips are protruding backward. Flex the knees, then vigorously extend them, pushing from the floor with the feet which will cause the hips to swing backward and slightly upward. Keep the hips flexed so that the feet are a few inches above the mat and let the body swing forward. At the end of the forward swing, arch the back (extend the feet forward as far as possible) and then quickly flex the hips to bring the feet to the bar. From there, kick as in the regular "Kip" and rise to a front support.

Hints: a. Keep the arms straight.

    b. Drop the hips as low as possible.

    c. Stretch the legs forward at the end of the swing.

    d. Recoil from the extension immediately.

    e. When *learning* the stunt, push off from the floor with one foot to bring the feet to the bar.

    f. Kick as soon as the ankles come to the bar. Don't hesitate.

    g. Pull with the arms (press the bar to the hips) and snap the wrists as in the regular "Kip."

FLEX HIPS RIGHT
AFTER EXTENSION

EXTEND

FEET GO
DIRECTLY
TO BAR

Spot: Spot as for the regular "Kip."

16. **Forward Hip Circle from Front Support**—Jump to a front support with the hands in an uppergrasp. (This is contrary to the general rule of undergrasp for forward circling stunts.) Raise the hips slightly so the bar rests low on the thighs. Lean forward and circle around the bar, returning to a front support position.

Hints: a. Lean forward keeping the body arched. (The legs rise behind.)

    b. The arms must be straight.

    c. Flex at the hips and tuck the head forward as the straight body passes the horizontal plane. This must be done very fast. Think of trying to put your head on your knees.

    d. As the head and shoulders pass under the bar, shift the wrists forward so the hands will come to the top of the bar. The legs are still on top of the bar when the wrists shift.

    e. The arms bend slightly as the body comes up.

    f. Maintain a backward pressure with the arms to hold the thighs against the bars.

    g. Finish with a nice backward and upward swing of the legs.

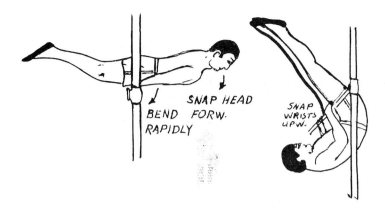

Spot: a. Stand on the *near* side and reach under the bar (bend the knees if necessary) to place your arm across the performer's back as he/she bends forward. Pull him/her around and then place your other hand on the back and lift upward.

       b. Gradually decrease the assistance.

17. **Forward Half Seat Circle**—Proceed as in the "Glide Kip" (No. 15) up to the arching of the back. After the extension, pike as before, but bring the feet *under* the bar (between the hands) and, as the body moves backward, shoot the legs up over the bar from the back side. The body follows the legs and finishes in a seat on the bar. This can be used for a dismount too by pushing off with the hands just before the upward and forward momentum is lost.

Hints: a. Follow hints *a, b, c,* and *d* in stunt No. 15.

       b. If the *sharp* recoil is made at the *end* of the stretch, the resulting action will be a vigorous backward swing in a pike position.

       c. Flex the hips as tightly as possible to get the feet under the bar. If *needed*, the knees may be bent a little.

       d. A sharp, partial extension of the hips as the body rises on the back side will help. Don't extend completely. A sudden cessation of the extension is important.

       e. Pull with the arms and keep the head forward.

       f. For the dismount, simply push off with the hands before momentum dies.

Spot: Stand at the performer's left on the *near* side and as the legs pass under the bar, place your left hand on the buttocks and pull toward you as you push upward on his/her back with your right hand.

Note: This may also be done starting from a seat on the bar. With legs straight, lift the body off the bar by straightening the arms (the body is in an "L" position). Lift the legs till the body drops backward (head is tucked) with the hips remaining flexed. Wait till the momentum from the drop has ended and, as the body begins to swing in the other direction, follow hints *d, e,* and *f*.

18. **Forward Seat Circle**—Start from a seat on the bar, hands in an undergrip. Straighten the arms to lift the seat off the bar, tuck the head, and rotate forward around the bar to return to the starting position. The body is in a pike position all the way around.

    Hints: a. When lifting the seat off the bar, hunch the back, draw the hips upward and backward, and keep the knees straight.

    b. The head is *up* during this phase. Think of reaching forward with the shoulders as much as possible.

    c. Now, as balance is lost, tuck the head sharply.

    d. Hold on tightly as you hit the bottom of the circle and pike as tightly as you can. Good hip flexibility is important.

    e. From here, follow hints *d, e,* and *f* in stunt No. 17.

    Spot: a. Two spotters stand on the *near* side of the bar. The one on the left reaches under the bar with the left hand turned so the knuckles are toward him and grasps the performer's left wrist. Pull down, around, and up on the wrist.

    b. Reach for the performer's left upper arm as it starts up from under the bar with your right hand and lift upward and push forward.

    c. The spotter on the right does the same, but with the opposite hands.

19. **Reverse (Back) Kip**—Use the preliminary move used in stunt No. 17. As the feet pass under the bar with the body swinging backward, partially extend the hips and reach upward with the legs (body in semipike, back to the bar, and legs and hips moving upward). As gravity brings the body down again, deepen the pike and then quickly extend again to force the head and shoulders up above the bar on the far side (legs are now pointing downward) to a rear support.

    Hints: a. The greater the forward swing at the beginning, the easier the stunt.

    b. Keep the legs as straight as possible when bringing them under the bar.

    c. Extend the legs upward fast (but without a snap). Don't extend completely and keep the head forward.

    d. Pike very deeply as gravity brings the body downward.

    e. As the bent hips pass under and forward of the bar, extend the body by lifting the head and chest. This extension is done with a forceful snap. The legs are thrust downward and backward.

    f. With the snap, bear downward hard with the arms and snap the wrists upward.

    Spot: Stand at the right, place your right hand under the chest and lift as the body extends.

Beginning Routine:

From a side stand frontways with uppergrasp, kick up into a backward hip circle (No. 9), bring the left (or right) leg over the bar and do a single knee circle backward (No. 6), bring the other leg forward over the bar and do a double knee circle backward (No. 11), change the left (or right) hand to an under grip, pivot on the left (or right) arm to a front support and do an underswing dismount (No. 2).

Intermediate Routine:

From a side stand frontways with uppergrasp, glide kip (No. 15) to support, backward hip circle (No. 9), drop kip (same as No. 12 except it starts from support instead of from a stand), forward hip circle (No. 16), squat from front support to rear support (No. 8), change the left (or right) hand to an undergrasp and pivot around that arm to a front support, do another forward hip circle to an immediate squat (or straddle) dismount (No. 4 or No. 5).

25

High Horizontal Bar

As with the *low* horizontal bar, girls can work the *high* bar if an uneven parallel bar is not available for them and boys can use the high bar of the unevens if there is no horizontal bar.

All of the stunts learned on the low bar can be performed on the high bar with the exception of the "Glide Kip." After they have been thoroughly learned on the low bar they may be used in combinations on the high bar. The bar should be high enough to permit a free hang (toes do not touch mat).

It is very difficult to give assistance on the high horizontal bar unles a suspended safety belt or spotting table is used. The ropes from the belt run through pulleys attached to the ceiling and are controlled by a spotter on the floor.

In the absence of the belt, the spotters must be prepared to "tackle" (catch the performer around the waist) if he/she is in trouble for most of the stunts. When dismounting from a swing, always release the bar at the *end* of the *backward* swing. Drop off just at the "dead point" when you are neither going forward nor backward.

Magnesium carbonate should be used on the hands to prevent them from sweating. The bar should be sanded regularly to remove the caked magnesium. The bar must be between the thumbs and fingers in all grasps. Unless you are using the high bar of the unevens. Hand guards may be worn.

1. **Wide Arm Chinning**—Jump to a hang with an uppergrasp and the hands spread wide apart. Pull with the arms and tuck the head forward to touch the bar with the back of the neck. Straighten the arms completely and repeat as many times as possible.
   Hints: Pull slowly, lower rather rapidly.
   Note: This is not a "stunt." It is done to develop needed strength. It develops other muscles than those used in customary chinning.

2. **Skin the Cat**—From a hang using the uppergrasp, raise the legs and pass them under the bar between the arms. Continue backward and bring the hips through between the arms also. Extend the legs downward. Return to a hang by reversing the movement.
   Hints: a. Pull with the arms and flex the knees and hips.
         b. Lean backward with the shoulders. (Push forward and downward with the hands.)
         c. Keep the knees close to the chest until the hips have passed through the arms and gone down as far as possible, then extend the legs toward the mat.
         d. Tuck the head forward, draw the knees to the chest and raise the hips to return.
         e. Round the back (pull the shoulders forward) at the same time.
   Spot: a. Stand to the right of the performer and push upward on the hips with your right hand *if* he needs help to raise the legs. Use the left hand to make sure he has his knees close to the chest.
         b. Assist his return if he needs help by lifting on his knees or abdomen with the left hand and supporting his upper back with the right.

3. **Knee Hang**—Jump to a hang and bring the legs upward, pass them between the arms and hook the knees over the bar. Release the bar with the hands and lower the body to a hang with the head down, the body being supported at the knees. To return, reach upward, regrasp the bar, bring the hips between the arms to a "Skin the Cat" position and drop to a stand.

Hints: a. Lower very slowly when releasing the hands.
   b. Keep the head forward. Extend the hips gradually.
   c. Keep the hands up (close to the body) until the hips are fully extended.
   d. Tuck the head forward first when starting to return to the bar.
   e. Then reach upward with the hands before flexing the hips.
   f. Don't drop off until maximum extension is reached in the "Skin the Cat" position.

Spot: a. Stand directly under the bar and have your arms right below the performer's shoulders, ready to support the shoulders should the knee hold loosen.
   b. Be prepared to brace from behind for the dismount.

4. **Front Pullover**—Jump to a hang, raise the legs upward, and at the same time flex the arms so that the waist will strike the bar. Continue on over the bar, pivoting at the waist, and come to a front support. Return to a hang by reversing the movement.

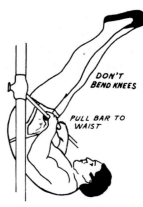

Hints: a. Flex the arms and raise the straight legs (flex the hips) at the same time.
   b. Lean backward with the shoulders when the arms are about half flexed.
   c. At the same time bear downward with the hands. Try to push the bar towards the thighs. This will draw you toward the bar.
   d. As the waist hits the bar, flex the hips more (let the legs drop over the bar) and continue to pull with the arms. Do not bend the knees. Bent knees will put added weight on the wrong side of the bar.
   e. To return, flex the hips (drop forward over the bar) and slowly lower the legs.
   f. Keep the head forward.

Spot: Assist by pushing upward on the performer's hips if help is needed. Gradually lessen the assistance.

5. **Swinging Turns**—Jump to a hang at the right side of the bar and obtain a swing. (The spotter may push the performer to produce the swing.) At the end of the forward swing, release the right hand and execute a half turn left, pivoting on the left hand, and regrasp with the right. The left hand is now in an undergrasp while the right is in an uppergrasp. Swing forward and release the left hand, execute a half turn around the right arm, regrasp with the left and swing forward again. Continue, turning at the end of each swing, to the other side of the bar. Drop off at the end of the swing just after *completing* the final turn.

Hints: a. Keep the back arched during the first half of the forward swing.
   b. When passing under the bar, thrust the feet forward (bend at the hips) slightly.
   c. Then arch the back again (thrust hips forward) just before forward momentum is lost.
   d. At the same time, turn the head and twist the hips. Don't turn before the *end* of the swing.
   e. The back is arched and remains so till the middle of the next forward swing.

       f. Try to keep the legs together at all times.

       g. Regrasp as soon as the turn is completed. The forward swing is just beginning and one hand is in an overgrasp, the other in an undergrasp, shoulder width apart.

Spot: a. Stand at the performer's side and move with him/her, ready to tackle if he/she slips off.

       b. Grasp the hips and twist them at the proper time if there is difficulty in turning.

       c. A second spotter stands at the far upright to keep the performer from banging into it.

6. **Knee Swing Up**—Jump to a hang and obtain a swing. As the legs swing forward bring the left leg upward, hook the knee over the bar to the left of the left hand and swing the right leg vigorously downward and backward to propel the body upward to a seat on the left thigh. The body circles upward supported by the hands and the left knee.

   Hints: a. Bring both legs up toward the bar just before the end of the forward swing.

       b. Hook the left knee as the body is ready to swing backward.

       c. Swing the *straight* right leg downward and backward as the left knee is hooked.

       d. Pull with the arms and lean forward when rising.

       e. It can be tried first without the swing. From a hang, bring the leg up and hook it, and then kick downward with the other leg. Keep the kicking leg *straight.*

   Spot: Stand directly under the bar and grasp the right ankle as it swings downward and push back and lift on the leg.

7. **Hock Swing Dismount**—Assume the "Knee Hang" position and obtain a swing. The spotter may aid in the swing. At the end of the forward swing unhook the knees and drop to a stand on the mat. *Do not attempt this stunt without a spotter present.*

   Hints: a. Flex the hips and tuck the head while swinging backward.

       b. Arch the back and raise the head when swinging forward.

       c. The arms lead the swing in both directions.

          1. Swing the arms backward when tucking the head and flexing the hips.

          2. Swing the arms forward just as the backward swing ends.

       d. Release the knees at the height of the forward swing.

       e. The back must be arched, the head up (look forward), and the arms reaching upward and forward.

       f. Don't whip the legs off of the bar. Simply straighten the legs and drop off.

Spot: a. Grasp the performer's right arm close to the shoulder with both hands and help to get the swing. Move with him/her, retain grasp on both forward and backward swings.

b. Lift upward on the arm as the legs are released.

c. Be prepared to support the body in case of a too early release of the performer's knees.

d. Use two spotters if they are inexperienced; one on each arm.

8. **Underswing Dismount from Support**—Mount to a front support using either the "Front Pull Up" or the "Knee Swing Up." Swing the legs backward slightly and then forward toward the bar. At the same time, lay backward keeping the arms straight. This causes the legs to shoot upward on the far side of the bar. Now arch the back so that the feet describe an arc (upward, outward, and downward). The head and shoulders follow the path of the feet. Release the bar as the body starts downward. This is similar to No. 6 on the low horizontal bar. (See page 188, stunt No. 2.)

Hints: a. *Don't* bend the arms.

b. Keep the hips close to the bar until you begin to arch the back.

c. Flex the hips slightly as the legs swing forward and upward.

d. Bear down on the bar with the hands as the feet start the downward part of the arc and the hands are overhead.

Spot: a. Use two spotters. One stands fairly close to the bar and lifts on the performer's back if the arc is too flat.

b. The other stands further in front to protect the performer against an overthrow which would cause him/her to fall forward. Be prepared to catch an arm or brace the chest of the performer.

9. **Underswing Dismount with Half Twist**—Mount to a front support as above and proceed as before. The half twist occurs just before the arch is completed. The legs are still moving upward and the hands still grasp the bar. Land in a side stand frontways.

Hints: a. Start the twist by turning the head and shoulders in the direction of the twist.

b. The arch and twist occur at the same time.

c. If the twist is to the right, release the left hand a fraction of a second before the right. Both hands should be released just before the twist is completed.

Spot: a. Use two spotters. One stands fairly close to the bar to spot the performer's shoulders if the performer does not twist or twists only one-fourth of the way.

b. The other spotter stands further away and guards against the performer falling backward when landing.

10. **Obtain Swing**—Stand about three feet from the bar, jump to a hang, and let the momentum of the jump carry you forward. As the return swing begins, pull on the arms and raise the legs. Just as the next forward swing begins, lean backward with the shoulders, straighten the arms and extend the legs upward and forward. Arch the back. Let the forward swing bring the whole body forward. Swing backward with the back arched and dismount at the end of the backward swing. Basically this is an underswing dismount (No. 8) without releasing the hands, but is more difficult because it starts from a hang instead of a support.

Hints: a. Just hang as the body swings forward following the jump.

b. The flexing of the arms and hips and the subsequent straightening of the arms and arching of the back occur in one smooth, continuous movement.

c. As the arms are straightened, bear downward and forward with the hands to draw the hips close to the bar.

d. At the same moment, lean backward with the shoulders. The body should approach a horizontal position.

e. As the body moves forward and upward, pull backward (force the straight arms over the head) with the arms.

f. Arch the back as you approach the end of the forward-upward swing.

g. At the *end* of the back swing, bear downward slightly with the arms to bring the body into a vertical position and drop off. Do this at the "dead point" of the swing.

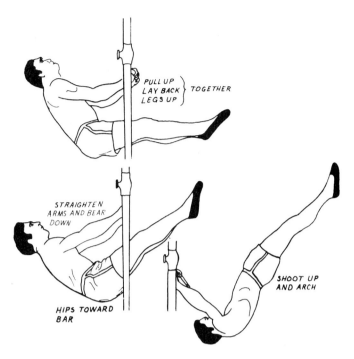

Spot: a. Stand to the performer's right on the far side of the bar. Place your right hand on the hips and push upward as he/she arches. Also place your left hand on the right shoulder and pull forward.

b. Then step to the near side of the bar to "spot" the dismount.

11. **Kip**—Jump to a hang and obtain a swing as described in No. 10. At the end of the forward swing, flex the hips and bring the feet to the bar. As soon as they reach the bar, extend the hips (kick upward and outward at a 45° angle). At the same time, pull with the arms to bring the body up to a front support. Dismount with an "Underswing Dismount."

Hints: a. Practice the "Kip" on the low horizontal bar first.

b. Do not take too large a swing. A medium swing is best. Try the stunt on the first or second swing.

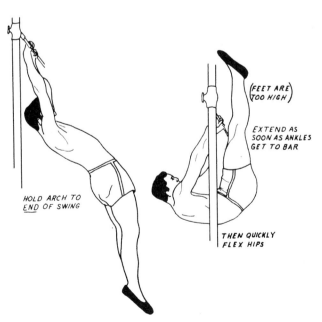

    c. Arch the back while swinging forward and keep it arched till the *end* of the swing.

    d. Flex the hips quickly at the very *end* of the forward swing.

    e. The hip extension (kick) should occur as soon as the feet come to the bar. It should be forceful.

    f. The arm pull is really a downward pressure on the bar. Keep the arms fairly straight.

    g. Snap the wrists forward as the body rises to a support.

Spot: a. Stand beneath the bar and to the right of the performer. Place your right hand on the buttocks and your left hand on the back as the hips are flexed.

    b. Push backward and upward as he/she kicks.

12. **Hock Dismount with Half Twist and Regrasp**—Jump to a hang, raise the legs and bring them between the arms, hooking the knees over the bar. Bend and straighten the arms rhythmically to produce a swing. At the end of one of the backward swings, release the hands, throw the arms over the head, and swing forward in the "Knee Hang" position. At the end of the forward swing release the knees, execute a half turn and regrasp the bar with the hands.

    Hints: a. Learn the "Hock Swing Dismount" first.

    b. Keep the back round and the head forward while working up the momentum.

    c. Bring the chest to the bar when flexing the arms.

    d. When momentum has been achieved, fling the arms overhead and extend the hips to throw the body away from the bar.

    e. Arch the back and lead the forward swing with the arms.

    f. Keep the head up.

    g. Just as the height of the swing is reached, reach to the left and upward with both hands and twist the head to the left. This starts the body to twisting.

    h. Bend at the waist as this is done.

    i. At the same time release the legs.

    j. Grasp the bar with both hands.

Spot: a. Use two spotters. One stands on the near side of the bar and is prepared to catch the performer if he falls as he throws his body backward away from the bar.

    b. The other spotter stands on the far side of the bar just to the right of the performer as he swings forward. Be prepared to catch the performer's shoulders as he twists and reaches for the bar in case he releases the legs too soon or misses his grasp with the hands.

13. **Drop Kip**—Mount to support by doing a "Kip" (No. 11). Then drop backward with straight arms while flexing the hips to bring the feet to the bar. Pause while the hips swing forward. Then as they start to swing backward, kick upward and outward at a 45° angle with the legs as in the regular "Kip" and rise to a support.

    Hints: a. Lean forward and swing the legs backward slightly.

    b. As the body returns to the bar, drop backward with the arms straight (shoulders lean backwards) and flex the hips (knees straight). The head drops forward.

    c. Drop the hips low. Work for complete flexion.

    d. Extend the hips slightly and flex them again immediately in a rocking motion.

    e. This provides proper timing for the kick.

    f. Kick as the hips start backward.

    g. The most common error is extending too early. *Wait* till the hips start back.

    h. All other hints are the same as for the "Kip."

Spot: Spot as for the "Kip."

14. **Half Turn and Kip**—Jump to a hang and obtain a swing. At the end of the forward swing release the right hand and execute a half turn, regrasping the bar as in the "Swinging Turns" (No. 5). Swing forward and "Kip" at the end of the forward swing. The hands are in a mixed grasp.

    Hints: a. Arch the back as soon as the half turn is completed and swing forward in the arched position.

    b. **Don't break the arch until the end of the forward swing.**

    c. Follow all the rules and hints for the "Kip."

d. Snap the left wrist forward (turn the knuckles downward) as the body rises to support. Snap the right wrist as in the regular "Kip."

Spot: Spot as for the "Kip."

Note: This can also be started from a support position. Start an "Underswing Dismount with Half Twist" (No. 9) but as the arch and twist begin, release *one* hand, pivot around the other and *regrasp* with the hand you had released. This occurs as the body swings upward and outward. Now swing forward and Kip as above.

15. **Back Uprise**—Jump to a hang and obtain a large swing. Pull with the arms on the backward swing and draw the body up to a front support. The body should remain straight.

    Hints: a. Get a very large swing as described in "Obtain Swing" (No. 10).

        b. Do the stunt on the *first* back swing.

        c. Begin the arm pull soon after the body passes the middle of the backward swing.

        d. Lead with the heels; keep the heels moving upward and the back arched.

        e. The arm pull is actually a downward pressure on the bar with straight arms which raises the body upward and toward the bar.

        f. A slight hip flexion and immediate extension executed near the height of the swing will aid beginners. Advanced performers will keep the back arched all the way.

        g. Go right into a "Backward Hip Circle from Front Support" (See Low Horizontal Bar Stunts, No. 10) to prevent banging against the bar with the abdomen.

Spot: a. Assist by pushing backward and upward on the performer's abdomen when passing under the bar.

        b. Be ready to tackle around the waist on the downward swing if the attempt has been unsuccessful.

16. **Kip with Undergrasp**—Jump to a hang with the hands in an undergrasp and obtain a swing. At the end of the forward swing, flex the hips and bring the feet to the bar. Then kick forward and outward as in the regular "Kip." Rise to a front support.

    Hints: a. Follow the hints for the regular "Kip" except for the wrist snap.

        b. As the "kick" is made, revolve the hands on the bar by snapping the wrists upward and forward. The thumbs must come to the top of the bar.

Spot: Spot as for the regular "Kip."

THE REGULAR KIP AND THE KIP WITH UNDERGRASP MUST BE WELL LEARNED BEFORE THE FOLLOWING KIPS ARE ATTEMPTED.

17. **Half Turn on Back Swing and Kip**—Jump to a hang with overgrasp and obtain a medium swing. On the back swing execute a half turn right (release the left hand and turn around the right) to regrasp in an undergrasp with the left hand. Both hands are now in an undergrasp. Bring the feet to the bar and kip to a support.

Hints: a. First, practice the turn only and use a *small* swing. As proficiency is achieved, increase the size of the swing.

b. Execute the turn in the middle of the back swing and regrasp instantly.

c. Bring the left hand downward, across the body to the right, and upward in a smooth motion as you turn. Just hang on with the right.

d. When you have confidence in the turn, begin flexing the hips (bring the feet to the bar) *as* the turn is made. This is fairly difficult but very important. Try to keep the knees straight.

e. For the kick, follow all the hints for the undergrasp kip (No. 16) except the arching out at the end of the forward swing.

Spot: a. Stand at the performer's left and reach for the hips with both of your hands as he turns. Be ready to support if he/she slips off during the turn.

b. Push upward on the hips as he/she kicks. Stay out of the way of the legs as they swing back after getting to the support.

c. If he/she can't get the feet to the bar, place your left arm under the lower back and right hand under the thighs as he/she turns and lift your right hand to help get the legs up.

18. **Kip with Hop-Change of Grasp**—From a medium *forward* swing with overgrasp, release both hands, change to an undergrasp, bring the feet to the bar, and kip to support.

Hints: a. First concentrate on the hop-change without thinking of the kip.

b. Start bending the hips (bring feet to bar) when passing under the bar.

c. A strong, sharp arm pull at this moment is required.

d. Release the hands while the body movement (from the pull) is upward.

e. Turn the palms toward you and regrasp immediately. Catch with bent arms.

f. Straighten the arms and extend the body forward, then swing back and drop off.

g. When the change becomes smooth, continue the upward movement of the legs as the catch is made and kip as soon as the feet get to the bar.

h. The hips drop slightly as the feet come to the bar. Keep the knees straight.

Spot: a. Stand under the bar to the left as he/she passes on the forward swing, step directly behind and grasp the hips.

b. Support (lift up) on the release and change. Step sideward as he/she swings backward.

c. Gradually reduce the aid.

d. When the change can be made without aid, assist the kip in the usual way.

19. **Forward (Front) Three-Quarter Giant Swing**—From a front support with *undergrasp*, cast upward into a handstand and continue forward over the bar (body extended, feet leading). Continue on down and around to a back uprise to a front support.

Hints: a. Practice first on a very low horizontal bar (one foot from the mat, if possible) and kick up to a handstand using an *undergrasp*. Two spotters (one on each side on the *far* side of the bar) catch and support the legs and body as he/she passes over the bar. They *lower* the body to the mat.

b. Keep the arms straight and the head up as the "kickup" is made.

c. As the handstand is reached, tuck the head and stay stretched away from the bar. Extend the body as much as possible. Trust the spotters to give support to the body.

d. Now raise the bar to shoulder height, jump to a front support with *under*grasp, obtain a "beat" (bend arms, swing legs forward while leaning forward over the bar), and vigorously thrust the legs backward and over the head while straightening the arms to a handstand.

e. Tuck the head forward, push away from the bar (stretch) and allow the stretched body to start downward with the feet leading. Spotters will again support the body and lower it as before.

f. The shoulders are ahead (forward) of the bar as the legs start upward, but must be brought back directly over the bar as the handstand is achieved.

g. The "beat" must be very vigorous and a strong push made with the arms. Keep the head up during this phase.

h. When this can be done fairly easily, raise the bar high enough to make the performer jump to reach it. He mounts to a support (kip, back uprise, front pullover), obtains an *undergrasp,* and repeats what he did on the the shoulder high bar.

i. Stay extended (stretch away from bar) during the downward swing.

j. Do not lead with the shoulders. Let the feet lead.

k. As the body passes under the bar, follow the hints found for the "Back Uprise" (No. 15), except that the wrists will have to be snapped forward. Also, do not go into a back hip circle because the hands are still in an *undergrasp.*

Spot: a. Use two people. They spot as directed in hints *a* and *e* above. They stay close, place their near hands on the performer's shoulders *as* he/she kicks up and the far arms under the hips as *soon* as he/she reaches the handstand position. Support as he/she passes beyond the handstand.

b. When on the high bar, be especially alert. If the shoulders lead and he/she is not fully extended, stop the person under the bar.

c. If he/she is in good position, push backward and upward on the abdomen on the way up.

d. If he/she fails to come to a support and starts to swing downward and forward, stop him/her under the bar. One must not swing forward with an undergrasp.

20. **Backward (Back) Three-Quarter Giant Swing**—From a front support with overgrasp cast backward into a near (not quite vertical) handstand, swing downward with stretched body. Continue the swing, passing beneath the bar, moving forward and upward. As the body moves upward, draw it to the bar by moving the arms closer to the body. Circle the body over the bar and return to a front support.

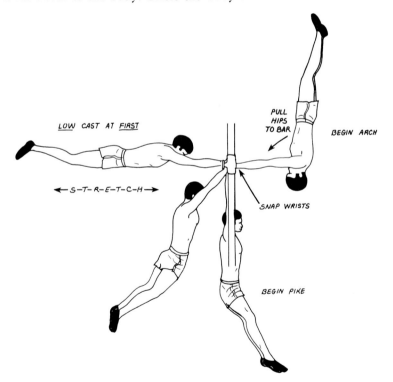

Hints: a. This is essentially, a "Front Pullover" (No. 4) but done with a swing.

b. Try from a swinging hang first, gradually increasing the amount of swing.

c. Drive the legs forward and upward (flex the hips) just after passing under the bar.

d. At the same time, pull with the arms. Keep the eyes fastened on the bar throughout.

e. Just before the body drapes over the bar, snap the wrists to the top (rotate the hands on the bar).

f. As more momentum is provided by a higher swing, the wrist snap becomes more important, more forceful, and earlier.

g. When trying from a support, start with a flat (low) cast. Do not throw to a handstand but *do* stretch away from the bar. The arms, body, and legs should be in a straight line.

h. When working from a big swing, arch the back after flexing the hips. This occurs when the hips are higher than the bar.

i. The wrist snap is executed at the same time and the head is raised.

Spot: a. Two spotters stand on spotting tables (or horses), one on either side of the gymnast.

b. In the early stages, each places his/her hands on the performer's back and hips and lifts.

c. When he/she casts from support, the spotter on the left grasps the students left wrist with the right hand (thumb pointing down) from under the bar. Keep a firm grip on the wrist and use the other hand to push the hips upward. (The other spotter grasps right wrist with left hand.)

d. Shift the hand on the wrist to support performer's thigh as it comes over the bar to keep it from crashing on the bar.

21. **Backward Free Hip Circle**—Basically, this is like the backward hip circle from front support. (No. 10 on low horizontal bar) and should be *learned* on the low bar. It is an advanced form of the movement. Start with a high backward cast of the legs as before. As the body returns to the bar, lay back with the shoulders and circle around the bar *without* touching it with the body. The body should shoot upward toward the ceiling (it can be done to a handstand) before lowering to a front support.

Hints: a. Obtain a "beat" by bending the arms and swinging the legs forward while the shoulders remain forward of the bar.

b. Drive the legs backward and upward while straightening the arms. The shoulders remain forward.

c. As the body returns to the bar, lean backward with the shoulders to begin the rotation around the bar.

d. Slightly flex the hips as they approach the bar and drop them below the bar.

e. As the shoulders drop beneath the bar, the pike increases.

f. As the shoulders begin to rise on the other side, sharply extend the hips upward and throw the head back.

g. At the same time, snap the wrists (rotate the hands on the bar) upward. The arms bend *slightly* to facilitate the wrist snap.

h. Try to force the arms over the head. This "pull" on the bar will shoot the body upward.

   i. The arms remain straight except for the slight bend at the time of the wrist snap.
   j. Keep the shoulders slightly forward of the bar as the straight body lowers to the bar.
   k. Get the concept of a very high underswing from support (No. 2 on low horizontal bar) in your mind.

Spot: a. On the *low* bar stand to the right on the far side of the bar and place your left hand on the right shoulder as it drops under the bar. Pull forward and upward and place your right hand on the buttocks as he/she arches upward. If the arch is too soon, be prepared to catch the body as it descends.
   b. On the *high* bar, stand at either side and be prepared to stop the downward and backward swing directly under the bar if he/she extends too early. Do not let the swing go past the middle because of the overgrasp.

Routines:

Since many of the stunts in the following routines are not listed in the *high* horizontal bar stunts, these stunts will have LHB after their specific number.

Beginning Routine:

Stand slightly to the left (or right) of center, jump to a hang with overgrasp and execute a Front Pullover (No. 4). Continue with an Underswing (No. 8) but do not dismount; maintain the grasp and swing backward in a hang. On the forward swing do one Swinging Turn (No. 5) around the right (or left) arm. Swing forward and do a Knee Swing Up (No. 6) with the left (or right) leg. Take an undergrasp with both hands and execute a Forward Single Knee Circle (No. 7 LHB). Change the right (or left) hand to an overgrasp, support on the right (or left) arm and swing the forward leg back under the left (or right) hand, regrasping in an overgrasp in a front support. Now, Underswing with Half Twist (No. 9, plus see *Note* for No. 14) and swing forward in a hang to a Front Pullover (see hints *a* through e for stunt No. 20) to an immediate Underswing Dismount (No. 8).

Intermediate Routine:

Jump to a hang with an overgrasp and Obtain Swing (No. 10), Kip (No. 11) on the forward swing to a Backward Hip Circle (No. 10 LHB), to a Drop Kip (No. 13), then a Forward Hip Circle (No. 16 LHB) to an Underswing (No. 8, but do not dismount; maintain grasp). Swing backward in a hang to a Back Uprise (No. 15); now Underswing with Half Twist (No. 9, but regrasp with *under-grasp* and keep hold; don't dismount). On the forward swing, flex the hips to bring the straight legs up under the bar between the arms to a Forward Half Seat Circle (No. 17 LHB), to a Forward Seat Circle (No. 18 LHB), then pivot around the left (or right) arm to a front support and Drop Kip (No. 13) to an immediate Straddle Dismount (No. 5 LHB).

26

Balance Beam

Working the balance beam might be described as doing floor exercise on a mat approximately sixteen feet long and four inches wide . . a rather limited area at best! Most of the tumbling, dance, and balance skills which are done on the beam are fundamental floor exercise movements made considerably more difficult on beam by the confinement of the event. In almost every case, these skills should be learned on the floor exercise mat before they are attempted on the balance beam; and they should be mastered on the low beam before graduating to the high beam. A low practice beam is indispensible in a safely conducted class or competitive gymnastics program.

If enough mats and/or crash pads are available it is prudent to build mats up almost as high as the beam on both sides. This is especially wise when working on stunts requiring an inverted or a summersaulting position.

1. **Support Straddle Mount**—Jump to a front support position with hands beside the hips and the arms fully extended. Spread the legs and turn the body to the right, lifting the right leg over the beam to a straddle sitting position. Release the left hand and place it opposite the right hand on the left side of the beam.

2. **Squat Mount**—Place a mounting board at right angles to the beam. Stand on the board with the hands across the top of the beam. Bounce upward, press down against the beam to raise the hips as high as possible. Then bend the knees and pull them into the chest between the arms to arrive in a squat stand. Do not bend the arms and keep the shoulders forward until the feet get to the beam. Do not look down.

Spot: The spotter stands on the far side of the beam, directly in front. He supports the performer's upper arms with both hands.

3. **Straddle Mount**—Begin as for the previous stunt and bounce upward; however, do not bend the knees. Instead, spread the legs as wide as you can and bring the feet to the beam outside the arms.

   Spot: Stand at the other side of the beam facing the gymnast and place one hand in front of each shoulder to prevent falling forward.

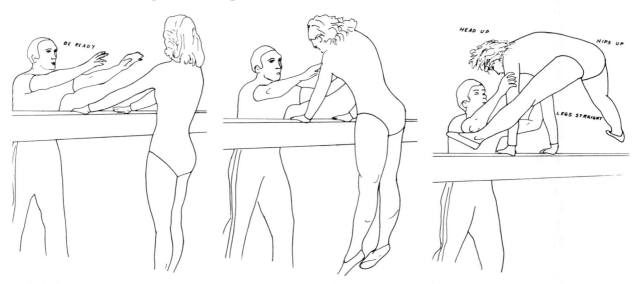

4. **Walking on Beam**—When walking on the beam stand straight, keep the head aligned with the body, and focus your eyes on the end of the beam. With each step point the foot to the side of the beam down toward the floor, then place it on the beam turned slightly outward. Keep the arms extended straight out to the side.

5. **Walking Backward on Beam**—As in walking forward, focus your eyes on the end of the beam and stand upright. Since you cannot see the beam with each step, feel it with the balls of your feet. It also helps to position the toes on the outside of the beam as the foot is securely placed across the beam.

6. **Walking with Dip Step**—Walk as you would normally walk, but bend the supporting leg to approximately 90° with each step. Extend the other leg and swing it forward with each step.

7. **Chassé**—Step forward with the right leg straight, weight on the left leg and left foot turned slightly to the left. Shift the weight to the right leg, push with the right leg swinging it forward again, and bring the left leg forward to replace the right leg. Continue this movement down the beam. (One leg "chases" the other.)

8. **One Half Turn (180°)**—From a walking step with one leg forward, rise to the toes of both feet and turn on the balls of the feet in the direction of the back leg. Turn 180°, then lower from the toes. Keep your arms extended over your head, or out to the side (for better balance).

9. **Arabesque**—Step forward on one leg and raise the other leg to the rear as high as possible without bending at the knee. Arch the back, lift the head, and extend the arms to the sids.
   Note: Try several different arm positions. Experiment to find your favorite position.

10. **Squat Turn**—This stunt is similar to the previous turn except that it is done from a squat position. Begin standing at the middle of the beam with one leg in front of the other. Slowly lower to a squat support with the arms extended to the side, then pivot on the balls of the feet to complete the 180° turn.

11. **Forward Roll**—Standing upright with arms extended overhead, bend forward at the waist keeping the hips well raised. Grasp the beam with one hand on each side of the beam as you lower the upper body by bending the arms. Press the head down to the chest, raise the hips and duck the head under to roll across the back of the head, neck, and rounded back. Pull the knees to the chest in a tucked position and roll forward. Complete the move by rolling to one leg, allowing the other leg to extend down beside the beam and come to a stand on the supporting leg.
    Spot: The spotter stands to the side of the low beam, supporting the hips as she rolls forward. Then grasp the near arm for support as she completes the stunt.

12. **Forward Roll Mount**—This mount is done from the end of the beam with the aid of a Reuther board. Take several running steps forward, bounce on the board, and at the same time place the hands on the end of the beam (on top with one hand on each side). Push down with the arms, duck the head as the hips rise overhead, and do a forward roll as you would on the mats.

Note: Maintain a grasp on the beam as long as possible for better balance.

This stunt may be completed in several different ways. You can finish in a sitting position—continue rolling forward to a stand—or straddle roll forward to a squat.

Spot: Spotter stands beside the beam facing the performer (see picture). Reach across the beam and grasp both hips as the gymnast begins to duck her head. Guide the hips downward to control the movement. You may then reach under the beam to help with the balance after the roll is completed.

13. **Backward Roll**—Assume a supine position grasping the beam with the hands beside the ears. Keep the elbows in and press the palms to the side of the beam. Raise the legs by piking at the waist. Bring the legs back until they touch the beam behind the head, then bend the knees, tuck and come to a squat stand to complete the stunt.

Spot: Stand to the right side at the performer's hips and reach across under her left hip with your right hand. Place your other hand under her right hip. Support both hips as she raises the legs up and over the top of the roll.

14. **Cartwheel (Roundoff) Dismount**—Before attempting to learn this skill on the beam master it first on the mats, i.e. do not try a cartwheel dismount off the beam until you can do a good cartwheel on the floor!

Stand one step back from the end of the beam leaving just enough room for the hands on the beam. Throw the arms down, one in front of the other, and simultaneously kick the back leg and push with the front leg to provide enough momentum to clear the end of the beam as you cartwheel over to land on the mat at the end of the beam. You may execute a 1/8 turn to land facing the end of the beam for better balance (roundoff).

Hint: As your hands contact the beam, push down hard to keep the straight angle between the arms and the trunk. Try to prevent the shoulders from sagging forward.

Spot: Spot as for the cartwheel on the floor.

15. **Straddle Swing to Squat**—Although this is a basic move in itself, it is also a leadup skill for several other more advanced moves including the straddle roll to handstand and the straddle forward roll.

Sit in a straddle position on the beam with the hands on the sides of the beam (palms facing in). Raise the legs quickly, then rock them downward and drive the heels up in back as you push down against the beam with the hands. When the hips are off the bar, pull the knees into the chest and place the feet on the beam between the arms.

Spot: The spotter stands at either side with one hand on the shoulder and the other hand lifting the near thigh of the gymnast.

16. **Forward Roll—Straddle Swing to Squat**—This is the combination of the forward roll (described earlier) with the previous stunt (straddle swing to squat).

Do the forward roll as previously described except do not bend the knees as you pass over the top of the roll. Instead, keep the legs straight throughout, but spread them wide before beginning the downswing (when upside down). Then reach forward to place the hands between the legs for the swing to a squat.

17. **Handstand on Beam**—Even the beginner can practice learning the handstand on a low beam. It is the most important of all gymnastics moves and one that should be practiced frequently. Practicing on a low beam allows greater safety and more repetitions.

   Stand to the side facing the beam with both hands on the beam at about shoulder width. Practice bouncing upward off both feet, raising the hips as high as possible, and then raising the heels to an extended handstand position. If you do not make it all the way up, simply return to the starting position and try again. If you over-turn (go too far) pivot on one hand and do a roundoff to the mat on the other side.

   Hint: If you have difficulty bouncing off both feet and getting the hips up, try kicking to the handstand with one leg forward (to push) and the other in back (to kick).

   Spot: The spotter stands at the other side of the beam to prevent over rotation. He should be at the side opposite the way you twist on the roundoff so as to avoid getting hit if the stunt is overturned.

18. **Stride Leap** *(baby split leap)*—When the stride leap is done to its fullest and the gymnast arrives at a full splits position in the air, (see picture) it becomes a split leap. This is a more advanced move and takes considerable practice. Begin slowly and continue gaining height as you gain confidence.

From a regular walking step with the arms extended to the side, swing the back leg forward and push off the supporting leg. Keep both legs straight while they are in the air and bend only as you land on the front foot.

19. **Combinations**
  1. Squat mount—turn and stand—step forward to chassé—squat turn and stand to—regular turn—step forward to—cartwheel dismount.
  2. Straddle mount—turn to splits—turn to stand—chassé and bring the back leg forward to—forward roll—straddle to squat stand—step to stride leap—and cartwheel dismount.

27

Uneven Parallel Bars

This is a woman's and girls event but boys can work it as well. As indicated in the Low Horizontal Bar (Chapter 24) the low bar skills for the unevens could be learned on a horizontal bar if the unevens are not available.

Most of this work is done on the low bar because less strength and skill are required than when working on the high bar or transferring from one to the other. Of course, some high bar work and transferring is included but it should be understood that these skills can be done on both bars.

The low bar height should be approximately chest high. The grasp is usually the "hook" grasp (thumbs on same side of bar as fingers) and an undergrasp is used for forward revolving work while an uppergrasp is required for circling backward.

1. **Single Leg Cuts from Front to Rear Support**—Jump to a front support position with arms fully extended and the bar resting comfortably at the thighs. Lean on the left arm, push off from the right and bring the extended right leg forward under the right hand to rest in a straddle support. The right hand regrasps as soon as the leg passes. Then repeat the procedure with the other leg and end up in a rear support position with the head up and the back arched.

2. **Cast**—Begin in a front support position on top of the bar. Pike the body around the bar, then vigorously extend by driving the heels upward and pushing down against the bar with the arms. Continue pushing and release the hands to land on the mat facing the bar.

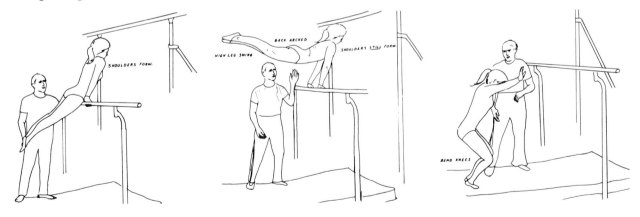

3. **Pull Over**—Stand facing the bar with the arms extended forward and the hands in an over grip. One leg is beneath the bar and the other is under the body. Kick the rear leg forward and jump with the other leg joining it and simultaneously pull the hips to the bar as you circle upward. Continue pulling until you arrive in a front support position on top of the bar.

Spot: The spotter stands in front of the bar to the performer's right side. He reaches under the bar with his left arm to support and lifts her shoulder. As her legs come upward to the bar, he pushes up with his right hand under her hips to help complete the stunt.

4. **Back Hip Circle**—Jump to a support, hands in an uppergrasp, and swing the legs backward for momentum. Bring the body back to the bar and circle around it (bar at the hips) and return to a front support position. Drop to a stand.

 Spot: From the right side reach under the bar with the left hand and place it on his/her hips as they come to the bar. Pull forward and keep the performer close to the bar.

5. **Underswing—from a Stand**—From a side stand frontways with the hands in an uppergrasp on the bar, take a slight jump, and bring the thighs to the bar. At the same time, lean backward with the head and shoulders and allow the hips to swing forward and upward. As the hips move forward, extend the legs upward and forward on the far side of the bar by arching the back. The shoulders and head follow the path of the legs and hips and the hands release the bar before the feet complete the arc to the floor. Land in a side stand rearways. Repeat the stunt with the addition of a half twist while the body is in the air. Land in a side stand frontways.

 Hints: a. Stand with the feet fairly close to the bar. The body should be leaning backward when the arms are straight. Keep the hips extended.
 b. Push off from the feet and drop straight backward with the shoulders as the thighs are brought to the bar.
 c. *Keep the arms straight.* Bending the arms may cause you to hit your head on the bar.
 d. Bear downward with the arms to bring the hips close to the bar. The body should be almost horizontal. Do *not* drop the hips.
 e. Drop the head backward as you arch the back.
 f. A backward thrust with the arms as the back arches will give greater height and distance.
 g. Release the hands as the thrust is made and the arms are as far back as they can go.

Spot: a. Stand in front of the bar to the performer's right and reach under the bar to grasp her right wrist with your left hand (palm facing downward).

       b. Pull forward on her wrist as she brings her legs toward the bar.

       c. Place your right arm under her lower back and lift upward as she arches her back.

       d. Maintain the grip on the right wrist to prevent her falling forward as she lands.

Note: A towel or sponge rubber pad can be taped to the bar between the hands as a safety precaution to prevent injury in case the arms bend and the head hits.

6. **Underswing—from Support**—Begin in front support position on top of the bar. Slowly lean rearward, keeping the arms straight and as the shoulders begin to drop, pull the hips to the bar. Arch the back and pull backward with the arms to finish as in the previous stunt.

    Spot: The spotter stands behind the bar to the performer's left side. His right hand is behind shoulder and his left hand is at the near hip of the performer. With this position of the hands he guides the performer through the movement. A second spotter may be used in front of the bar to prevent over-rotation.

    Note: It is a good safety precaution to tape a piece of foam rubber around the bar between the hands in case the gymnast should inadvertently hit the bar with his/her head.

7. **Underswing with One-Half Twist**—Execute as if to do the underswing but as you begin the forward flight, turn the head to look over one shoulder. Pull with the arms behind the head and turn the hips in the same direction. Release the opposite hand to complete the turn and land facing the bar.

    Spot: The spotter stands in front of the bar at the side to which the performer will turn. He has both arms at the back of the performer so that the body is cradled and supported at the completion of the turn.

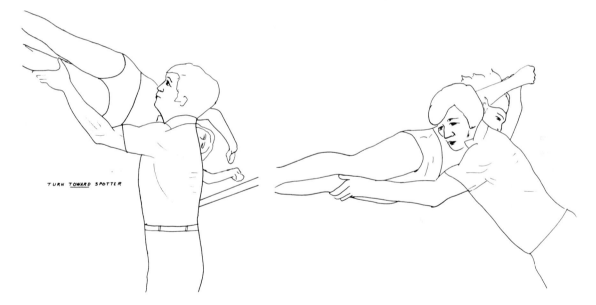

TURN TOWARD SPOTTER

8. **Single Leg Swing Up**—This stunt can be used as an elementary mount or a separate stunt. Raise the bar to shoulder height and *begin by running forward,* bent knees but arms straight. At the front of the swing bring one leg under the bar between the arms and hook it on the bar. Swing the other leg downward and back, pulling with the arms and finish in a straddle support position on the bar.

    Hint: Try to keep the arms extended and in line with the body as you bring the leg to hook the bar. Do *not* allow the head to go back or drop the shoulders.

9. **Single Leg Circle Forward**—Jump to a support and place the left leg over the bar between the hands. Sit on the left thigh. The hands are in an *undergrasp.* Lean forward, circle under the bar supported by

the hands and the left knee and return to a seat on the left thigh. Swing the right leg over the bar and dismount with a quarter turn left to a cross stand left.

Hints: a. Raise the hips (take the weight on the arms) and hook the left knee when leaning forward.
  b. Tuck the head to the chest.
  c. Bend the arms slightly.
  d. Swing the right leg upward and forward as the circling begins.
  e. Then whip the right leg downward and backward very vigorously.
  f. Flex the arms slightly and lean forward when coming up again.
  g. Also, move the bar from the knee back to the thigh.

Spot: a. Stand on the *near* side of the bar to the performer's left. Reach under the bar to grasp her left wrist with your left hand (knuckles toward you).
  b. Reach under the bar with the right hand too (palm turned toward you) and place it on her left knee as she raises and leans forward. Pull back with your right hand to help her hook the knee.
  c. Pull downward and toward you as she circles under the bar and shift your right hand to her left upper arm as she comes around to help lift her up to the seat on the left thigh.

10. **Mill Circle**—Begin in a forward split position with the hands in an undergrip. Lift the body by pressing down with the arms. Lean forward with a straight upper body, push the chin out and rotate forward with the bar pressed against the front of the rear leg. From the bottom of the circle as you begin to rise, push the front leg against the bar, pike at the waist, and pull down against the bar. Return to the beginning position.

Hint: Remember—in any movement circling the bar you gain momentum by lengthening the body as you swing down and shortening the body as you swing upward against gravity.

11. **Sole Circle Underswing**—With the bar at chest height grasp the bar in an over grip and begin at an extended arms length away. Jump upward, spread the legs and place them outside the hands on the bar. Keep the arms and legs straight as you swing downward. As you begin the upswing pull the arms behind the head as if to throw the bar rearward, release the feet from the bar and extend the body. Finish as for a regular underswing.

Note: This stunt can also be done with the legs together. It is slightly more difficult this way, but it is easier to spot.

Spot: Two spotters are necessary for this stunt. The first spotter stands approximately five feet in front of the bar to prevent over rotation. The primary spotter is on the other side in front but outside the performer's legs. The near arm goes to the performer's shoulder and the far arm

goes under his/her near hip. The spotter lifts with both arms and follows the performer through the complete movement.

12. **Sole Circle Underswing with One Half Twist**—This stunt is identical to the previous stunt except that in beginning the upswing, look over the shoulder and turn the hips to complete the turn.

 Spot: Spot as for the previous stunt but make sure the close spotter is at the side in the direction of the turn. That is, if the gymnast turns to the left the close spotter should be to her left. Spot as for the previous stunt and the performer will turn into your arms.

13. **Penny Flip (Hock Swing) Dismount**—Begin by hanging by both legs below the bar. Swing back and forth until the swing is approximately level with the bar. Then, at the top of a predetermined swing (front), release both legs and drop to a stand in front of the bar.

 Hint: Learn this stunt with the help of a spotter. The spotter stands in front and to the left side of the bar. He/she assists with the swing by pushing with the left hand against the performer's chest. The other hand reaches over the bar and presses down against the gymnast's legs to insure that they do not slip from the bar. On a count of three—on the front swing— the legs are released and the stunt completed.

14. **Cast to Single Leg Squat Through**—Cast upward from a front support position and as the hips rise bend one leg at the knee and pull it down and between the arms to a straddle support position.

    Spot: Determine which leg will squat through and stand in front of the bar on the opposite side. Reach under the bar with the near arm and help raise the hips. The front hand is at the performer's shoulder to keep her from falling forward.

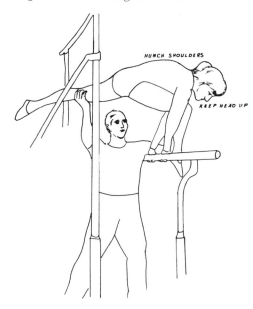

15. **Front Hip Circle**—Jump to a front support with the hands in an uppergrasp. (This is contrary to the general rule of undergrasp for forward circling stunts.) Raise the hips slightly so the bar rests low on the thighs. Lean forward and circle around the bar, returning to a front support position.

    Hints: a. Lean forward keeping the body arched. (The legs rise behind.)

    b. The arms must be straight.

    c. Flex at the hips and tuck the head forward as the straight body passes the horizontal plane. This must be done very fast. Think of trying to put your head on your knees.

    d. As the head and shoulders pass under the bar, shift the wrists forward so the hands will come to the top of the bar. The legs are still on top of the bar when the wrists shift.

    e. The arms bend slightly as the body comes up.

    f. Maintain a backward pressure with the arms to hold the thighs against the bars.

    g. Finish with a nice backward and upward swing of the legs.

    Spot: a. Stand on the *near* side and reach under the bar (bend the knees if necessary) to place your arm across the performer's back as she bends forward. Pull her around and then place the other hand on her back and lift upward.

    b. Gradually decrease the assistance.

16. **Kip** (running)—Raise the bar to shoulder height and stand behind the bar at arms length. Keep the arms straight as you run forward (knees bent). Run forward until the body is fully extended, then pike at the waist and bring the shins to the bar. Swing to the rear in this position, extend the body, and press down against the bar to arrive in a front support on top of the bar.

    Spot: The spotter stands in front of the bar to the left side. As the gymnast runs forward the spotter places his right hand behind the left shoulder and his left arm under the hips. He rides forward then backward in this position and lifts to help complete the stunt.

16. (a) **Glide Kip**— This stunt is similar to but more difficult than the previous stunt. Stand facing the bar just over an arm's length away. Jump upward off both feet and at the same time reach forward and grab the bar in an overgrip. As you begin to glide forward keep your feet as close to the mat as you can *without* touching. Stretch to an arched position at the front of the swing, then pike at the waist and bring the shins to the bar. Continue the kip as you did in the previous stunt.

    Note: At the front of the swing the body should be in a straight line from the hands to the toes. A slight arch in front will make it easier to pull the legs into a pike.

    Spot: Spotter stands to the side of the performer in front of the bar. Her/his near arm supports the near arm of the performer and his/her far arm is placed under the performer's near thigh. The spotter guides the kip movement forward, then lifts as the performer begins to pike and carries the gymnast through the movement.

17. **Drop Kip**—From a front support position with straight arms, slowly drop rearward holding the bar to the body. The bar slides from the waist to the shins as you swing forward under the bar. Maintain this position as you swing forward, then rearward, and complete the skill as in the previous stunt.

    Spot: Spot as for the previous stunt except that you stand behind the bar and guide the gymnast through the range of motion.

Combinations:

    a. Cast—single leg squat through—single leg circle forward.

    b. Running single leg swing up—mill circle—cut rear leg forward.

    c. Front pull over—back hip circle—drop kip—underswing dismount.

    d. Running kip—front hip circle—cast to—back hip circle—drop kip—cast to straddle sole circle underswing dismount.

18. **Sole Circle**—Cast upward raising the hips as high as possible and bring the straight legs down between the arms to rest on the bar. Fall backward and allow the momentum to carry you 360 degrees around the bar.

    Note: The stunt can also be done in a straddle position. It may be easier this way, but it is considerably more difficult to spot.

    Spot: Use two spotters—one on each side in front of the bar. Both spotters reach under the bar and grasp the wrists of the performer. Then, as she begins to rise, reach in with the other hand and push up against the gymnast's chest to help her complete the stunt.

19. **Sole Circle Dismount**—Instead of riding to the top of the bar (360°) as in the sole circle, the gymnast releases the bar just before arriving at the top and jumps upward and forward to land in front of the bar. This can be done with the legs together or apart and outside the hands.

    Spot: Spot by grasping upper arm.

20. **Front Seat Circle**—Take a rear support position with the hands in an under grip. Press down on the bar raising the hips and fall forward in a tight piked body position. Maintain this position on the downswing but as you begin to rise from the bottom, pull down against the bar and extend the hips to finish in a rear support position.

    Hint: Lift the hips as high as possible to begin the downswing and try to establish a straight line between the arms and back.

    Spot: One spotter is in front of the bar supporting the chest. Spotters stand behind the bar, one on each side, reaching under with the near hand and grasping the gymnast's wrist (thumbs down). As the gymnast rotates down and begins the upswing, the spotter places his other hand under the back and helps him/her rise to the top of the bar.

Transitional Moves from Bar to Bar

21. **Fake Kip**—Begin sitting on the low bar in an arched position, reaching back and grasping the top bar. Bring one shin up to the top bar keeping it straight and at the same time bend the other leg bringing the bottom of the foot up on the lower bar. Simultaneously, push with the lower leg, extend the upper leg along the top bar, and pull upward with the arms bringing the top bar to your waist. Finish the stunt in a front support on the top bar.

    Hints: To learn the "kipping" action, practice the movement of extending the bottom leg and pulling upward *without* pushing off the lower leg. Once the rhythm of the movement has been learned this will help in learning the more advanced kips.

    Spot: The spotter stands under and between the bars with hands under the thigh and hips of the performer. Push upward as the gymnast kips, then provide support for balance on the top bar.

22. **Beat Swing for Stomach Wrap**—This is not a stunt in itself, but it is an important fundamental skill for several more advanced movements. Take a front support position on the low bar facing the top bar. Reach up and grasp the top bar with both hands in an overgrip. Pike slightly around the low bar, then quickly extend the heels upward. This will cause you to rise off the bar. Maintain your grasp of the top bar, and pike slightly as you return to the bar. This pike will cushion the blow to the abdomen —it will also put you in a slight pike ready to do it over again. Continue until you can get considerable height off the bar.

    Spot: No spot is necessary for this stunt.

23. **Beat Swing to Back Hip Circle**—This is the same as the previous skill except that as you return to the bar, release the hands, bring them to your sides on the bar, and use the momentum to do the back hip circle.

    Spot: The spotter stands under and between the bars facing the performer's right side. The spotter's left hand goes to the back, right hand under the near thigh. Press the performer's body into the bar as he/she does the circling.

24. **Stomach Wrap**—The previous skill is a leadup for this stunt and it is similar except that for the "wrap" you begin by hanging from the high bar while facing the low bar. Take several practice swings, piking as your hips contact the bar. When this can be done smoothly with a good swing simply release the hands as you touch the bar with your abdomen and bring them to low bar beside hips. The momentum from the swing will allow you to rotate around the bar in the back hip circle position.

    Note: Spend considerable time in developing swing from the "beat swing." The more swing you have the easier the stunt will be. The stunt is generally done from a cast off the top bar. This makes the stunt easier, but it also makes it more dangerous. Proceed cautiously!!

    Spot: Spot as for the previous stunt.

25. **Underswing One-Half Twist to Wrap**—From a front support position on the high bar facing the low bar slowly allow the shoulders to drop backwards and at the same time pike at the waist bringing the legs up in front of the bar. As you reach the bottom of the bar turn to one side (left) and release the other hand (right). Extend the body outward as you complete the turn and regrasp the right hand in a mixed grip to the right of the left hand. As you drop to the lower bar continue the extension of the body until you contact the lower bar. Then, pike and do a back hip circle, with hands beside hips in overgrip.

   Hints: Practice the underswing with 1/2 twist on the low bar before attempting this stunt.

   Spot: Two spotters are required for learning this skill. The spotters stand in front of the lower bar facing each other at a position where the performer will land on the lower bar between them. Spotters reach up and lower the performer to the lower bar as she/he begins to descend. Initially the spotters bring the student to a complete halt on the low bar. Then, gradually allow more momentum until there is enough to do the back hip circle.

26. **Hip Pull Over** *(from low to high bar)*—Sit on the low bar with your back to the high bar. Reach up and grasp the high bar in an overgrip and at the same time flex one leg and bring that foot up to the low bar. Push down against the low bar with the flexed leg, and keeping the other leg extended, kick it upward toward the high bar. At the same time pull the high bar in and toward the waist with the arms. Finish in a front support on the top bar.

   Spot: The spotter stands under the high bar facing the gymnast. In spotting from the performer's right side the spotter holds the near upper arm with her/his left hand. The spotter's other hand goes under the lower back and lifts upward as the gymnast kicks.

27. **Underswing Dismount from High Bar** *(over lower bar)*—This stunt is the same as the underswing dismount from support which was described earlier except that it is done from the high bar. Begin in a front support position on the high bar facing the lower bar. Keeping the arms straight slowly allow the shoulders to begin falling rearward and at the same time pike and bring the legs (shins) up to the bar As you reach the bottom of the swing pull evenly with both arms, extend at the hips, and arch over the lower bar.

   Note: The spotting is the same as previously described except that the spotter stands between the bars and places both hands on the performer's back as he/she extends over the low bar. Two spotters may be used. If so, the second spotter stands in front of the low bar on the opposite side from the other spotter. This second spotter spots the landing by extending one arm in front and the other arm in back of the gymnast as she/he clears the low bar.

28

Trampoline

The trampoline is probably the most popular piece of apparatus in the eyes of participants and one of the most questioned on the part of uninitiated administrators. Potentially, the trampoline is dangerous, and strict adherence to safety rules and precautions are absolutely necessary. If the trampoline is treated with respect, however, it is reasonably safe and takes its place as a valuable and enjoyable part of the complete gymnastics picture.

Recently trampolining has faced a lot of unfavorable publicity which has caused many persons to discontinue the activity. The first problem arose from increased insurance rates for liability coverage for programs that included trampoline work. Then the American Academy for Pediatrics published a statement recommending that the trampoline be banned from competitive sport *and* from all physical education programs because of the number of quadriplegia cases resulting from trampoline accidents.

In 1905 President Theodore Roosevelt considered the proscription of football because of the violence, injury, and death connected with the game. As a result, those interested in continuing football introduced rules, regulations, and safety equipment that greatly reduced (but didn't eliminate) the dangers of playing the game. Tremendous numbers of automobile accidents occur every day. The loss in lives and property is extremely high. Yet nobody suggests banning cars or stopping football.

No one would advocate an activity that is sure to result in injury. Trampolining can be reasonably safe. Many schools have conducted programs for thousands of man hours of participation without a single major injury. Of course, this does not include sprained ankles and scraped elbows and knees. But remember, its possible to get the same results from stepping off a curb or slipping on a banana peel.

It isn't the trampoline itself that is dangerous; it is the unsafe practices that are often permitted because of lack of knowledge or because of indifference. As stated earlier, when the prescribed safety rules, regulations, and conditions are strictly adhered to, the trampoline can and should be used in all physical education programs.

It should be emphasized that the American Academy of Pediatrics, when confronted with the above argument by the AAHPER did agree that the use of the trampoline in well conducted and supervised programs did *not* constitute an *unreasonable* risk of serious injury.

Special Precautions for Trampoline

Spotting on the trampoline differs from spotting for other events. For the most part, trampoline spotters are not in actual contact with the performers. Another difference is in the number. For high school competition, a minimum of four and a maximum of six is required. When four are used, one should be at each side and end of the trampoline, and for six, two should be at each side. Some teachers advocate more than six for class purposes if they are available. However, too many can get into each others way. Also, when spotters are too close together, sometimes no one will take the initiative to spot, expecting the one next to him to do it. All spotters must remain constantly alert, ready to move as needed in order to support or catch a performer who is falling from the trampoline.

The quintessence of trampoline spotting is to watch every move of the trampolinist (especially when he/she is in the air) to determine if he is off balance and if he is, to decide which way he is apt to go when he lands. In other words, it is imperative to *anticipate* the probable trajectory and station oneself at the proper point, ready to support the performer. A good spotter will actually foresee a bad bounce and act accordingly.

In addition to general spotting there is specific spotting, both by hand and by using an overhead belt, for special stunts. This spotting will be dealt with in a special section in connection with the stunts described later.

The best safety practice is rigid adherence to a strict order of progression and sufficient practice of each of the basic stunts to assure basic control so that no one will fall off the trampoline. There is a natural tendency for participants to try to go as high as they can while bouncing. This inclination must be kept under control until the time comes when the performers can work without loss of balance and without drifting away from the center of the bed while bouncing at a moderate height.

Mats are now required on the floor all around the trampoline during competition. It is a good idea to do the same thing for class use of the trampoline as well.

Spotting tables may be used. They should be about four feet long, three feet wide, and forty-two inches high for the large trampoline and thirty-nine inches high for the smaller one. These tables can be easily and inexpensively made from one-inch pipe covered with three-quarter inch plywood. They will serve not only as fine spotting stations but can also expedite quick exchanges of performers.

Since mat burns on knees and elbows are frequently "acquired" by beginners, it is a good idea for the class members to wear sweat suits. This suit should not be loose and baggy. If sweat suits are not available, the teacher might well keep a good supply of Band-Aids in his pocket!

Trampoline work requires a somewhat different type of organization than that used for the other events. The usual procedure is to have a student try a stunt once or twice before he is followed by the next squad member. On the trampoline it is recommended that quite a number of repetitions be allowed before giving way to the next participant. Take care, however, that not too long a period is permitted without a change. For most of the beginning material a time limit of about one minute per individual is best. If a longer period is allowed, the performer becomes too tired. In addition, if the period is longer, there is too much sustained inactivity for the remainder of the squad members. If each person gets five minutes at a time, the last member of a squad of six will have to stand and wait for twenty-five minutes before getting the first and only chance to bounce. It is better to give individuals five chances of one minute each. Use a stopwatch to keep from giving some too long a time and others too short. Have one of the class members check on the time so that you will be free to supervise the work.

Set up a definite rotation in each squad so that no time is lost in changing participants. For elementary youngsters a stool can be provided at one end to aid and speed up their mounting to the bed. As soon as the signl to change is given, the next person should be ready to go. Caution students, however, not to get on before their predecessor stops bouncing. When dismounting, they must not *jump* from the bed. Their bodies by this time will have become conditioned to a surface that gives. When leaping onto the unyielding surface of the floor, the shock is sometimes unexpected and can cause injury. To prove that the body quickly becomes accustomed to the resilient surface of the bed, suggest that immediately after each one dismounts carefully, he try to jump from the floor as he had been doing on the bed. The unexpected feeling connected with this should convince the students that it would be unwise to jump off the trampoline. In dismounting, a hand should be placed on the frame before carefully dropping off.

Learn the stunts first from a stand. Then try a little jump before doing the stunt and return to the feet. Next, see if the jump can be maintained after landing on the feet. When a number of repetitions of the stunt can be done with two or three bounces between, try a series of stunts with only one intermediate foot position. For example, from a bounce, drop to the seat, to the feet, to the seat, and to the feet.

After several of the beginning stunts have been learned in a series (one foot position between each trick), it is wise to put two, three, or more of the stunts into a little sequence or routine. This creates a greater challenge, involves quick thinking, requires (and develops) better control and body position and is more fun. Also, it keeps class members interested in the simpler stunts for a longer period of time and this practice will satisfy the impatient ones who say, "I've learned that, now let's do something harder." Actually, the combinations increase the number of safe, beginning activities that can be presented to the beginning pupils and will allow them to become more familiar with trampoline work before going on to more advanced work. Another device to lengthen the time spent on "easy" material is the game of *Add One* which is explained in the chapter on games (Chapter 9). This game adds the fun and thrill of competition to the learning of the stunts and their combinations.

When starting to work on the trampoline, it is a good practice to walk around on the edge of the bed to get the feel of its giving underfoot. Then go to the center of the bed (where the two lines cross) and stand with the feet about shoulder width apart and the eyes focused on the edge of the bed. Now begin bouncing up and down with the arms held loosely at the sides without allowing the feet to *leave* the bed. In other words, *ride* the bed up and down. Keep the body loose and relaxed rather than tense and stiff. This preliminary work should be done for control and confidence before starting with Stunt No. 1.

There are several sizes, styles, and price ranges of trampolines manufactured by a number of good, reputable equipment companies. It is suggested that for high schools, the large (10′ x 17′ frame) trampoline be used while the smaller (9′ x 15′ frame) be used for junior high and elementary schools. In either case, a web bed is recommended over the solid canvas or solid nylon bed. Though it is more expensive, the action of the web bed is so superior (it actually creates a softer landing surface due to the lessened wind resistance which results from the holes in the bed) that it is well worth the added cost. The suspension system—either exercise cable (rubber cords) or springs—is an individual matter. The springs are less expensive and are quite satisfactory. In fact, they are required in most competition.

1. **Straight Jump**—Start by rising on the toes and lifting the head and chest (stretch upward) as the arms are brought slightly upward in a forward and sideward direction. Follow this movement immediately by suddenly bending the knees and leaning slightly forward from the hips as the arms thrust backward and downward in a circling motion. This movement depresses the bed and as the bed rebounds, forcibly extend the knees and ankles and circle the arms upward as the body stretches upward. Circle the arms downward as the body descends and bend the knees slightly as the feet contact the mat. As the bottom of the descent is reached, start the upward movement as before.

   Hints: The following hints are general and pertain to the bouncing for all stunts. If deviations are recommended for a specific stunt, the fact will be noted in the hints for that stunt.

   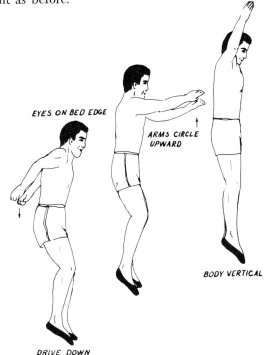

   a. Keep the feet comfortably spread (about shoulder width) when landing.
   b. Keep the head up. The eyes should focus on the edge of the bed. Do *not* look at the feet.
   c. Keep the body relaxed during the flight and not tight and tense.
   d. Keep the body in a straight, vertical alignment.
   e. Bring the feet together in the ascent and spread them again just before landing.
   f. Circle the arms upward on the ascent and downward on the descent. The timing of the arm movement is very important and should be smooth and continuous.
   g. Drive the arms downward forcibly as contact with the bed is made to further depress the bed.

h. Bounce in the center of the bed. Use the "Break Bounce" (see No. 2) if the body drifts away from the center.

i. BOUNCE AT A MODERATE HEIGHT UNTIL GOOD CONTROL OF THE BODY IN FLIGHT IS ACHIEVED.

Spot: The following spotting hints are general and pertain to spotting all stunts. Where "extra" spotting is required or suggested, it will be noted specifically.

   a. At least four spotters are needed (one to each side and to each end). If six are available the extra two should be responsible for one-half of each of the sides.

   b. If more than seven are working on one trampoline (one performer and six spotters), the others should keep back. When too many are around, there is the danger of everyone expecting the "other fellow" to do the spotting and consequently no one does.

   c. The four (or six) spotters must remain alert and keep their eyes on the performer at all times. Even before he starts to bounce off they should be able to anticipate his direction from his body position while in the air.

   d. In most instances, all that will be necessary is to put the hands up and brace the person to keep him from falling off.

   e. In some cases the person may be high in the air coming toward the spotter. The spotter must *remain calm, watch* the performer for the best place to grab, push, or hold, and then do whatever has to be done. He must resist the temptation to close the eyes or duck.

   f. The performer must cooperate by making as few movements as possible. THE MORE ONE KICKS AND SQUIRMS, THE HARDER IT BECOMES FOR THE SPOTTERS.

2. **Break Bounce**—This is not actually a stunt, but rather a safety device used to "kill" or stop an off-balance bounce. It should be practiced often in the early stages of trampolining so that it can be used when needed.

   Bounce as in the "Straight Jump" (No. 1) and after three or four bounces, bend the knees sharply as the feet contact the bed on the descent. This will absorb the momentum and kill the bounce.

   Hints: a. As the knees bend, lean forward slightly from the waist.

   b. At the same time, place the arms sideward and slightly forward for balance.

   c. Be sure to keep the head up.

3. **Tuck Jump**—Start with two or three straight jumps, then as the body ascends, draw the knees up toward the chest and grasp the shins with the hands. As the body descends, release and lower the legs and resume bouncing. As proficiency is gained, try tucking every other bounce and finally on every bounce.

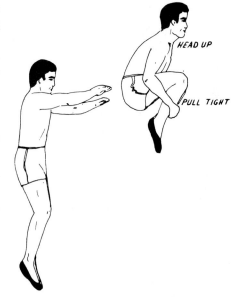

   Hints: a. Keep the back fairly erect. Don't lean forward.

   b. Keep the head up.

   c. Bring the knees up as the arms swing upward for the ascent.

   d. Release the legs and straighten them downward at the peak of the jump.

   e. As the legs straighten, swing the arms downward too.

4. **Pike Jump**—Again take two or three straight jumps, then as the body ascends, flex the hips (bring the legs up so that they are approximately parallel to the bed) to touch the toes with the hands. The legs may either be spread or together. Lower the legs as the body descends and rebound. As proficiency is gained, pike every other bounce and then every bounce.

HEAD UP

LEGS PARALLEL

EARLY LEG LIFT

Hints: a. Keep the head up and the back erect.
   b. Bend the knees at first if necessary, but try to keep them straight.
   c. Start the leg lift as soon as the ascent begins and combine it with the arm lift.

Extra—Alternate pike and tuck jumps without intermediate bounces.

5. **Seat Drop**—On the way up, begin flexing the hips to raise the legs. Drop to a sitting position on the bed and rebound again to a stand.

Hints: a. At first, start from a stand and keep the legs loose and relaxed, the legs slightly bent as they are raised. (If legs are kept rigid and heels hit bed first, body will be thrown backward.)
   b. The seat should land exactly where the feet had been.
   c. The heels, seat, and hands should hit the bed at the same time.
   d. The hands land beside and slightly behind the hips with the fingers pointing *forward*.
   e. Allow a very slight backward lean of the upper body.
   f. Push with the hands as the rebound begins.
   g. At the same time, bring the legs down.
   h. After a few trials from a stand, try it from a low bounce.
   i. As proficiency is gained, keep the legs straight and together.
   j. When returning to the feet from the seat, the arms should be driving downward so that they can lift for the ascent.
   k. When good, solid, controlled seat drops are achieved, try doing them in series. (Seat, feet, seat, feet, etc.)

NOT YET IN FULL PIKE

STARTING DOWN

STARTING UP

HIT SAME TIME

PUSH OFF

6. **Jump, One-half Twist**—After two or three straight jumps, execute a half turn or twist on the way up and land facing in the opposite direction.

   Hints: a. Keep the body straight and vertical. Don't lean in any direction.
   b. Take off and land in the same spot.
   c. Bring one arm upward and the other across the body at the height of the hips.
   d. Wait till feet have left the bed before starting the twist.
   e. When this can be done easily, try a full twist.

7. **Tuck Jump to Seat Drop**—Start as in a regular "Tuck Jump" (No. 3) but when straightening the legs, extend them forward (hips still flexed) instead of downward and land in a seat drop. Return to a straight jump as from the regular seat drop. Try this in series.

   Hints: a. Start at low or moderate height.
   b. As hands release the legs and the legs shoot forward, bring the hands beside the hips so they can contact the bed at the same time the hips and heels land.
   c. At the same time, lean very slightly backward with the upper body.
   Extra—Combine Pike Jump (No. 4), Jump One-half Twist (No. 6), and Tuck Jump to Seat Drop (No. 7).

8. **Knee Drop**—From a straight bounce, bend the knees to bring the lower legs behind you (rest of body remains vertical) and land on the knees. As the rebound occurs, straighten the knees and land on the feet.

   Hints: a. Learn this from a standing position instead of a bounce, but be sure to take off from both feet and bend both knees at the same time.
   b. Keep shoulders directly over the hips and knees. Do not lean forward or backward. Do not look down.
   c. A very slight bend at the waist should be made by beginners to avoid a whiplash action which would be produced by an arched back and a backward lean of the shoulders.
   d. Extend the toes backward. Land on the instep at the same time the knees hit.
   e. Drive the arms downward as the knees contact the bed to increase the downward momentum.
   f. With the rebound, circle the arms upward.
   g. Try to land on the same spot with the knees and then the feet.
   Extra—Go from a knee drop directly to a seat drop. Then go from a seat drop directly to a knee drop. Finally put the combination together in a series (knees, seat, knees, seat, etc.)

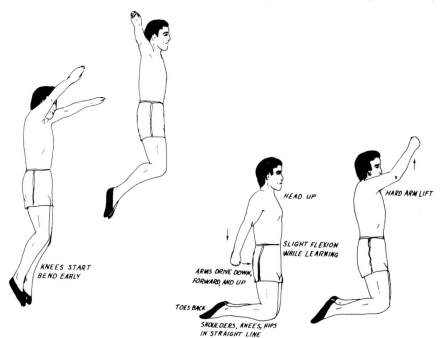

9. **Jump, One-half Twist to Seat Drop**—This is a lead up stunt for the "Swivel Hips" (No. 10). From a bounce, execute a "Jump, One-half Twist" (No. 6) and as soon as the twist is finished, flex the hips and do a seat drop.

   Hints: a. Be sure that the body is straight as the twist is made.

   b. Flex the hips only after the one-half twist is completed.

10. **Swivel Hips**—Execute a seat drop and as the body rises, bring the legs downward, raise the arms upward, turn the head in the direction of the twist, twist one-half turn and execute another seat drop.

   Hints: a. As soon as the push off from the hands is started, swing the *straight* arms forward and upward and *as the arm lift finishes,* pull the left shoulder back and turn the head to look over the left shoulder (if the twist is to the left). This movement is *part* of the arm lift.

   b. At the same time, drive the legs downward (force an extension of the hips).

   c. As the twist is made, the body should be in a straight, stretched position, arms up and legs down.

   d. Flex the hips again as the twist finishes. The flexion is the last part of the twist.

   e. Don't forget to place the hands beside the hips on *both* seat drops.

   f. If difficulty is experienced in extending the hips (if the twist persists in a pike position) try the stunt as a seat drop with one-half twist *to a stand* several times before going back to the swivel hips.

   g. Another aid to proper execution is concentration on keeping the feet directly in line with the longitudinal center stripe on the bed as the legs are brought down.

   h. Still another aid is to think of throwing the straight legs down, underneath the body and behind it before turning.

11. **Front Drop**—From a straight bounce, lean forward, raise the legs backward and land on the chest, abdomen, thighs, forearms and hands. The arms are bent, elbows at about shoulder level and hands beside and a little forward of the head. To rebound, push downward with the arms, raise the chest, and land on the feet.

Hints: a. Start from a standing position, hips and knees partly flexed and forearms resting on the thighs.

b. Depress the bed slightly and as it rebounds, swing the legs backward and upward to straighten the body (the chest must remain forward) and drop to the front drop position described previously.

c. The belt line should land right where the feet had been (in the center of the bed).

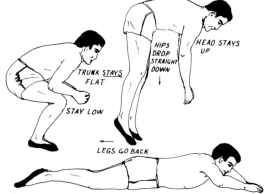

d. All points of contact land simultaneously. The head is up.

e. As the bed rebounds, push downward with the hands, raise the chest, and bring the feet under the body to a stand in the center of the bed.

f. Work on this form of the front drop four or five times to get the feel of it. The crouched position, the lack of height, and the fact that the upper body is already almost parallel to the bed assures that no injury will result from hitting either the chest before the thighs or vice versa.

g. After a good, flat landing has been made several times in succession try it from a more erect position—still without a bounce.

h. Lift the hips upward and backward (pike the body) on the ascent and flatten out just before the landing is made.

i. *Do not* bring the elbows under the body or reach for the bed with the hands.

j. After success has been achieved from an erect stand, try the stunt from a *low* bounce. Again pike the body on the ascent and flatten out for the landing.

k. *Do not* dive forward. The belt must always strike the transverse line on the bed.

l. Now try a series of front drops (front, feet, front, feet, etc.). Remember to lift with the arms and shoulders and pike at the hips when going from the feet back to the front drop.

12. **Front Drop—Seat Drop**—Execute the "Front Drop" (No. 11) from a bounce. As the push for the rebound is made, draw the legs forward, pass them under the body on the ascent and on through to a seat drop on the descent. Return to the feet as from a seat drop.

Hints: a. As the push from the "Front Drop" is made, lift the head more vigorously than for the regular "Front Drop."
  b. The chest is also raised.
  c. As the legs are brought forward, bend the knees till the upper legs are parallel to the bed. Then straighten the knees to thrust the legs forward.
  d. This can be done with straight legs, but it is more difficult and should be attempted after the bent leg variety has been done several times.
  e. Be sure to use the hands on the seat drop.

13. **Seat Drop—Front Drop**—Execute the seat drop from a bounce and as the push-off is made, lean forward with the chest and shoulders and extend the legs backward to land in a "Front Drop" position. Return to the feet from the "Front Drop."
  Hints: a. Lean forward as soon as the rebound starts. Also, push off with the hands.
    b. Draw the knees to the chest at the same time and draw the hips backward.
    c. Keep the knees and hips flexed until the body is parallel to the bed.
    d. Extend the body into the front drop position.
    Extra—Series of "Seat and Front Drops": Start with a Seat Drop and then continuously alternate between Front Drops and Seat Drops.
    Extra—Series of "Knee Drop," "Seat Drop," "Front Drop." Start with a Knee Drop, go to a Seat Drop, then to a Front Drop and back to a Knee Drop. Continue.

14. **Seat Drop with Full Twist to Seat Drop**—Execute a "Seat Drop" and on the rebound, execute a full twist and return to a "Seat Drop." Then rebound to a stand.
  Hints: a. As the rebound from the seat drop begins, lean backward about 45° with the upper body.
    b. At the same time raise the hips to straighten the body. The body is now fairly straight and about 25° above parallel with the head higher than the feet.
    c. At the same time, the right (left) arm is thrown across the chest and the head is turned to the left (right) to initiate the twist.
    d. Also, bring the left (right) elbow downward and behind the back.
    e. All of the above hints are done in one smooth, flowing, coordinated movement.
    f. As the twist is completed, flex the hips, bring the upper body forward, and land in a seat drop with the hands on the bed on either side of the hips.
    g. Push to the feet as in a regular seat drop.
    h. As the twist is done, keep the body in alignment with the longitudinal stripe on the bed.
    i. *Do not start the twist until the rebound has started* and the body has left the bed. The body will be thrown in the direction of the twist if it is still in contact when the twist begins.

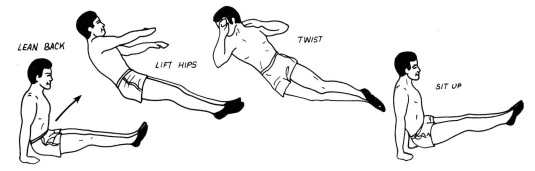

Spot: a. The spotter on the side toward which the twist is done must be ready to brace the performer if he/she starts to twist while still on the bed.
  b. To learn, the performer can move to one end and do a seat drop with the ankles just over the edge of the bed. The spotter grasps the ankles just before the performer sits and turns him/her as he/she rises. The spotter must know the direction the performer wants to turn. (Remove a spring or two to protect the spotter's hands.)

15. **Half Turn Table**—This is executed from a "Front Drop" and should not be tried until a good "Front Drop" can be performed. As the rebound occurs, push toward the left (right) with both hands, look over the right (left) shoulder, draw the knees toward the chest, and spin around a half revolution before extending the body again to land in a "Front Drop" facing the opposite direction. The front surface of the body is always toward the bed.

Hints: a. Land in the "Front Drop" with a firm body. A relaxed landing will kill the rebound.
   b. Do not *raise* the head and chest as the rebound begins.
   c. Push *sideward* with the arms as soon as the body *begins* to rise.
   d. Bring the knees to the chest (flex the knees and hips) and round the back (double up in a tight ball) as the push is made.
   e. Keep the shoulders level. Don't raise the right (left) shoulder as the head is turned to look over it.
   f. Lean or throw the head sideward to look over the shoulder rather than twist or turn it.
   g. Hold the drawn-together position till the half turn is almost completed, then extend quickly to the "Front Drop" position.
   h. The chest remains parallel to the bed at all times.

16. **Full Turn Table**—This is the same as No. 15 except that the body makes a complete revolution in the tucked position before it is extended for the landing. Finish in a "Front Drop" position facing in the direction of the original "Front Drop."
   Hints: a. More height for the "Front Drop" is needed plus a more vigorous push-off and a tighter tuck.
   Note: Advanced performers can do a one and one-half and even a double "Turn Table."

17. **Combination**—Do a "Swivel Hips," go directly to a "Front Drop," and then into a "Half Turn Table," and return to the feet. Try several of this series in succession.

18. **Back Drop**—From a "Straight Jump," flex the hips as the body rises and lean backward slightly with the upper body so that a landing on the back is achieved as the body descends. The contact is made on the *rounded* back with the legs pointing upward and the arms sideward but free of the bed. The rebound is to the feet.
   Hints: a. To learn, start from a stand in the center of the bed with one leg raised. Keep lifting the leg higher till the body is thrown off balance backward.
   b. Keep the head forward (chin on chest) and hold it firmly in that position (tighten the neck muscles) so that it isn't snapped backward as the back contacts the mat.
   c. Keep the shoulders forward and the back rounded.
   d. Raise the supporting leg to join the free one as the balance is lost.
   e. Keep the body "tight" and firm for the landing. If relaxation occurs, the rebound will be killed.
   f. A slight, partial extension of the hip joint as the rebound begins will aid in coming to the feet.

LIFT LEG
WHEN
FALLING

TUCK
HEAD

BACK ROUND

    g. After several successful "one-foot takeoffs," try the stunt from a low bounce and a two-foot takeoff.

    h. If the hips hit first, lean back a *little* more on the takeoff, and lift the hips a *little* higher.

    i. Remember, it is better to be a little short (insufficient rotation) than a little long (too much rotation). Play it safe.

    j. The back should land a little behind the spot from which the feet took off.

19. **Front Drop to Back Drop**—From the "Front Drop" landing, push off hard with the hands, lift the head and shoulders, and pull the knees in to the chest to start the backward rotation of the body. As the back approaches the bed, tuck the head forward and shoot the lower legs forward and upward.

20. **Back Drop to Front Drop**—From a good, solid "Back Drop" landing, shoot the legs upward and forward vigorously by a quick, *partial* extension of the hip joint. Accompany this with a forward lean of the body as the rebound occurs. With the forward rotation of the body, tuck the knees to the chest, continue to lean forward, and when the rotation reaches the point where the chest is toward the bed, extend the legs backward to a "Front Drop" landing.

    When this can be done easily and well, combine No. 19 and No. 20 and continue back and forth from "Front Drop" to "Back Drop" to "Front," etc. Try for five or six in succession. Good timing and firm landings are required.

21. **Half Twist to Back Drop**—On the ascent from a bounce, lean forward (body straight) and raise the legs backward so the body is about a 45° angle with the bed. Twist so that the back is toward the bed and land in a "Back Drop" position. Rebound to the feet.

Hints: a. Arch the back slightly as the legs move back and the shoulders go forward.
   b. As the peak of the rise is reached, throw the left arm under the body and to the right.
   c. At the same time, bend the right arm, raise the right elbow, and turn the head to look under the right shoulder.
   d. The head is down as it turns and remains forward for the landing.
   e. When the body twists, pike at the hips, bring the legs up, and land in the "Back Drop" position.
   f. Don't pike too soon—wait until the twist is almost completed.

22. **Cradle**—The "Cradle" starts from a "Back Drop." As the body rebounds and moves toward a "Front Drop" landing, execute a half twist and land in another "Back Drop" at the other end of the bed, facing in the other direction. This can be repeated immediately, returning to the original "Back Drop" landing spot and then continue indefinitely.
   Hints: a. Don't try to twist too soon. Wait until the body is past the midway position.
      b. Don't kick or squirm to get around. Just relax and execute the twist as learned in Stunt No. 21, above.
      c. To repeat, be sure to get a solid, firm "Back Drop" landing position.

23. **Half Twist to Front Drop**—As the body moves upward from a bounce, lean backward slightly and bring the legs forward slightly (do not flex the hips) so the body approaches a 45° angle with the bed. Execute a half twist and land in a "Front Drop" position. Rebound to the feet.

Hints: a. Instead of starting from a jump as described above, it can be learned from a stand by raising the right foot forward, leaning backward, and turning to the left.
   b. Pivot on the left foot and as the body starts to drop, raise the left foot to join the right.
   c. After a few successful tries from one foot, try it from a low bounce.
   d. Thrust the hips upward and forward when leaning back. Keep the body straight and in line with the center stripe and the arms up.
   e. Look to the feet momentarily and, as the body loses its upward momentum, turn the head sharply to the right.
   f. At the same time, bring the right arm across the body hard and the left arm down along the left side. The head and hips twist right.
   g. As the twist is completed bring both arms to the front of the body for the "Front Drop" landing.

24. **Full Twist to Back Drop**—Same as No. 23 but execute a full rather than a half twist and land in a "Back" rather than a "Front Drop." Rebound to the feet.

Hints: a. Review Stunt No. 14 ("Seat Drop with Full Twist") a few times.

b. Then work on the "Full Twist to Back Drop." It starts as No. 23, but a higher bounce is required.

c. Also, a more vigorous throw with the arms must be made and the head remains turned longer.

d. As the twist is completed, the head moves forward.

e. Don't kick, squirm, or fight to get around. The twist will be smoother with a relaxed body.

f. As the full twist is completed, flex the hips and bring the legs upward. Keep the legs straight.

g. Land on the upper, rounded back, head forward, and arms and legs upward.

25. **Front Drop, Full Twist to Front Drop**—On a rebound from a "Front Drop," throw the right arm under the body and turn the head to the left. The left elbow is lifted to aid in turning the body a complete revolution to land again in the "Front Drop" position. Rebound to the feet.

Hints: a. Keep the body parallel to the bed. Do not push downward with the arms and do not raise the head and chest.

b. Make the entire twist in one movement, though it is wise to practice the "Half Twist to Back Drop" first (Stunt No. 21).

c. Concentrate on a smooth, effortless twist without kicking and squirming. Keep the legs straight and together.

d. Bring the right arm close to the chest and keep reaching to the left with it until the twist is completed, then bring it right sideward for the landing.

e. Be sure to *wait* till the body leaves the bed before starting the twist or else the body will be thrown sideward off the trampoline.

Front Flip Progression:

Though most teachers believe the "Back Flip" to be easier than the "Front Flip," the "Front Flip" is almost always taught first on the trampoline. This is due to the easy progression that is possible, leading up to the execution of the "Front Flip." Start by doing a simple forward roll just as on a tumbling mat. The next step is to drop to a hands and knees position and flip over onto the back or seat. Then it is tried from a "Knee Drop" position over to a "Seat Drop." After several successful attempts have been made to a *controlled* "Seat Drop" (performer actually knows where he is and isn't landing blindly), it can be tried from the knees to the feet. Practice an intentional "short" landing (incomplete spin with feet landing slightly forward, causing loss of balance backward) to prevent the chance of overspinning and landing with the weight forward. When the trampolinist can land consistently with control and accuracy, he is ready to start all over again with a takeoff from the feet.

Starting from the feet, turn over to the back, then to the seat, and finally from the feet to the feet. Always work each progression until the "feeling" for the landing is achieved. When working from feet to feet, remember to land "short" for a period of time as a safety measure to prevent falling forward on the face.

26. **Front Turn Over from Hands and Knees Drop**—From a low bounce, lean slightly forward and raise the hips behind to land on the hands and knees. On the rebound, keep the hands in contact with the bed, tuck the head, raise the hips, and turn over to land on the back. As the hips pass over the head, remove the hands from the bed.

Hints:

a. The hands, knees, and feet should land at the same time with the toes extended backward.

b. The shoulders should be directly over the hands, the hips over the knees, and the head up. The hands should be in front of the cross lines and the knees behind.

c. Tuck the head sharply as the rebound begins. Do *not* turn the head to either side.

d. At the same time, press downward with the hands to help raise the hips.

e. Keep the chin against the chest and take the hands off the bed to allow the drop to the upper back. Keep the body tucked.

f. When this can be done easily, bounce a little higher and turn over to the seat.

g. The regular "Seat Drop" position should be attained—legs straight, hands on bed beside hips, shoulders over hips. (If the knees are bent, there is a chance of hitting the face against the knees.)

27. **Front Turn Over from Knee Drop to Seat**—From a small bounce do a "Knee Drop" and on the rebound, tuck the head, flex and raise the hips, and turn over to a landing on the seat.

   Hints: a. A *very slight* forward lean is required for the "Knee Drop."

   b. Do *not* collapse at the hips when landing in the "Knee Drop."

   c. Hold the bent arms in front of the body, hands about shoulder high, elbows down. (This is *not* like the regular "Knee Drop" landing.)

d. As the rebound begins, reach upward, forward, and downward in a circular motion with the hands. Do *not* thrust the hips backward.

e. Don't lower the upper body to create "spin." Instead, think of raising the hips over the head.

f. At the same time, tuck the head forward. Be sure it does not twist to either side.

g. Don't tuck the head as soon as you land on the knees. *Wait* for the rebound.

h. Combine a lift of the hips with the other movements.

i. Then throw a little higher and a little harder and turn over to a "Seat Drop."

j. Work for a controlled "Seat Drop" landing. It should be so controlled that a "Swivel Hips" can be done from it.

28. **Front Flip from Knees to Feet**—Start as for No. 27 but bounce a little higher and throw a little harder.
    Hints: a. Tuck up tighter (knees to chest) after the hips lift.
    b. Open for the landing by reaching for the bed with the feet.
    c. Look forward when opening. Do *not* keep the head tucked.
    d. Open a little early—land short—to keep from overspinning. (Drop to the seat after feet hit.)
    e. When the "feel" of the landing is acquired, eleminate the "short" landing (feet too far in front) and try to keep balanced.

29. **Front Turn Over from Feet to Back**—From a *low* bounce, tuck the head, lift the hips, and turn over forward to a landing on the back. Rebound to the feet.
    Hints: a. Lean *slightly* forward on the takeoff. Don't bounce high.
    b. Think of bringing the hips over the head rather than bringing the head under the hips.
    c. Keep the arms low. They need not be used.
    d. Keep the body tight when landing on the back and keep the head tucked forward.
    e. Work on this phase until you know where you are as you land.

30. **Front Turn Over from Feet to Seat**—Same as No. 29 but turn over a little further and land in a controlled "Seat Drop."
    Hints: a. Use a little more height than in No. 29. Don't lean *too* far forward on the takeoff.
    b. On the takeoff, carry the hands in front of the shoulders, elbows low.
    c. Reach upward, forward, and downward in a circular motion with the hands.
    d. At the same time, lift the hips and tuck the head.
    e. Land in the "Seat Drop" with the legs straight to avoid hitting the face against a raised knee.
    f. Keep practicing till complete control in the "Seat Drop" is achieved.

31. **Front Flip**—Same as No. 30 but land on the feet instead of the seat.
    Hints: a. Bounce relatively high just behind the cross lines on the bed.
    b. Lean *slightly* forward on the takeoff.
    c. Reach with the arms as in No. 30.
    d. Raise the hips and tuck the knees to the chest as the head tucks.
    e. Imagine a wall or rope just in front of you about shoulder high and do the flip *over* the barricade. Do not just bend forward.
    f. Open early and land "short" with the feet out in front of the hips.
    g. Raise the head from the tuck position and look straight ahead when opening for the landing.
    h. Practice the "short" landing until sure of your position. Then try to land on balance.
    Spot: This stunt should have special spotting. Stand to the performer's right with the left foot on the frame and the right foot on the cross line. The left foot bears most of the weight and the right foot is raised just before the performer lands and is replaced when he becomes airborne. As the gymnast goes for the flip, step onto the bed, place the right hand on his neck or upper back and push downward, to the left, and upward in a circular motion. The left hand goes to his abdomen and lifts upward. As he lands, be ready to grasp his right upper arm with both hands to prevent a possible overspin.

Teaching Technique

Beginners frequently tend to lean too far forward on their takeoff for the "Front Flip." This causes them to travel forward. Knowing this, they like to move to the back end of the trampoline so that if they do travel, they will still land on the bed. Because they are aware of the room in front of them and know that there is no room behind, they unconsciously lean forward more than usual. Thus, a bad habit can develop. Instead of letting them work from the back end of the trampoline, insist that they take off from the center. This will keep them from leaning forward too much.

32. **Back Flip**—From a bounce of medium height, reach upward with both hands as the body ascends. Look back with the head and draw the knees upward to the chest and turn over backward. Grasp the shins with the hands as they pass over the head. As the revolution is completed, open and reach for the bed with the feet.

   Hints: a. Don't lean back and look back when leaving the bed.

          b. The arm lift is directly upward.

          c. Do not start the tuck too early. Drive downward with the legs first to gain height.

          d. Bring the hips forward and the knees up to the chest. Do not bring the chest down to the knees. Leaning forward with the chest to achieve a tuck position is one of the common faults.

          e. Grasp the shins or knees at the top of the flight (body upside down) to insure the tuck position.

          f. Keep the head back. The second most common fault is to tuck the head immediately after throwing it back.

          g. Keep the eyes *open*. When the bed is seen after three-fourths of the flip, don't reach for the bed with the hands. Continue to lift with the head and chest until the revolution is complete.

          h. Look forward to the edge of the trampoline.

          i. Open up (extend the legs downward) and place the feet on the bed directly below the hips.

          j. Do not move to the front end of the trampoline in order to have plenty of bed space upon which to land. This only encourages backward leaning takeoffs. A good technique to use on a person who does lean backward too much is to move him toward the back end of the bed. This should cure his tendency to travel backward.

          Warning: Spot very carefully and closely in this situation.

   Spot: No one, not even those who have already done back flips off diving boards, should begin to learn this stunt without special spotting. Basically, there are too approved methods of spotting. Some experts advocate one, some another. These spotting techniques must be practiced. Ideally, the spotter should practice spotting on a gymnast who is already capable of doing the "Back

Flip" unaided. If this is not possible, spend a great deal of time working with somebody who just does straight bouncing. Do not have him try the flip until you become competent on the belt or hand spotting technique.

Overhead Spotting Belt:

This rig should be considered a "must" for any advanced tricks. It consists of one single and one double pulley attached to the ceiling (or overhead girder) with a rope running through the pulley so that one man can operate a safety belt. The distance between the two pulleys is determined by the height of their attachment. The higher the attachment, the greater the spread that is necessary. In all events, the spread should be enough to give the performer complete freedom from entanglement with the ropes.

The problem in operating the system lies in keeping the ropes tight enough at all times to prevent their flopping loosely and interfering with the performer's movements and yet not get them so tight that he will either be pulled up, held up, or "lowered" downward by the ropes. The spotter must know when it is *necessary* to hold or support the gymnast to prevent his being injured. An "artist" at spotting can use the device as manual manipulation to actually *aid* in the performance of a stunt. This is effected by giving the exact amount of pull or lift at the precise moment it is needed to turn the person over.

A portable overhead spotting rig that can be attached to the trampoline is available, but it is not as satisfactory and is more exepensive than the beam-supported rigging. Of course for outdoors or in a gym where it is not possible to suspend pulleys, the portable rigs will do.

To start, the spotter stands directly under the double pulley, takes a single wrap around the right (left) hand with the rope so that when it is tightened and the performer is standing in the center of the bed, the spotter's right hand is about chin high. The other hand is held loosely around the rope and is stretched overhead. As the performer springs upward, the spotter pulls downward with his right (left) hand so that the ropes remain semitight. The rope slides through the upper hand. As the performer begins the descent, bring the lower hand upward at the same speed he/she descends so that the ropes remain taut but the drop is not slowed by the pull of the ropes. As the gymnast sinks into the bed, the spotter's hand is going to have to reach over the head. The spotter must *anticipate* both the ascent and descent—especially the ascent. Beginning spotters frequently wait for the rise to start before making their downward pull. This will cause the ropes to become loose and floppy and frequently the spotter will still be pulling downward when the gymnast starts down. When this happens, the man is being "carried." A spotter must sense or feel the bouncer's timing and react in perfect accord with it. Only after this rapport has been established between the two should the back flip be attempted.

In addition to this exact timing of up and down strokes, the spotter must decide when the performer needs to be supported. Remember, it is better to support him/her too soon or when support really isn't needed, than to be too late or fail to give support when it is needed. The knowledge of when a gymnast is safe comes with experience. Until this experience is gained, if you must err, err on the side of giving support when it is not needed rather than the other way around.

This method of spotting, though good, is somewhat time consuming because the spotting belt must be taken off and put on others. To reduce this wasted time as much as possible, have two belts, one being worn by the person on the trampoline and the other by the next one up. When the change is made, simply unsnap the ropes from the one belt and attach them to the other. Then, while the second person is bouncing, the first can take the belt off and the third one can put it on.

Hand Spotting:

Hand spotting is just as safe as belt spotting when done by *practiced*, capable spotters. It has the advantage of saving time because the belts do not have to be put on and taken off. As soon as one is done, the next hops up and is ready to go. A second advantage lies in the fact that with the spotter right there, the performer is apt to have more confidence. Thirdly, the spotter can actually assist the learner by turning him/her over no matter how he/she goes about doing the stunt. Success, no matter how much of it is due to the spotter's help, encourages the beginner and he/she is able to "go" for the next attempt in a much more relaxed frame of mind.

Though hand spotting is superior to belt spotting when done by experts, it is harder to learn and less sure in the hands of inexperienced men. It is urged, therefore, that one engage in much practice before attempting to hand spot a beginning gymnast in the "Back Flip." It should also be understood that for many truly advanced stunts, the belt technique is the only practical one to use. For example, it would be sheer folly to attempt to hand spot a one and one-half twisting double forward somersault (Rudolph Flifis).

To hand spot a "Back Flip" stand at the performer's left side, facing him. Grasp trunks, shirt, and supporter with the right hand (thumb and little finger on outside of trunks, other three fingers inside waistband). Both performer and spotter start bouncing. They must time their bounces perfectly, each one going up exactly the same distance at exactly the same time. With practice, this can be done.

When the bouncing is perfectly synchronized, the trampolinist attempts the flip. As he goes for it, the spotter lifts with the right hand, twists the wrist to the right to induce spin, and pushes upward with the left hand on the performer's left leg if needed. If the performer follows directions (which is usual when he/she has confidence in the spotter) all will go well. If he/she panics and straightens out early, tucks his head forward, or fails to "go" for the stunt, the spotter must be prepared to catch and lower him/her to the bed. Almost always it is possible to turn the performer over far enough with a strong push on the leg combined with a strong lift and turn of the right hand. It is for the few times that the student can't be turned that the spotter must be prepared to catch.

When everything goes well and the trampolinist turns over easily, the spotter must be prepared to guard against an overspin. If the spin is too fast or there is no opening up, be alert and prepared to release the right hand and grasp his /her upper arm with both hands or place your right elbow and shoulder against the back as he/she lands.

Remember: practice, Practice, PRACTICE with just the bouncing. If a person is available who can do the back flip unaided, practice spotting that one. If not, take the most adept person in the class and practice with him/her outside of class time. There is no substitute for practice.

This lengthy discourse on spotting and the continued emphasis on practice and care may seem to imply that the front and back flip on the trampoline are too dangerous to use for class. This is not the case. Hundreds of youngsters have learned these and more difficult stunts without any spotting whatsoever. But, the possibility of an accident is always present, and it is to guard against this possibility that the spotting is stressed.

33. **Layout Back Flip**—When the "Back Flip" has been well learned, as described in No. 32, it can be tried "laid out" (body extended). The mechanics here are different. Obtain a relatively high bounce. When ready for the flip, swing the arms upward as the body rises, circle them sideward and raise the chest to arch the back. Tilt the head back at the same time. Revolve with the body extended and land on the feet.

Hints: a. Lean slightly backward with the shoulders when rising and thrust the abdomen forward.
    b. Don't throw the head and shoulders back while the feet are still on the bed. Establish the upward direction first.
    c. Use a powerful upward, then sideward, swing of the arms.
    d. Thrust the chest upward as hard as you can. Think of putting your chest against the ceiling right above the feet.
    e. Lay the head back as far as it will go.
    f. Arch the back as much as you can.
    g. Consider the arms as an axis around which the body revolves.

FORCE CHEST UP

ARCH

ARMS SIDEW.

ARMS UPW.

Spot: a. Use an overhead spotting belt if one is available. If not, use the following procedure: Stand to the performer's left with your left foot on the frame and your right foot on the red line. For the preliminary bounces shift your weight to the left foot and remove the right when he/she *lands,* and step back with the right when he/she is in the air.

 b. At the take off for the flip, step onto the bed with both feet, place your right hand under the lower back and lift. The left hand can push up on the legs if more spin is needed.

34. **Barani**—This is almost like a "Front Flip" with a half twist. It can also be compared to a "Round Off" (No. 15 in Individual Tumbling Stunts) without using the hands for a push-off. Start the "Front Flip" and when half way through, execute a half twist. This is usually done in pike position rather than tucked. Of course, the "Front Flip" must be well learned before attempting the "Barani."

Note: There are three main methods of teaching the "Barani"; each has its own merit. Some learn more quickly with one method while others do better with another. Try one, and if little success is found, switch. The three methods follow: (1) Do a piked "Front Flip" and twist just before landing. Continue, and try to twist earlier each time. When the twist is done while the hips are above the head, you are doing a "Barani." (2) Do a "Round Off" from a "Knee Drop." Repeat, putting less and less weight on the hands until it can be done without touching the hands to the bed at all. Then try the same series from a foot takeoff instead of from the knees. (3) Proceed as follows: (a) From a "Knee Drop," turn over to a *flat* lying position on the back (body must be extended and not in the regular "Back Drop" position). (b) Repeat, but just before landing on the back, twist over to a *flat* "Front Drop" position. (c) Repeat, but just before landing as before, draw the knees in and land on the hands and knees. (d) Repeat, but this time land on the knees only. (e) Repeat, but land on the feet. (f) Now take the same stages through but start from the feet instead of from the knees. It is important that you *not* try a succeeding stage until you feel comfortable in the preceding one.

The mechanics of the true "Barani" follow:

Hints: a. Start from slightly behind the cross lines on the bed.

 b. Start the pike front flip *first.* Do not start the twist from the bed.

 c. Bend slightly at the waist and lower (but don't *tuck*) the head at the takeoff. Keep the eyes on the cross lines.

 d. The hips rise rapidly, the shoulders are square (level), the arms are slightly spread and reaching downward and forward. The entire body is still moving upward.

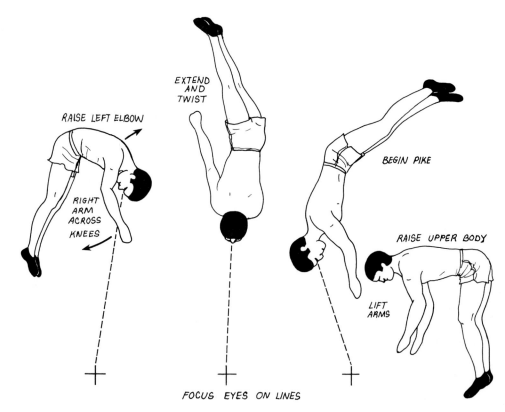

e. As the hips come above the head, the head is raised. If the eyes are kept on the cross lines, this will happen automatically.

f. Begin to diminish the amount of pike (extend the body gradually) before the body is vertical.

g. As the body extends, drop the right shoulder and sweep the right hand across the knees while the left arm bends and is raised sideward.

h. At the same time, turn the head left (eyes still on cross lines).

i. As the twist is completed (the body is now descending), flex the hips again to bring the feet under the body.

j. The eyes remain fixed on the same spot till just before the landing. As the body pikes, raise the head and shoulders and focus the eyes on the end of the trampoline.

Spot: a. A "twisting belt," a device that enables a performer to twist around his longitudinal axis at the same time he is rotating around his transverse axis and still be suspended by the overhead rigging, is almost a necessity for many of the very advanced moves. Its use makes spot-the "Barani" very easy. If one is not available, stand for the preliminary bounces as in No. 33.

b. As he/she starts the flip, step onto the bed, grasp the left hip with your right hand, the right hip with your left hand, and lift and twist. He/she should not bounce very high while you are helping.

29

Sample Demonstrations

The value of a demonstration has been mentioned before so this chapter is concerned only with actual samples of demonstrations and techniques of preparing and presenting them.

The following factors are important and need to be considered when planning a demonstration program:

1. The ability of the class (beginners–advanced).
2. The length of time the performance is to last.
    Is it part of a long program or is it to be the entire program?
3. The condition of the area in which the demonstration is to be given.
    a. Is there sufficient room for a run?
    b. How many pupils can work without crowding?
    c. Will mats be available?
    d. Where will the audience sit? (On one side? On three sides? Surrounding the performance?)
    e. Will the performance be on a raised platform (stage) or floor level?
4. The availability and amount of practice time.
5. The type of audience.
    a. Children
    b. Adults
    c. Parents
    d. Physical education instructors
6. The age of the performers.
    a. Elementary
    b. Junior high
    c. Senior high
    d. College

The first number on the program should be very good. It should move rapidly and include all members of the cast. The last number should also be spectacular. The audience is prone to remember its first impression and the last one sticks too. If there are any mediocre parts in the demonstration, they should be placed in the middle where the audience will be most likely to forget about them.

Do not wear the audience out by too much repetition or too lengthy a demonstration. If the entire class is to do a forward roll, have them all roll together across the mat or roll in two or three lines going in opposite directions. Have something going on at all times. Avoid pauses. Arrange the stunts so that the finish of one places the performers in a position for the next. Attempt to develop different floor patterns. Have the performers work from various angles and formations. If possible, arrange for them to work on different levels by constructing platforms raised above the original height of the demonstration area.

There are three main types of demonstrations, namely: (1) class demonstrations, (2) demonstrations by skilled performers selected for their outstanding ability, and (3) clown or comedy work. Following are a few examples of demonstrations. They are merely suggestions and idea stimulators. Each instructor will no doubt prefer to develop his/her own because the individual peculiarities of every situation must be considered.

Class Demonstrations

(Elementary School)

1. Class marches in along the side of the mat, halts, and faces the audience on command of instructor. Participants should be lined up according to height.
2. Half face left and other half face right and go to left and right ends of mat; each does series of forward rolls one after another. Those on left use outside edge of mat; those on right use inside edge. Each walks behind mat to the end of the mat he/she began from as soon as finished rolling.
3. As soon as the last ones start their forward rolls the first follow with backward rolls. They again return to place.
4. They pair off and those on the left do forward double rolls while those on the right do backward double rolls. This time they stay on the side of the mat where they finish.
5. With the same partners used in the double rolls, they move back across the mat with the front line doing the camel walk and the rear line doing the elephant walk. (The second pair get ready while the first pair start out. Line up at rear of mat as soon as finished.)
6. Build a simple pyramid and return to position behind the mat.
7. All drop to a front support and do a seal crawl forward across the mat. Straighten to stand, and face about.
8. First one steps in front of one on right and every other person does the same. Form wheelbarrows and go back across the mat, stand up and turn around forming a single line.
9. First three on the left form centipede on front edge of mat and the next three form centipede on rear edge of mat. Race to other end of mat. Next sets of threes get into position while first two sets are racing. Stand at back of mat when finished.
10. Every other person does headstand. Return to stand and the others do headstand. (If all can't do it alone, have partners assist.)
11. Half go to left side and half to right again. Those on left do bobbin backward in pairs on front edge of mat; those on right do bobbin forward on rear edge of mat. They remain at the side where they finish.
12. Five from each side do a skin the snake and return to a stand and then five more.
13. All do cartwheels. Half from right, half from left. Form line to rear of mat when finished.
14. Build simple pyramid. Return to line back of mat.
15. Build four six-man squash pyramids, squash, all get up and form line at back, face left and run off.

Demonstration by Eight Advanced Performers

The mats should cover an area about 12′ x 24′.

1. The performers enter running, side by side, four from each end, and do simultaneous cartwheel flips and land facing each other.
2. Each then does a backward roll to a headstand, pushes up to a handstand and snaps down to a stand.
3. Immediately each does one mule kick and retreats to the ends of the mat. (Four to the left end, four to the right end.)
4. The first two on the left do a back-to-back pullover along the front edge, followed by the second pair and the four on the right do the same along the rear edge of the mat.
5. A student from the left does three rolling snap ups along the front edge of the mat and then does a forward roll to a lying position on the back. As he/she starts the third one, another from the left follows and does one rolling snap up followed by a forward roll to a lying position. The same thing occurs on the back edge of the mat with pupils from the right.

6. The two remaining on the right do foot-to-pelvis front flips over the two lying on the front edge of the mat, and the two on the left do the same thing over those lying on the rear edge of the mat.

7. The four on their backs simultaneously do snap ups to a stand and bend forward, placing their hands on their knees.

8. The two on the right do a neck lift front handspring over the two in the front row and at the same time, the ones on the left do the same over those in the back row.

9. The four standing on the mats do front leap to handsprings (those in front going toward the right and the ones in the rear going to the left) to the end of the mats.

10. Three from the left do three-man jump and roll (each one does four rolls) and stop, going to the rear of the mat, and three from the right do the same.

11. The one remaining on the left and the one remaining on the right each do a round off and back handspring and then line up at the rear with the others.

12. All step forward onto the mat and the two end pupils do a tip up, the next two do a headstand, the next two do a forearm stand, and the middle two do handstands.

13. Two of them step to the center of the mat (back to back) and the others are tossed into toe-pitch back flips, two at a time. All return to the rear of the mat.

14. All build a pyramid. Return to rear.

15. Seven of the students build a pyramid and hold it while the eighth does a round off, back handspring, back flip in front of the pyramid.

16. The pyramid dismounts, the performers line up and march off.

Clown Tumbling (Three People)

1. #1 does forward roll toward audience.
   #2 does dive roll over #1 from the left.
   #3 does dive roll over both of them from the right.

2. #3 holds arms out and #2 runs toward him/her and dives for the arms. While in the air, #1 grabs #2's leg which causes a fall.
   #1 runs toward #3's arms and jumps for them. As he/she is in the air, #3 waves at the audience and #1 crashes to the mat.
   #2 stands at end prepared to catch #3 who runs toward him/her. Just as #3 jumps, #1 jumps into #2's arms, #3 bumps into #2 and all three go down.

3. They get up and #1 does a handspring, #2 does a one-arm handspring and #3 does a handspring but fails and lands on his back.

4. #1 and #2 lift #3 to his feet (stiff) and turn to shake hands.
   #3 fall forward (dead man's fall).

5. #1 and #2 turn #3 over and #1 runs over him/her (stepping very lightly).
   #3 sits up and #2 runs from the other direction and knocks him/her over again by stepping on the chest.

6. #3 falls back and draws feet close to buttocks as he/she falls.

7. #1 runs toward #3 and does a knee shoulder spring and lands facing #2.

8. #2 places a foot in #1's hands and jumps upward, assisted by a lift from #1's hands and straddles over #1's head, landing astraddle of #3.

9. #3 gets up and swings fist at #2 who ducks forward so that #3 falls across his shoulders and is thrown into a neck lift front handspring.

10. #3 faces #2 and they do a shoulder straddle from floor into an assisted front flip.

11. #3 and #1 then do a double cartwheel.

12. #1 and #2 then throw #3 into a double toe-pitch back flip.

13. #2 and #3 then throw #1 into a double toe-pitch back flip, but #1 goes straight up, screams, and is caught by #2 and #3 as he drops. They lower him to the floor in a faint.

14. #2 grasps #1's ankles and #3 grasps #1's head and they carry #1 off (stiff).

Combination Demonstration

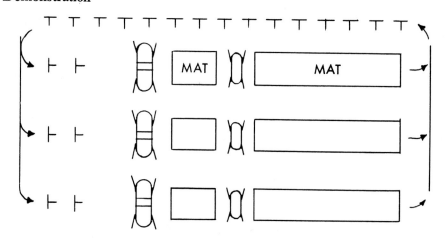

SIDE HORSE	BUCK	TUMBLING MAT
1. Knee spring dismount from kneeling position in saddle	1. Straddle vault with quarter turn.	1. Cartwheel
2. Squat vault	2. Straddle vault with half turn	2. Backward roll
3. Straddle vault	3. Straddle vault	3. Handspring
4. Jump to a stand between pommels and leap forward to buck and	4. Straddle vault	4. Two forward rolls
5. Flank vault to right	5. Flank vault to left	5. Cartwheel flip to a forward roll
6. Jump to straddle stand and jump forward to mat and	6. Squat vault	6. Two forward rolls
7. Thief vault	7. Jump to a stand and leap forward with flexing hips and touching hands to toes	7. Forward roll
8. Straddle vault	8. Scissors vault	8. Backward roll and snap-up to a handstand
9. Sheep vault	9. Sheep vault	9. Forward roll and head-spring
10. Thief vault	10. Dive roll over buck	10. Forward roll
11. Straddle vault	11. Neck spring vault	11. Handspring
12. Jump to a stand between pommels and leap forward with a full twist	12. Handspring vault	12. Round off to a back hand-spring

BALANCE BEAM

BALANCE STUNTS

FLOOR EXERCISE

See "Floor Exercise Stunts and Transitions" under **Simple Stunts**

HIGH HORIZONTAL BAR

LOW HORIZONTAL BARN

PARALLEL BARS

POMMEL HORSE

RINGS

SIMPLE STUNTS

TRAMPOLINE

TUMBLING STUNTS

UNEVEN PARALLEL BARS

VAULTING